A skyscraper project utilizing walls of glass and sheet-copper supported on inner concrete piers.
Frank Lloyd Wright, architect. [See page 309]

# THE NEW WORLD ARCHITECTURE

## By *Sheldon Cheney*

*Author of "A Primer of Modern Art," "The Theatre" etc.*

WITH 389 ILLUSTRATIONS

TUDOR PUBLISHING COMPANY

NEW YORK          MCMXXXV

CHENEY

THE NEW WORLD ARCHITECTURE

PRINTED IN THE UNITED STATES OF AMERICA

## AUTHOR'S ACKNOWLEDGMENT

IN THE text and the captions I have made note of the more usual obligations incurred in the preparation of a book of this sort. But I should like to say a word of direct thanks to certain architects who have given me freely of their time and their ideas: most particularly Frank Lloyd Wright, Bernard Maybeck, and Eliel Saarinen in America, Joseph Hoffmann in Vienna, and Walter Gropius in Berlin. I have also had advice and help from Dr. Werner Hegemann, editor of *Wasmuth's Monatshefte für Baukunst*, from Joseph Urban, Ely Jacques Kahn, and H. Th. Wijdeveld, editor of *Wendingen*, Amsterdam. But my greatest debt is to Frank Ernest Hill, of Longmans, Green & Company, for friendly if serious criticism, and for suggestions that led to re-arrangement and rewriting. My wife has aided not only with suggestions but with constant co-operation in the preparation of the final manuscript.

For illustrations, I am especially indebted to Hugh Ferriss for permission to reproduce six of his drawings; and to Frank Lloyd Wright for the fine series of photographs of his earlier and later work. Frederick Kiesler, Walter T. Steilberg and Claude Bragdon have generously helped me to obtain photographs of buildings not their own; while the editors of *L'Architecte*, Paris, have been generous in permitting reproductions from that publication. I wish to thank, too, Miss Pearl Chase of the Plans and Planting Committee of the Santa Barbara Community Arts Association, and my brother, Charles H. Cheney: they supplied the photographs of buildings in the California style, and afforded opportunities to study that so attractive phase of conservative progress in the pleasantest of fashions.

To the many architects in the United States and Europe who have responded to my requests for photographs of their works, I can only say a general and sincere " Thank you " — and hope that my treatment of their contributions will seem adequate and fair. I disavow, however, any intent to attempt a detailed view of the new architecture, with every contributor properly noted and " placed "; I shall be content if I am judged to have made clear the main roads in what is still an uncharted, if not chaotic, field.   I may add that if I seem too insistent upon certain fundamental principles, which are now axiomatic to us all, the fact that the book has been two years in the making, is at least a partial explanation. What seemed insurgent and revolutionary two years ago is now the accepted and standard basis for merely progressive thought — so fast moves " Modernism."

S.C.

*Gland, Switzerland, June,* 1930

# CONTENTS

# THE NEW WORLD ARCHITECTURE

From a drawing by Hugh Ferriss

# CHAPTER I

## THE NEW WORLD ARCHITECTURE

AFTER civilization, what? The question is not an idle one. Granted that civilization is what we have, humanity is about ready to move on to something else. Signs are not lacking that the present generations are living at one of the three or four major turning-points in human history. The latest centuries-long slope has brought us to a summit. Almost suddenly a different prospect widens before us. An old age, a human epoch, and its methods of organization and its beliefs, have proved their utmost. As we look back at the achievements that men prized most during the last five hundred years of that age — the military victories, the regal pomp, the arts, the religions — we begin to discern that these were less important than the incidental building of foundations for a different unforeseen world. A new faith, a new power, and a new way of living have been born. The new conception of Space-time has found wide acceptance.

1

An object lesson in the new and the old architecture: the Nineteenth Century *Credit Suisse* building in Geneva, Switzerland.   [See plate opposite]

Architecture is a fixation of man's thinking and a record of his activity. Thus it may be locally circumscribed or broadly expressive, mean and cramped or imaginatively aspiring, tricky or honest, timid or bold, shallowly pretentious or truly glorious.   We may be sure that the future will judge the architecture of the half-thousand years prior to 1900 as bad: weak, unoriginal, vacillating, showy.   For the spiritual chaos and the will-to-power and the strife of those centuries are truly mirrored in the buildings.   Since Catholicism, having conquered all Europe, became corrupt, giving birth to a conflict from which neither the One Church nor revolting Protestantism has ever risen to world power, to more than narrow

Model for the new *Credit Suisse* building in Geneva, showing typical stripping back to simple forms.
Maurice Turrettini, architect.

sectarian influence, there has been no unity, no plan, no spiritual outlook in the life of the Western world. It is the disunity, the conflict, the short-sightedness, that architecture faithfully reflects. But the text of my book is this: just as a new life was stirring beneath or beyond what men *called* true life at the end of that five hundred years, just so, beside the orthodox architecture of disunity and pretension and commerce, the foundations of a new architecture were being established; and that new architecture begins to raise its head today, throughout Europe and the Americas, as the first creative manifestation in the art since Michelangelo (who came a century after his time) laid down his tools.

The new architecture is still so bound up with the problems of civilization, so related to the struggle to escape from the limitations of civilization, that this first chapter will be concerned with humanity and the world as much as with the art of building; with the background of man's economic, social, and cultural life, out of which I hope will emerge for you a clearer understanding of machine-age building.

The social historians mark three general periods in man's tenancy of the world up to this time: savagery, barbarism, and civilization. The period now drawing to a close, civilization, began when men came together in certain places for trading, formed cities, then states, and gradually created means for extending and protecting manufacture and barter — all designed to increase the hold of a human group, a tribe or nation, on the three essentials, food, clothing, and shelter; and it arrived at its final phase in the network of mass production, salesmanship, financing, and credit which we see today, dependent upon a substructure of political states held together by patriotism on the part of the peoples, and a competent but judicious aggressiveness on the part of governments.

The building up of this civilization toward the present wonderfully efficient but appallingly unstable edifice has included the development of those cultural institutions, the religions and the arts. After flourishing several times under favoring conditions, these have become mere accretions to the civilized structure of society. Particularly since the separation of the Church from the business-state, the trader (business man) has not troubled to understand either art or religion — they have been side-issues; though the recorders of civilization, discovering that the arts have a way of surviving as the only tangible and admirable phenomena from phase to phase of history, have been facile in parading these as the more imposing bolsters or achievements of the civilized establishment. But we shall do well to remember that the name " civilization " is political, and the reason behind it is economic, commercial, and — at the present conjunction — nationalistic.

As I implied at the start, however, civilization is not final; nor is its architecture. Like barbarism it is a stage ultimately to be outgrown. And with the expansion of the business-state until no part of the world remains unexploited for raw materials and markets, with the most advanced nations each with a world-wide network of commercial initiative and privilege, of administration and exploitation, the end is in sight. The next phase — in assuming the rôle of prophet, I go not so far as to venture a name for it — will be not a *state* organism, but somehow a *world* unit. If the word " world " and the word " human " be not in the title, at least those will afford foundation-ideas of the time. It is for this reason that we hear it stated that there is now " a world will to peace " or a world-conscience.

The universe-idea will, of course, extend over from social organization to religion and the arts in the new establishment; under recent civilization, religions have been not only conflicting and expedient, but usually for a nation or a race, and the arts have been national and often for a class within a nation (as Roman architecture, with the trail of the proud conqueror and the boaster over it, or sentimental English middle-class painting, or French " decoration," fit only for the love-nests of sophisticated kings and courtesans, for whom, indeed, it was first invented).

In the new time, religion — if what takes the place of that is not too inclusive to wear the name — will be broad enough for the whole world, or suffer recognition as only a survival from the civilized age; while the arts will have world-wide application, as against the national " styles " of recent centuries. It is relevant that the first outcroppings of Modernist art, including architecture, have had more affinity with primitive — i.e., barbaric — practice than with any civilized style: for there is a universality about savage, barbaric, and even early civilized work that is absent when a national culture has, as we say, " flowered," and always a hardness, a precision, and a reliance on basic proportion and geometric relationships, that civilization has generally lost in favor of a softer ornamentalization, a prettified art.

The radicalism of Frank Lloyd Wright, more than any other factor, has tended to eliminate the high and often spiky roofs of the Victorian era, in favor of lower and less restless forms. Above, Wright's own house at Spring Green, Wisconsin, fitted in line and materials to the low rolling Western country. Below, an object lesson in a simple reposeful house, by Wright, beside the more usual product.

Now if you happen to be of that softer persuasion, and if you have not wakened to the heralds of the new dawn, you may see all that I have said as a reason for holding to what is termed civilization, to the world structure as it exists, somewhat shakily, today. (After all, there is nothing wrong about it, except its foundations.) Visualizing all primitive art as bare or ugly — certainly it is different from the things of Raphael and Reynolds and Donatello we were told in school to reverence as beautiful — and being comfortable in your place in civilized social adjustment, feeling that nationalism is the safest and best thing you know, you decide again that "Modernism" is more dangerous than what you have. You prefer to believe that civilization is riding along to an evolutionary betterment: that the faults will have been worn away without too much disturbance of your particular little fenced-in field. As a point of fact, until very recently, at any rate until the opening of the World War of 1914, most people were with you in denying the actual change that was taking place, undermining the foundations of your beliefs, your security, and your arts, clearly foreshadowing the end of civilization as known. Even now, when millions have crossed — in allegiance, at least — the vague border-line between civilization and a later world-order, a new creative world-organism, nine-tenths of our neighbors are actively resisting modern progress in one direction or another.

And indeed we ourselves, whichever side of the border our thinking places us, live strange mixtures of old and new habits and actions. We are in an age when mechanical genius has revolutionized the pattern of living, the fabric of doing and thinking, of going and coming, of securing and selling, of work and play, which is the individual human life. In addition to the watch and pocket-knife that used to be the personal mechanical equipment of the ordinary man, I carry fountain-pen, permanent pencil, mechanical lighter, and, at night, electric flash. I step to a crystal-clean wash-bowl to wash my hands in hot or cold running water, warm my feet at a steam radiator, and look with satisfaction at a floor vacuum-cleaned. I step from my door into a self-propelled vehicle that almost noiselessly whisks me over perfectly smoothed roads to the railway station. There I get into an electric train; but if that seems slow, I quit it at the next large city, get into an airplane and fly. And most of these mechanical improvements are all-pervasive: that is, I am not thus favored because I belong to a class. The farmer and worker have their automobiles and may utilize railways and street-cars; fountain-pens and flashlights are the commonest possessions of schoolboys; and (in America, at least) there is no building that omits sanitary plumbing and central heating, and the housewife expects as a matter of course to have electric iron, electric cook-box and vacuum-cleaner (and you're lucky if she doesn't put you down for the still-somewhat-expensive electric refrigeration). We communicate by typewriter, telephone, and wireless. We are entertained by phonograph, radio, and moving picture. We are essentially a world of machine-users, and the whole pattern of our existence has changed, as compared with that of our grandparents.

*But,* machine-users that we are, ninety-nine one-hundredths of us live in houses of the merely civilized, not the machine-age era. That plumbing, that running water, that heating plant and vacuum-cleaner and automatic refrigerator — they all are mere incrustations upon the " civilized " house. Beyond the polished floors, everything is a survival: the furniture is stuffed, ornamented, imitation-hand-carved, the doors are Colonial-panelled, the window-frames ornamented with mill-work Neo-Classic mouldings, the windows themselves are broken into small panes (because, forsooth, once large areas of glass were expensive, and later house designers, looking at the substitutes, thought them " picturesque "). And indeed, the whole house, in its larger aspect, is historically flavored: it is in an accepted " style," Colonial or English-cottage or Spanish or what not. Our living, our tool-work, our transportation, our communication, are new; but we cling to, or are caught in, old houses, inefficient, stylistically smelling of the past.

We sometimes wonder why our dwelling-place couldn't have been conceived and built as cleanly, as efficiently — and as beautifully — as

New factory forms, gaining from new materials and methods of construction, and from machine-mindedness. Laboratory building in a group designed by Norman-Bel Geddes for the Toledo Scale Company, Toledo, Ohio. Concrete and glass construction with cantilevered floors. The corner projections designed to eliminate glare from the rounded glass corners.

our automobile: *that* has just the combination of mechanical efficiency and comfort, of cleanliness and pleasurable brightness, of mechanically perfect shelter and of beauty out of proportioning and structure, that we should relish in a house. But we never liked to embarrass the architects by asking.

Let us not infer hastily that *all* architecture today is like that. As a matter of fact I leave my historic dwelling-house and ride into town to work in a building that is a well-nigh perfect business-machine. It is simply a series of cubicles piled thirty stories high, with efficient communication lanes between offices and to the street: electric elevators up and down, scientifically calculated halls and aisles; steel frame sheathed with baked clay; concrete floors, tile-and-plaster walls, metal doors and window-frames; plumbing, central heat, central vacuum-cleaning, electric lights. And the architects have mercifully left out all Gothic, Greek, and Baroque ornament; only around the main doorway, and in the elevator grills, is there any thrust toward decoration, and here there is something not unpleasing and quite appropriate to the uprightness and sheerness of the building, to its machine aspect.

This business building brings us back to civilization and to what is coming after: to civilization because in use, as a business building, it belongs to the culmination of the commercial state; and to what may come after, because here is a new sort of universality, a stripping clear of all the historic styles, a mode of structure so elemental that it is the obvious thing that a landlord puts up in Berlin or Panama or Tokio, if he wants extensive space enclosed. And indeed, my historic house and my machine-age office seem to me like the closing of the last chapter in the story of the styles of civilized architecture, as of the civil state, and at the same time the opening page of a world architecture and a world-slope of thought and action.

The record of man's progress through savagery, barbarism, and civilization is to be read most vividly in his architecture, in his solutions of the problems of *shelter:* his achievements, his glorious flights, are memo-

Old architectural forms became meaningless when this beehive problem was met. A business building in New York, by Ely Jacques Kahn.
[Sigurd Fischer, photo]

rialized for all time in buildings; and hardly less permanently, his lies and evasions. Aye! there is a sad truth in that, almost terrifying. Architecture, good or bad, is inescapable; its revealment of the soul of those who conceived and built it, inevitable. It puts on record, indestructibly, the spiritual or material habit of mind, the originality or timidity, the daring creativeness or the cringing imitativeness, of architect, of owner, of the age. The painting or sculpture of the same time may be put away if its superficiality or falsity condemns it; the building remains inescapable, till its usefulness is completely exhausted.  In the Parthenon or in Rheims Cathedral there is an immortal reminder of the stirring flights of the human spirit.  But the Paris Opera, the New York Public Library and the Reichstag building may achieve as great longevity and flaunt their weakness, vulgarity, and superficial decorativeness almost to time's end.  One who has come to read great faults in nineteenth century civilization, and to recognize the signs of architectural dishonesty in buildings, may find the showier streets of Paris or London or Rome a distressing confession; and almost any home suburb a discouraging reminder of weakness.

And yet, the world over, wherever imperialism and nationalism have come to highest expression (and therefore nearest to an end) — in western Europe or the United States or Japan — the beginnings of a consciously different world architecture are apparent, not only in business skyscrapers and factories, but in homes, studios, schools, even churches. While reflecting faithfully the old age, the building art heralds the new. And the most notable fact — when one assembles all the evidences of the new architecture — is that it has freed itself of every trace of the styles expressing civilization.  Outside the one background chapter of history, and a very few pictures introduced for purposes of contrast, you will find in all the 389 illustrations in this book not a single Greek column or Gothic buttress or Romanesque portal or English-Palladian window; not because I made exclusion of historic elements a basis of choice, but simply because buildings grown organically out of machine-age materials and methods of structure, out of modern needs and modern living, and out of honest creativeness, arrive free of stolen trappings.  Moreover, it seems to me that the capabilities of the new mode are so broad, the invention so fundamental, that for the first time humanity touches on an architecture that may conceivably be for all the world, for all types of building, not merely for a nation, or for churches alone, or palaces or temples.

" And even churches . . ." The *Stahlkirche* at Cologne. Professor Otto Bartning, Berlin, architect. [From *Die Stahlkirche,* by Dr. Paul Girkan]

In the chapters that follow you will find that I spread forth in pictures the most significant evidences I have been able to gather of the beginnings of the new art of building; and that, describing them, I state definitely my belief: (1) that a new mode *is* established, constituting an architectural revolution more fundamental than any in seven centuries; (2) that the principles and methods underlying are nearer to universal than any that have previously governed building art, and that, therefore, this is

Canvas and wood, used in accord with "the feel of the desert country," give rise to unorthodox but interesting architectural forms.  The camp of Frank Lloyd Wright in Arizona.
Frank Lloyd Wright, architect.

the beginning of a world-slope, not merely a racial or national phase; and (3) that nothing to be accomplished hereafter in the "historic" styles known to civilization will really matter — not even a Cathedral of St. John the Divine or the next Greek Lincoln Memorial.  (I except those minor modes, peasant cottage building, etc., that are so fundamental to the soil that honesty ever brightens them.)

You have talked, you tell me, to one hundred practising architects, and ninety-nine of them profess faith still in revival or adaptation of the "accepted" styles, or in what they call Eclecticism — appropriate "choosing" from the past.  You ask me, then, why I speak so positively about a different architecture, and particularly about the passing of historic styles; for this is a thing architects should be wise about if anything.  Quite undismayed, I shall answer you in three ways.  First, the devoted (shall we say enslaved?) professional in any art or activity is the last man to get a world perspective on his work: he is in a groove, he is bound by traditions, rules, ethics, and he is too busy on detail to relate his profession to new world currents; he has to be blasted out of his rut, out of his conceit and his ignorance, every so often, by social cataclysms or revolutions in thinking, or loss of his job. As a matter of fact, the new budding architecture of today has arrived less through the architects than through engineers, the masters of the machine which is at the heart of the social revolution. Second, when you found even *one* architect in the hundred committed to an art of building wholly different from civilized styles, you had before you a striking proof of progress; for ten years ago you would have had to run through a thousand before encountering a man who would dare profess a vision beyond Neo-Classic, Gothic, or Beaux-Arts. And third, I answer that not all the clinging to what was " Art " or " Beauty " yesterday can stay the human spirit from going on to new conceptions and new forms when life is moving on. And I have sought where youth is dreaming, where the spirit is aroused, where disillusionment with the old has already given place to imaginative speculation and experimentation and the poetry of daring; among those who hold that it is within the power of the human soul to create, to mould living, to shape new functions to new forms of beauty. There I have found — I believe — architecture that speaks, that answers to an æsthetic need of the human spirit, as unmistakably, as appropriately as did the Greek or the Byzantine or the Gothic.

Because the new architecture is so different, because in practice so little of it can be seen in any one place, as compared with manifestations of the old, I suggest that the reader glance rapidly through all the illustrations in the book, before continuing with the text. I hope that he will come back to the reading with the sense of certain qualities consistently achieved: geometric simplicity; absolute honesty in the use of materials and " motives "; total independence from known styles of decoration; a new massiveness and precision; clean lines, hard edges, sanitary smoothness; resistless *drive*. A very few creative designers have entered into a second phase of the new building: beyond the simplification, the honesty and the massiveness, they arrive at new modes of ornamentation, appropriate to our age — and the illustrations are chosen with that further advance in mind.

UPON the hill above Stuttgart is a village — a suburban development might better suggest its dependency upon the city — wherein all the buildings breathe a strange geometric unity.  In the entire group, houses and apartments, there is not a shred of applied ornament, and not a column or arch or gable that can be marked as inheritance from a " style " of the past.  The walls rise beautifully bold and clear.  They have windows and doors in them, of course; but the stripping away of all the other common impedimenta — pilasters, cornices, ornamented window-frames, cartouches, brackets, fanlights, mouldings, etc., etc. — permits the building itself to stand out startlingly clear, with clean-cut outlines and great reposeful areas of unbroken surface.  There is the peace of simplicity here, the fundamental beauty of sculptural proportioning, the stirring pleasure of masses and directions manipulated boldly and honestly for abstract formal values.

As for the windows, where they occur they are large, seldom broken into small panes, disposed for fundamental compositional effect; and above all, bespeaking generous light and air within.  (Some of them seem to work with the simple ingenuity of the glasses in your motor car, with a precision and a responsiveness seldom known in mere house-windows.)  There isn't a sloping roof in all the suburb — partly, no doubt, a point related to some new æsthetic of machine-square cubes and planes, but also indication of a conviction that in living the open life we should make more of the tops of our houses.  There are porches, decks, terraces, bespeaking purpose to profit by outdoor living space: sun-traps, shaded verandas, sheltered sleeping quarters, air-baths, spaces half garden and half sitting-room.  If there is anything that can be marked as consciously added to the architecture for decorative effect, it is to be found in the

Houses in the Weissenhof suburb, Stuttgart, Germany. The one above by Walter Gropius. Below, house at left, by Mies van der Rohe; at back, by Gropius; at right, by J. J. P. Oud.

manipulation of railings, awning supports, and ladders (a little flavor of steamship design, there is here), or very rarely a pergola or decorative lamp.

Honesty, openness, economy, brightness, direct thinking, faith in a new life, consideration for one's neighbors, these breathe in the very air of this experimental " development," projected consciously to give the dreamers of new worlds opportunity to crystallize their ideas in concrete and glass and metal.

The skyscrapers of New York tower higher and ever higher, until the mid-city has the aspect of mighty honeycombed cliffs, deep-cleft with canyon-streets. Huge masses of steel, stone, and glass are thrown skyward, signalizing the indomitable push and the irresistible lift of the creative human spirit at work. These terraced crags, these monumental up-ended pigeon-cotes, these soaring pylons and towers and piers, overwhelm us with their expression of daring, of lawlessness, of inspiration. This is at once a new Babel and a City Divine. By day it thrills us with its stupendous engineering feats, its aspiring finials, its stirring masses and directions and outlines; by night it enchants with the loveliness of amber lights patterned on huge screens hanging from the sky, or with a tower of flame or an opalescent glow of color projected on gigantic walls.

At times the layman sees the skyscraper naked — for the structure itself is in the standing steel skeleton and the monolithic floors. The metal posts rise; the cross-beams are set in; and then the building stands, stone floor above stone floor, with only posts between — and the wise ones know that a new architecture has been born, not an art of piling up masonry, and only secondarily a thing of walls: an architecture of work-floors and living-floors suspended in air. A sheath-like envelope of glass and terra cotta or metal or brick is hung on the skeleton; and in its shaping, its design, the architect expresses (or blankets, denies) the power, the lift, the inspiration.

The straight new skyscrapers, the expressive ones, rise among many others wherein the height is dwarfed, the daring engineering squeezed

A typical New York crag-like skyscraper. Drawing for the Western Union Telegraph Building, by Voorhees, Gmelin & Walker. The exterior shell is of varied shades of brick, affording a carefully calculated effect of colorfulness.

into old stylistic envelopes, the lines weakened, the stirring proportions masked. But even the chaos of the jumbled good and bad is exciting: the early evasions and excuses form a frame for the later jutting crags and gloriously towering towers. And indeed, this whole, this patched-together design of the stirringly new and the weakened new, expresses an unparalleled up-push of human energy, an epic plundering of light and space, a beehive activity and an ant-heap concentration.

The accented lines of the houses in the Weissenhof suburb are horizontal; and one is tempted to frame the thought, " the new architecture is horizontal." But the soaring skyscrapers of New York give the lie to that generalization. They rise up with emphasis on the long hard edge, on the sculptural treatment of pylons and vertical ribs. The primary " motive " is the repeated pier-line, the chief relieving factor the occasional terrace. What the student may note, however — even so early in his experience of the new building — is that the American architects and engineers are capitalizing elemental mass, are piling up the same cubes, making the total design as geometric, as clean-lined, as machine-economical, as the builders of the elemental Stuttgart houses. The values of the reposeful, horizontal-accent home buildings are essentially an out-growth of a faith in those fundamentals so emphasized in the recent honest skyscrapers; are similarly a courageously honest answering to a new economic problem. In the one case the architect has arrived at a simple dwelling-machine, rationally contrived, close to the earth; in the other case, at a multiple business-machine, true to materials and to commercial purposes, upshouldering bulkily, defying the old laws of masonry construction.

The evidence of the skyscraper may be read in Chicago as well as New York, in Detroit or St. Louis or Cleveland or Seattle. But if we were to seek in America the nearest approach to the Stuttgart achievement, we should have to go to California. In two ways that state has claimed the attention of artists and students who look toward a revolution in house building. Inheritors of an old world style, from Spain

Trying to redeem the chaos of commercial New York. Below, a photograph looking into Wall Street from the air [by the Fairchild Aerial Surveys]. Above, a drawing by Chester B. Price showing, at right, the vertical accent of the new Irving Trust Company-One Wall Street Building; wherein the architects, Voorhees, Gmelin & Walker, try to establish the only uniformity of expression possible: a vertical one. [Copyright photos by courtesy of the Irving Trust Company]

through Mexico, a style long ago brought into agreement with the soil and the climate by native Amerindian and Spanish-settler adaptation, the Californian architects started on a course of simplification and rationalization; until, within the decade, one has been able to see the phenomenon of hundreds of houses attractively honest and simple, though born of an historic impulse: whittled down to a basic structure and pattern that would appear revolutionary and " new " if we did not recollect the " backward evolutionary " process behind it.    And indeed a few — a very few — of the houses in " the California style " could be set down in the Weissenhof group and seem to belong to the geometric pattern and honest modern expressiveness there.    A great many more illustrate the phenomenon of a Renaissance mode stripped back to elemental massing and rational functioning, with an unmistakable flavor lingering from the original historic source.    In general these too (though less significant to us just here) are logical house-machines, with a simple, direct beauty that marks them as tolerably of their place and of their time.

In California, again, are the latest achievements of Frank Lloyd Wright, the most important of radical architects in the world today: the rebel and the *bête noire* to all the comfortably conservative, Beaux-Arts-influenced, organized professionals in America, and something of a god to youthful Germany, youthful Japan, to Holland, to Russia — even to a few in his own America.    But not to put him ahead of the story, let us only pause to note that Wright has done more than any other individual to demonstrate that new methods and new philosophies of building have already displaced the old, wherever man has come to spiritual honesty and creative inspiration; and that in California he has recently built houses that answer boldly and stirringly the challenge of the new age.    You may mark some of these buildings as merely pleasingly simple, colorful, and logical, with more of decorative feeling than the typically " stripped " architecture of the associated Stuttgart designers or the New York engineers — but with no flavor of the past in the ornamentation. If you would read the entire record of Wright's thirty years of insur-

Examples of the "Californian Style" house. At top, cottage in Santa Barbara, by
Reginald D. Johnson. Middle, the Nelson house in Rancho Santa Fe, by Lilian
J. Rice. At bottom, a house in Carpenteria, by Reginald D. Johnson. [Top photo
by Jessie Tarbox Beals, bottom by J. Walter Collinge; by courtesy of Plans and
Planting Committee of the Santa Barbara Community Arts Association]

The Millard house, Pasadena, California.   An example of design by Frank Lloyd
Wright in pre-cast concrete slabs.   [1923]

gency, you would have to see isolated buildings from New York to Japan, with special attention to the group of his early works in the Chicago neighborhood (where he was pupil and helper to that earliest and most prophetic of the pioneers, Louis Sullivan); pause in Wisconsin; and then spend time with the several latest manifestations of his genius in the Far West.   In the suburbs of Chicago, incidentally, you will find his houses largely of wood and stucco, with long decorative roof-lines and horizontally accented masses; whereas the later houses are based solidly on the values that grow out of concrete: an elementally simple type of building expressing the heaviness and massiveness of poured concrete, and a more

Typical Viennese stylization. The Stoclet mansion in Brussels, by
Joseph Hoffmann. [By courtesy of *l'Architecte*, Paris]

open, colorful, and varied type born of the use of pre-cast concrete slabs.
In all three types the simply proportioned forms are enriched with an idiomatic ornamental language that is Wright's own, freshly invented.

In Vienna, and out where the Viennese Secession architects have
worked, there are perhaps the *smartest* examples of Modernism thus far
achieved. The Viennese seem to have made elegance a first test of success in revolting from earlier stodginess and academicism. They started
their insurgency without the Americans' passion for clean engineering;
and while they had to go back to simplified forms and clear-cut lines to
find a new starting-point, they were animated most by the desire to

The Austrian Pavilion at the Cologne Exposition, 1914.   Joseph Hoffmann, architect.

create a surface style.  *Stylization* has been their watchword, and you may read of their success in the grace, the smartness, and the restrained richness of their decorative touch.  Here are the less austere buildings of insurgents who feared bareness a little, who temper the bold mass and the naked line, who delicately relieve simplicity with exquisite touches of color, with precise outlining of masses, with sensuously lovely all-over patterns.  In Vienna — one of the world centres of Modernist practice and teaching — one thus sees a distinctive, stylistic, and exceptionally alluring phase of the new world building.

As one travels day after day, with eyes alert for evidences of an emerg-

School at Celle, Germany. Otto Haesler, architect. [By courtesy of *l'Architecte*, Paris]

ing twentieth century architecture, Germany affords more examples than any other country. The Weissenhof suburb at Stuttgart is merely the most concentrated group, the outstanding object-lesson; one finds the spirit of progressivism, of change, equally at work at Frankfort or Cologne or Düsseldorf, in Hamburg, Berlin, Dessau, and Dresden. Less brilliant, less striking than some of the Austrian, Dutch, and American manifestations, one feels, nevertheless, that the German evidence goes deeper, that Modernism here is no longer the radical thing, the wild experiment outlawed and ridiculed by the entrenched conservatives, the powerful professionals, but rather the new normal thing, of the very fibre of the nation. The honesty of construction, the massive forms, the confessed functioning, seem to set well with the forthright German nature, the Teutonic solidity of character. Anyway, you may see the challenge of the new architecture raised in every residential suburb from Breslau to the Rhine towns, and in department stores, schools, and apartments in every city.

Then let us imagine ourselves dropped down in a city in Holland. Immediately the new architecture asserts its presence — one or two Modernist buildings in the average downtown block, and entire suburbs of cliff-like apartment buildings or of box-like workingmen's homes. These Dutch suburban "developments" are the strangest to unaccustomed eyes: whole towns that look like play-patterns of geometric toy-blocks, or quarter-mile-long apartment façades, with the queerest jutting balconies, and interminable bands of windows, and extraordinary contrasting textures of brick and colored tile. It mostly has a catching decorative value too, though more "mannered," perhaps, than the German or American, more self-consciously different from the old styles of building. Here in Holland more than anywhere else Modernism has full official sanction, so that the schools we see are direct and simple agglomerations of recitation rooms, assembly halls, and play spaces (without reference to Renaissance palaces or the Paris Opera or picturesque fortresses), the police stations and state railway stations are factory-sheer, and municipal housing groups are designed on rational human beehive forms. Long ago there was in this tiny kingdom a pioneer whose name you will find bracketed often with Louis Sullivan's: H. P. Berlage. He succeeded in corrupting the younger generation of students, in leading them away from the fold of orthodoxy and imitation, more quickly and more thoroughly than any radical leader in any other country. And so for nearly a decade — until Germany actively resumed building and overtook her two or three years ago — Holland showed the most Modernistic face to the world of any of the nations. And for a new architecture with a most pronounced national or racial flavor you must even today go to the Dutch cities.

There is wide-spread evidence, then, a far-scattered concrete achievement in the new modes: in Germany and Austria (and one may add Czecho-Slovakia and that part of Switzerland influenced directly by Germany); in all the big American cities, and in some Middle Western and Californian suburbs; in Holland. These are the main scenes of a physical change that is apparent even to the casual eye. Russia is experimenting, even wildly, though the evidence that is available, in photographs, is less convincing. On the border-line, committed already

School at Hilversum, Holland, by Willem Dudok

to the new mode, one might say, but tempering the bareness of it, the simplicity, with some native idioms and traditional methods, are the Scandinavian countries. One knows the pleasantly simple flavor of that northern building, the Swedish particularly; and out of faraway Finland came one of the most brilliant of the radicals working in America today, a man already known throughout Europe as a leader: Eliel Saarinen.

And why is there no weighty evidence from France? As early as 1925, Paris spread out the buildings of the Exposition of Decorative Arts, avowedly to bring to focus contemporary French effort outside the traditional styles — and to bring world Modernism into agreement with the graceful French talent. But that affair, and sporadic outcroppings here and there, early and late, have only gone to show that outside a few inspired engineers and one or two imported radical architects, the impotent Beaux-Arts men still control France. Even the Exposition proved the French to be adapters of the Viennese thing, softening down the squared masses into sweeter and more graceful forms — with the sensuous delicacy of the Viennese touch a little spread toward the luxurious and grandiose. But occasional shop-fronts in Paris or Cannes are colorfully intriguing and assiduously new; and interior decoration of a lush Modernistic sort is coming to be known as Parisian.

In thus spreading a preliminary picture of the outstanding phases, I have set down a rough sketch of the geography of modern architecture. I might have chosen to tell the whole story by nations (though the German, American, and Dutch chapters would then be out of all proportion to some others — and the British hardly a page); but the internationalism of the new spirit, the universality of the creeping change, the creativeness that defies boundaries, seem to forbid a too strict nationalistic alignment. Rather our approach may be profitable if we proceed at first chronologically, from historical background to earliest emerging experiments, on to the first striking machine-age achievements, and then to the typical modern answers to the use-problems of the new age: in skyscraper business building, in factory, in a different sort of home.

We have caught a glimpse, outwardly, of a new architectural expression, have a bird's-eye view of a changing world and the first outcroppings of a new building art. Before accepting it, or analysing it, let us plunge into a consideration of the past.

Corridor in exposition building, Cologne. Adolf Abel, architect

# CHAPTER II

## *THE PAST AND ITS SLAVES*

WHEN those most spectacular and most vociferous of the Modernists known as Dadaists suggested, some years ago, that it would be beneficial to mankind, and favorable to the development of a truly modern art, if all the museums were burned, they did not suggest destroying all the cities of the past as a method of stimulating a modern architecture. And yet among conservative commentators a belief persists that "the radicals" want an absolute separation from the past; want architectural students kept ignorant of history; desire that the world's heritage of stored wisdom and contrived beauty shall be wiped out.

As a matter of fact, history is today affording to the architectural Modernists their chief solace and prop. From the monuments of the far past, rightly read, they are able to confound the pretensions of the Eclectics and to hearten themselves for the slowness of their own gains. They find that the trouble with history was the way in which late nineteenth and early twentieth century historians had distorted it, suppressing, overemphasizing, obscuring the total view by piece-meal enthusiasms. (One of the most salutary signs of contemporary cultural

progress — in spite of those who cry "superficial" and "emotional" —
is the prevalence of bird's-eye view outlines and dramatized "stories"
of every subject important to man's happiness and progress.    From
*The Story of Mankind* and *The Outline of History* to the full-view ac-
counts of religion, the arts, the occupations, and professions of humankind, this is an indication of a great desire for broader understanding, for
world outlook.)    Architecture was being written about, and taught, as
if it were exclusively a collection of decorative styles.    Architectural
history was peculiar, moreover, in that writers treated it as if creatively
it were complete: all styles had been invented, pigeon-holed, coded, and
the architectural student simply was told that he could reach into one
pigeon-hole or another for the decorative garment that seemed likely to
drape over a new structure with least twisting of its codified elements.
Undue importance was put on nineteenth century developments, particularly on certain phases of re-warmed "Renaissance" — most particularly the French phase.    Shadows of shadows were analysed as if they
were the real thing.

I have not yet encountered any bird's-eye "story" of architecture
from the modern view-point, though I hope that somewhere a just one
is being written, an account giving due proportion to what is creative
and what is imitative or merely ornamental.    But I have talked with
"radical" architects in many countries, and I know that they are progressing with constant reference to history; nay, fortified with the
certain belief that they have struck back to principles that underlay the
art in the periods of glorious building.    And they are sure that they
have escaped from a harmful perversion in turning their attention to the
great *structural* periods instead of remaining bound to Renaissance systems of façade-study.

Now I believe so strongly that the only safe departure-point for the
revolutionary is a knowledge of what is revolted from, that I want to
take even my readers back for a brief excursion into history: for how else
are we going to come at this thing intelligently, understandingly?    I want

Unity Temple, Chicago.  Frank Lloyd Wright, architect.  [1907].  Honesty, in outward forms and in expressiveness of materials: an example of organic as against " arranged " architecture.

to remind them of the great ages of building, in briefest summary; and then to point out the immediate contrast between Eclectic practice, at the recent end of historical endeavor, and the thing we have been studying under the vague name of " The New World Architecture "; and perhaps to establish certain likenesses of aim in the Moderns and in creative builders of primitive times, of early Greece, of Romanesque Christianity, and early Gothic.

As a preliminary we shall need to inquire just what is the thing we are studying, what is essentially architecture.  Shelter, of course, is the fundamental reason for the existence of the art.  Thus architecture is rooted in the material necessities of humankind as no other major art is: in that first economic prerequisite to cultural or spiritual advance, the gaining of food, clothing, shelter.  How the fundamental forms of the walls and the roof they support changed through thirty centuries of differing needs, new inventiveness, and varying abundance or scarcity of wood and stone, constitutes the story of the art; but certain principles of structure remain the same wherever roofs are lifted.  First, that *the building shall be an organism*.  Good building is structurally unified and expressive; when ornamentation or manipulated composition or any other sort of incrustation becomes more important than the structural truth that makes the building stand up, then one has come to a weak period in the story of architecture.

Claude Bragdon makes an illuminating distinction between two general sorts of architecture in the world: *organic* and *arranged*. In creative eras the architects never forgot the organism that grew out of foundations laid out to use, and out of expressing the forms and directions of the supporting and supported members; whereas in eras neglectful of the truths of the organism, architects artificially arranged walls over the skeleton structure, masking it with compositions ornamental or showy on their own account. The architecture as seen by the eye became an illustration of something different from the building itself. To the sort that Bragdon calls arranged architecture, others have given the name *manipulated* architecture. Still others have called it *stage-setting* architecture. At any rate, let us begin by remembering that a false front laid up against hidden supports and roof is not a manifestation of the building art; the supports and roof are the main thing.

The impulse to construct is basic to human nature, and no man should practise architecture unless he feels the inherent excitement of building, a sort of soul-pull toward structural expression. In the great eras only a man who had pushed to the top by devotion and service became master-builder: the one in whom the impulse toward construction was strong, and in whom the urge to self-expression in building was dominant. (There were no schools of architecture to attract "likely" boys to a dignified calling, then.) To such a one the blocked-out foundations afford a soul-satisfaction, the naked rising pillars are thrilling, the clean-proportioned wall is more stirringly beautiful than all the stylistic ornament ever arranged on paper and transferred to stone or wood or glass. For the foundations, supports, and walls are essential to the building art, whereas the reasoned façade decoratively masking those elements is only a secondary thing, the product of knowledge, of taste, dead of emotion.

The return to *beginning* with fundamentals. Model for the massing of a theatre, by Joseph Urban. [See also the drawing by Hugh Ferriss at the head of Chapter I]

If we call the setting-up of supports and roof " engineering," then we may say that only that ornament or decoration is alive which grows out of the engineering. It grows out of the constructor's imagination and inner vision and love, too; but it is valid to the beholder only if at least reflectively structural. Frame and garment are essentially one. What determines the character of the building is thus not the ornament, but rather the massing, the proportioning, the use of materials according to their virtues, and a certain rhythmic play over all these things.

Without pausing to inquire more deeply into the æsthetics of the matter, so early in our journey, it is relevant to note that any truly modern statement about architectural theory will begin with those elements, will emphasize *massing,* including proportion, profile, volume-relationship and contour (all essentially sculptural values). When one has got clear this primary fact (so long obscured by over-study of the encrusted elements), one may go on to the sequential fact that volumes, masses, mean surfaces; and, again, that on the flat, the proportioning and rhythmical distribution of the structural elements are the first assets toward decorativeness. Beyond all this, of course, is the totality, the indefinable thing called " architectural form," the sum of all the material and seeable elements, stamped with the quality or beauty or significance that is the individual designer's own unexplainable contribution. With so much and no more notice of the fact that there is a current revolution as regards the æsthetics of building, let us turn to our historical summary.

IF WE adopt the method of structure as first guide, we may go direct to the Greeks; for the Egyptians, though they had worked with the system of post-and-lintel construction that came to perfection in Greece, had done so clumsily, heavily, with the stamp of slave-mind and slave-labor on all building. There is very little, aside from the engineering of the pyramids, to give the student pause; the rest is largely variation in ornament.

But Greek builders picked up that most elementary of structural principles, a beam spanning space by virtue of support in two posts, and elaborated it into one of the great, simple, beautiful architectures of the world. In that few hundred years of reason, of love of beauty for its own sake, of emotional release tempered by intellectual restraint, of a new experiment in free living, the post was refined into pillars so *right* that they have been standard structural elements in more than half of the twenty-odd centuries since. (If, like all rigidly standardized things, they have become a curse in the end, we need not hold that against the inventors.)

In the two drawings of Greek temples one sees the system brought to flower. In the one, every stone is indicated, and we may note how close to the fundamental principle the builders have stayed — lintel across

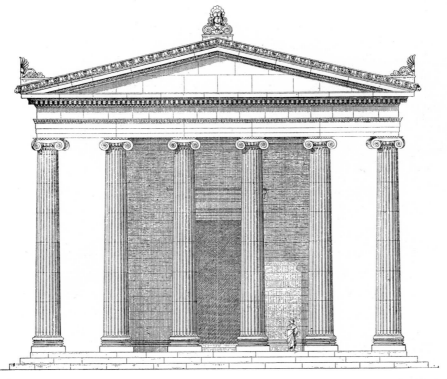

Ionic Temple. [This and the next three illustrations are from *Geschichte der Architektur*, by Wilhelm Lübke]

two posts, and then merely stone on stone — in spite of restrained and expressive ornament at a few transitional points. One might read into this essentially simple building (as distinguished from Roman arched and decorated structures, or Gothic vaulted and buttressed ones) a reflection of the clarity, poise, and ease of the Greek mind and life. Vitality and strength are there, generously, but subjected to æsthetic discipline and spiritual restraint.

A reconstruction of the Parthenon, after F. Thiersch

The Parthenon is generally accepted as the masterpiece of Greek building art, as a summary of the glories of elaborated pillar-and-lintel architecture. To some it seems to come a shade after the height had been reached, at a moment when applied ornament had begun to encroach a little, where only functional decoration had existed before. But if the first sign of the decadence was here — and the elaborately ornamental Corinthian mode was to follow very shortly — still this was a work of almost primitive strength, of magnificent mass and of masterly proportioning. The strong lift of the columns and the solid weight of the entablature have more to do with the " rhythm " or " form " of the building than has the sculpture or other frankly decorative features. There is truly profound rhythm, depth on depth of formal relationship: inexhaustible beauty. The building, we are now told, was once rich with colors — and thus quite unlike the Neo-Classicist sentimental visions of a white purity in all Classicism.

Even the tyro in the architectural field notes easily certain of the virtues in these Greek temples: how the long low steps lead the eye in a perfect transition from ground to structure, affording a sense of the building being firmly rooted and yet a separate growth; how the repeated full, round columns initiate the rhythm, how the entablature is held clear and solid, expressing the old function of the lintel, declaring the weight that rests on the columns, how the decorative flowering occurs at the top.

But deeper students, architects and critics, have brought to notice certain less obvious virtues and refinements. They point out how logical is the working out of the elementary pillar-and-lintel system into this vitally expressive composition of columns and entablature, externalizing in beautiful relationships the internal forces of support and down-pressing weight. They have even gone beyond the bounds of æsthetics, finding in the uplifting strength of the supporting members and the down-bearing mass of the supported bodies a spiritual and moral illustration of the Greek conception of life: the belief that stress and strain, common to any aspiring effort of mankind, if met with reason, fortitude, and understanding, result in a beautiful poise, a disciplined happiness. The columns rise upward in constant aspiration toward higher truth, toward perfection, to meet the bearing-down force of fate, calm, level, restraining, in order that there may be finality. And in this eternal balance of aspiration and restraint, in the poise of the magnificent reach brought under spiritual control, there is beauty. (Personally I do not believe that such direct symbolism or " lesson " is ever in the mind of the great creative artist; though he is seldom without vague consciousness of larger spiritual and social implications of his work.)

Other and more architectural refinements are brought to our attention by less moralistic critics: the way in which the fluting of the columns lightens the surfaces of the shafts, even while the direction of the grooving reinforces the sense of support; the perfection of the mouldings, each emphasizing structure, each filling a compositional need in softening the transition from one main mass to another even while adding to the sense of firmness, each beautiful on its own account; and the absolute rightness of the column-unit, the perfect unity of Doric shaft, cap, and "abacus," or of the Ionic base, shaft, and scroll-capital. (It is hardly possible that these are the only " perfect " solutions of the problem of free-standing supports, as some commentators declare, the only refinements of the post that ever will be characterized by so much of incidental and contributory beauty. It is rather that this was the only time in history that the problem of direct upright support was met by a creative and reasoning people who were also beauty loving and free minded — the Egyptians were slaves to the idea of building for death, not life.) Still other and subtler refinements have been discovered in the slightly uneven spacing between the columns, and the slightly curved " straight " fronts: both adjustments to correct optical defects of the human eye.

All this grew up as the flowering of that system of building that begins with a cross-bar set over two posts. The Moderns turn to this architecture of the Greeks for inspiration, for renewal of their belief in the simple, the direct, the logical thing as the beautiful thing — for confirmation of their faith that expressive form will flower where the passionate artist bases his designing on function and material and honest thinking. Beyond this, too, the new world architect feels an affinity for the Greeks: modern intense life, machine-age materials, and mechanical efficiency find the temples understandable and appealing in the new time. There is something in the audacity of the massive building, the long naked line, the sheer wall, that speaks spiritually to the artist of today. There is a heaviness tempered by absolute precision. There is too an *openness:* the Greeks built for the eye looking from without, and probably — for all we know — skimped the interiors; and now again humankind is escaping from the secretive hiding-away and mystery of the Dark and Middle Ages; and from the typical interior-decorator styles that followed with the half-revolution known as the Renaissance.

Roman architecture is notable for magnificent engineering feats, for roofing vast spaces, for constructing the massive bowls of theatres and amphitheatres, for daring aqueducts and bridges; but for the rest it is rather empty, rhetorical, and uncreative. What is finest in it is the structural use of the arch. Here is the world's second great system of building, of making a solid section of wall stand over an opening, and (with arch elaborated to vault) of making a roof stand over a void. The Romans had the arch from the Etruscans, who had inherited it from a still earlier civilization. But it was Rome that put the invention to work in a grand way.

Where the lintel over two posts had afforded a system of direct support to the down-bearing weight of wood or masonry, the arch brought in a more complicated method of *spreading* the weight of laid-up stone. The push was no longer directly downward, but was carried partially as a side-thrust into the masses of masonry on each side of the arched opening.

In constructing huge buildings with walls held up by story on story of arches, and in vaulting, and finally in raising great domes over immense spaces, the Romans exhibited a skill that stirs our emotions when we encounter the ruins of their structures today. The bewildering multiplication of arches that raised the immense bowl of the Colosseum, the daring piling-up of domed masonry that is the Pantheon, the great reach of the baldly engineered *Pont du Gard*, and the stupendous roofed spaces in the public baths — these things argue constructive genius, and illustrate courageous pushing of the arch-element to stupendous feats.

But the virtues of strictly Roman building almost end with the engineering. Over their structures the Romans put an ornamental envelope, seldom structurally true, often bombastic — and borrowed at that. They took Greek decorative forms, columns and cornices and entablatures, and stuck them on their buildings, inside and out, as ornament. They split the beautiful Greek columns in half and made them functionally useless. Often the fine proportions of the logically engineered building shone through the veneer of elaborate clothing; and a naked but

A reconstruction of the Colosseum

rhythmic engineering triumph like the *Pont du Gard* must always have been impressive.  But unfortunately it is the commoner envelope that has come to be known — and copied — in later ages as Roman architecture (just as the showiest element of any art or job is likely to mould the world's memory of it).

In the picture of the Colosseum you may see the cloaking process in its simplest and easiest understood form.  The breaking of the wall into

A reconstruction of the Baths of Diocletian in Rome

four bands is honest enough, and the superimposed rows of arched openings are logical and functionally decorative. But the engaged columns
are structurally unnecessary, are mere trimming — would never have
been there if the Romans had not seen columns on Greek temples and
admired them as " artistic." If the Colosseum needed any final touch
of ornament, beyond the rhythm growing out of structure, the Romans
were not creative enough to originate it in a language of their own.
They borrowed from the supreme artists of the time before them.

But that was only the beginning. In this second picture you may see
how the great engineering, still impressive in the Colosseum, soon became
less important than the superficial " stylistic " garment. If we may
believe in any of the accepted reconstructions, the Forum of a Roman
city was a riot of extravagantly decorated structures, rich with colored
marbles, statues, mosaics, gilt, and decadent Greek ornament; and the

vulgarest display of surface grandeur in the history of the world.    For architecture became elaborate without being honest, proud without noble birth.    If we return to our first-chapter idea of art as an index to living, we have here further proof: for this is characteristically the architecture of boastful conquerors, of ruthless, unspiritual material domination: of the powerful out on a holiday.    It is transparently the architecture of great fighters and great lawyers.    Magnificent plan and engineering ingenuity, yes — and sometimes the prodigious proportions and daring function persist expressively (the Pantheon); but in general the Romans preferred to dress their magnificently flung-up walls with columns supporting nothing, with fragmentary entablatures, with meaningless panels and niches and garlands.    Architecture had become embellishment, not building; display, not living.

In the East the next great style, the Byzantine, took form; not a new type of structure, but utilizing the arch and the dome with a new surface originality.    And indeed if the Orient-derived richness which here came into service, in combination with Roman structural elements, had been adopted in Rome, instead of decadent Greek forms, there might have been a far different story of achitecture then and in all subsequent times. The Byzantine is an enriched architecture; that is, the features of it that count first to the eye are the gorgeous areas of color and intricate tracery and pattern.    If this encrustation be not directly opposed to structure, if it *follow reasonably* the lines and directions of the functioning members, it may seem inherent to the organism — and therefore the whole be logical and convincing.    Such architecture is enchanting rather than soul-stirring, sensuously lovely rather than deeply characterful; though in the type-example, Hagia Sophia in Constantinople, the magnificent reach of Roman engineering is combined with the gorgeous sheath of Oriental richness.

Still, this is not a new style of construction, but rather a known style adapted and re-clothed (some say under late Greek rather than either Roman or Oriental inventiveness).    The enrichment was such that

we all remember Byzantine as one of the enchantingly beautiful phases;
but it is seldom mentioned in the list of leading architectures: Greek,
Roman, Gothic, Renaissance. In that it is like the minor visual arts
that contributed so to its charm, that never get mentioned with painting, sculpture, and architecture: mosaic, enamelling, carving in fine

Diagrammatic view of an early Christian basilica.    [From
*l'Architecture Romane,* by Édouard Corroyer]

woods, metal-work. Somehow these arts seem too colorful, too iridescent, too pretty, to be structurally important — the consciousness is
caught by the surface, the intellect is drowned under the delight of the
senses, the deeper view is obscured by the opalescent haze. At any rate,
Byzantine — think of Venice to visualize it — remains in the memory,
if not in the histories, as something appealing, even ravishing, if not
quite sober and solid.

It was rather the Romanesque — based more directly on Roman
tradition — that brought back architecture of imposing massiveness,
naked vigor, and constructive daring. Much of the Romanesque, par-

A German church of the Twelfth Century, in Romanesque style.
[From Corroyer]

ticularly in the North, was meagre just where Byzantine was rich, in the decorative elements; but the style — whether one counts it more important as a prelude to Gothic or as an achievement in its own right — has striking virtues, and essentially honest ones, in its fine proportioning, its occasional effective play of rich doorway against a severe massive wall, and in its aspiring vaulted interiors. The Romanesque builders almost succeeded where the Romans had failed: working always with the round arch, they almost brought to flower a completed and combined-functional-and-ornamental architecture out of the arch form. Certainly they gained more of variety and decorativeness out of true arch and vault developments than did their predecessors — using columns, to be sure, but always at least as an echo of functional lines.

For my illustrations just here I have chosen not the great monuments, which are to be found scattered from Italy to England — where they are called " Norman " — but rather two churches that will indicate the carrying on of structural traditions from ancient Rome to twelfth century France: an " early Christian " basilica and a church that derives its expressive form from the arch motive in various combinations, with typical high vaulting.  In this last may be seen the spring-board from which the mediæval builders soared into Gothic.

Now Gothic is not strictly a new system of construction; but so imaginative, so daring, is its adaptation of an old principle, so amazingly different in the combined functional and decorative features that grew out of the variation, that it affords the most dramatic chapter in architectural history.

The structural distinction is this: As the Romanesque builders raised the naves of their churches higher and higher, it was necessary to strengthen increasingly the walls on each side, to resist the side-thrust of the vaulting.  (You remember the massiveness of Roman walls wherever the arch is used, and the general heaviness of Romanesque.) The Gothic builders discovered a way to distribute the pressure by carrying part of the thrust from the directly supporting wall to buttresses set at a distance from the central structure.  The " flying buttress " really lies at the heart of the secret of the apparent lightness and delicacy of Gothic construction.  Through these half-arches spanning space — which the unthinking accept merely as a decorative addition to the building — the weight and thrust are distributed to a number of supporting piles of masonry.  The interior of the cathedral seems merely a composition of slender piers and glass; but the effect is gained only because the down-bearing weight of the roof is carried off outside by a series of flying buttresses springing from masonry supports.  For instance, this

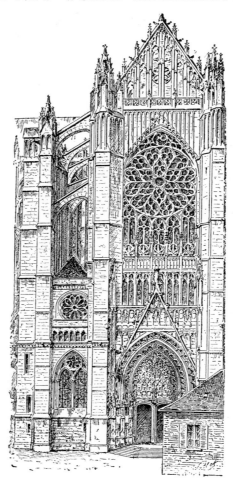

North façade of Beauvais Cathedral, showing lace-like main wall, and extra buttressing to sustain the roof thrust.  [From Corroyer]

lacy front of Beauvais Cathedral can exist only by virtue of the equilibrium of the main walls pushing out against the forest of buttresses across a considerable space; if the main walls supported the roof (which is 160 feet above the floor), they would necessarily be as massive and heavy as were those of Romanesque churches. The diagrammatic drawing opposite the bit of façade shows how the buttressing is accomplished. This is essentially an architecture of glorified props.

Diagram of a flying buttress. The pressure of the vault, at
right, acts outward against the nave wall, which is too
light to sustain it; the thrust is therefore carried through the
flying arch to the free-standing buttress at left.
[From Lübke]

Other features distinguish the Gothic style: the arch became pointed;
slender upright members were emphasized, giving a vertical accent in
place of the Classic horizontal one — the aspiring line passionately rising
heavenward, in place of the capping of the Greek column with the
restraining entablature; clustered columns took the place of solid individual shafts; and more complicated types of vaulting developed. But

it was the method of construction that conditioned all these things: the perfect organization of forces in equilibrium, the articulation of complex elements through which thrust and counter-thrust were balanced and supported; and this made possible the gorgeous flowering of intricate Gothic ornament.

There is no need here to recount the glories of mediæval architecture. We all know the great cathedrals — than which no buildings have ever been more exciting, more inspirational, more soul-stirring. That man should dare to raise aloft these skeletons of stone and walls of glass, seemingly so precariously poised on their lacy supports — that alone is thrilling. But then came the glory of color in the glass, adding richness to the already rich play of light and shade through nave and aisles and transept; and around the portals and on the buttress pinnacles and at the points of the arches, and over the altar, flowered the profuse sculptural ornament that magnificently dressed the frame. Some walls became great sheets of enchantingly colored glass; whole façades scintillated with a pattern of lace-like sculptured tracery, aisles took on the dim mysterious beauty of forest paths at dusk. And through it all the functional lines ran up, giving strength to the gorgeous fabric; proportioning was as carefully adjusted as of old, in Greece; honesty of intention conditioned all.

Or at least so it was while the Gothic impulse was fresh and strong. Later the proportions and the balance were lost, the vitality weakened, and ornament ran to excess. We have no time to explore the decadent phases, any more than the variations within the field of thirteenth and fourteenth century work; nor to note of secular Gothic more than that the pointed arch and the pinnacles and the distinctive ornament crept somewhat into the building of castles and guild halls and town gateways. But "vertical" architecture was doomed to go down to extinction when the amateurs and the artists of the Renaissance rediscovered classic styles.

It was the Renaissance scholars who gave the name "Gothic" to

Flying buttresses of the Cathedral at Rheims. [From *l'Architecture Gothique*, by Édouard Corroyer]

mediæval Christian architecture — in derision, as of something barbaric. And it was natural, as the leading thinkers of the time came out from under the domination of the Church, that the architecture of emotional aspiration and of mysticism should die along with many of the superstitions and naïve enthusiasms of the mediæval populace and clergy. For those short-sighted emancipators of the human spirit, the scholars of fifteenth and sixteenth century Italy, only a horizontal, coldly reasoned architecture would do. Gothic had made for mystery, complication, and passionate daring; now there must be revival of the calmness, logic, and unemotional thought of earlier eras.

The term " Renaissance " covers much: the early work included jewel-like palaces in Venice that borrowed enchantingly from the Byzantine, and massive palaces in Florence that took primary form from bald fortress-designs, and so on to a multiplicity of national variations, French, Spanish, English, etc. But the Renaissance created no new type of construction nor a new idiom in decoration. It built chiefly on the Roman arch system, and it borrowed Romanized Greek columns and cornices as ornamental units. It made these over into sometimes lovely patterns; and occasionally the finely conceived proportions of a palace or a church shone through the mask; but " Renaissance " meant essentially an intellectual rearranging, on the surface plane, of borrowed forms. It is the least creative of the " great " world styles.

Brunelleschi's dome stands up nakedly beautiful above all efforts at ornament, as an original creation; and so does many a campanile beside over-decorated churches in town or village of northern Italy. But the studied façades — and they spell Renaissance for most observers — are in general unmeaning patterns of contrived arches, pilasters, etc. — often a mere veneer. When occasionally we see a sixteenth century building standing up in fine solidity, gravely proportioned, in magnificent silhouette — like a Greek temple — or a long arcade that lulls us rhythmically with its Roman arches refined and set in harmonious composition, we are tempted to think that this style has indeed recaptured Classic proportion and mixed it with human intimacy. But the interior of St. Peter's, with its riot of vulgar ornament, its display arches and useless columns and false pediments, is nearer to the index of the style and the life that fostered it: cold intellectual research, deliberate pursuit of culture, princely wastefulness, and the mind enslaved to political control.

A special phase, baroque, meant little more than variation in profuse ornament: catchingly picturesque and delicate at its best, but in general a broken-up, nervous sort of thing — a clear sign of decadence. In Spain a happier mixture of Renaissance forms with Arabic and Gothic decoration (strange but true) gave birth to a fascinating sort of archi-

Interior of St. Peter's in Rome. [From *Geschichte der Architektur*, by Wilhelm Lübke]

tecture with massive construction relieved by richly delicate inlays. In France and England, as in Italy, Classic decorative forms were rearranged in compositions intellectually pleasing but never profound. The prettier phases in France ran into those minor styles associated with the Louis', which borrowed so much from the frills and luxuries of milady's boudoir.

And ever afterwards, up to 1900, architecture was Renaissance of one variety or another, with only an occasional ineffective challenge from Neo-Greek or revived Gothic. And indeed, the Modernists point out that when the early Renaissance designers dug up the elements of Roman construction and Roman-adapted-Greek ornament, instead of creating a new art for a new forward push of the human spirit, they initiated a sort of architectural slavery that persisted five hundred years.

Nor was the discovery, in the nineteenth century, of iron or steel as a structural skeleton for buildings a spur to new imagining; nor the enormous increase in the use of reinforced concrete, with its widening of available ways of building. In that century architecture was " set."

Architecture had become so professionalized, and the great mass of architects had become so obsessed with the faith that there are no good styles except the old ones, that the discovery of revolutionary ways of building — the only epochal discovery in seven centuries — was blanketed for near a half-century more under smug satisfaction with echoes and adaptations. Architects, who supposedly spend their days practising the art of building, missed entirely the significance of the greatest revolution in the course of the art since Romanesque was transformed into Gothic, a discovery of principle and method almost as elemental and epochal as Greek post-and-lintel and Roman arch. It was left for engineers — and two or three lone architects, outcasts among their associates — to pioneer in experimenting expressively with steel and concrete.

If the architects of the late nineteenth and early twentieth century had even been concerned with the fundamentals of the old styles, the wasting of fifty years would not now seem so much to their discredit. But what obsessed them was outward forms — usually quite divorced from function. Architectural æsthetics meant the theory of ornament. The study of building went no deeper than treatment of façades. One would think that the scientific era would have urged them back to a study at least as deep as the skeleton — but the fact remains that the architects more than any other profession or group of artists remained superficial and contented with tasteful masks and ornamental baubles. Fashion has washed them one way, then another — and they have not even created a fashion.

ECLECTICISM is the amiable name given to architectural incompetence in the period 1870–1920. Pickers and choosers from older forms of building, disputers for this or that style within the limits of impotency . and imitativeness, tasteful roamers, cultured repeaters of other men's

An awful example.  House design as practised about 1900.  [From a French art magazine of 1902]

architectural phrases — Eclectics!  They were so lost in their worship
of pilasters and cornices and acanthus leaves that they never emerged
into the fields of creativeness.  They studied their heroes and mentors,
Palladio and Vignola; they finished off at the Beaux-Arts School in
Paris, and added the true French flourish to their adaptations; they
usually considered deeply what surface fashion would best become a
library or a railroad terminal or a skyscraper; but it never occurred to
them, after steel and concrete came in, to approach the building as an
organism, to relate structural method to façade designing.  Correctness,
accuracy, pretty pattern, impeccable copies of stately colonnades and
lacy spires and picturesque staircases — all was provided in approved
museum fashion.  And indeed, here in America, in the period of McKim
and White and their associates, we had *everything* — except honesty,
courage, and creation.

I am speaking now of the time when the *nouveau riche* American
architecture of the mid-century and the Centennial era had given way

to the Beaux-Arts men and *tasteful* adaptation (though I find the French architectural magazines as late as 1900 full of the kind of junk-jug composition illustrated over-page — as inorganic, restless, showy, and futile as one can imagine). School training, conventional-mindedness, servile catering to imperialistic masters, lack of spiritual insight — these are prime reasons for the lack of creativeness in all the Western world in the period of Eclecticism. There is no reason, I suppose, why we should blame this body of Eclectics more than the eighteenth century men or any others in the long slave-minded period, except that the new principle in construction was there before them, denied by them.

The steel frame for high buildings came into use first in Chicago about 1890. Iron framing had been used in a limited way before that; but in 1891 a twenty-two story skyscraper built on a metal skeleton in Chicago was a world-wonder. Metal framing alone did not make the achievement possible: development of high-speed elevators, and of heating, lighting, and plumbing apparatus on a new scale, was a necessary accompaniment. But it was the invention of steel skeleton construction that afforded the point of departure for the most spectacular builders of modern times. Though obscured by exterior architectural practice through a quarter-century after, here was the revolution in structural engineering that was destined to change world building more than any other development since the invention of the flying buttress.

As we have seen — no understanding of modern architecture is possible until this has been emphasized and re-emphasized — there had been up to this time the three more or less distinctly separated types of building, based on materials and the ways of putting them together: three bases for architectural history. The post-and-lintel system was the simplest: a beam set across from the top of one upright to the top of another, to cover space. On it had been developed the glory that was Greek architecture. Second came the arch system: a method of spanning an opening by spreading the downward push sideways and along curved paths of stone blocks held apart by a keystone (an unscientific explana-

Neither post-and-lintel nor arch construction could make a building like this stand up; it is a result of metal introduced into construction, in this case as a core to the concrete members. Store at the Hook of Holland. J. J. P. Oud, architect. [By courtesy of *The Architectural Record*]

tion, but perhaps expressive if you visualize an isolated arch). The arch and its outgrowth, the vault, made possible Roman architecture; and the Gothic builders found a variation (wherein the arch's thrust was absorbed not by solid masonry walls but by slender piers buttressed for the necessary extra resistance), which permitted the daring achievement of the mediæval cathedrals. A third principle in building was introduced with the invention of the truss, for spanning wide spaces: a system in which a network of wooden or metal members in compression or tension came into use where the gap was too great for single beams. This last can hardly be termed a third great determining species of building, since it never gave rise to a style, as the other two did, and it may be used as auxiliary to any other method of construction.

But with the coming of the steel frame, a wholly new sort of engineering came in. Up to its appearance, the masonry at the bottom of a building had to support the weight of all the stories above. This was no great handicap in a church, which was all one great hall, or a fortress or a temple; or in any very low building. But as business exploitation of city land values drove buildings up in the air, as story on story was added, the necessary thickening of the walls at the base, to carry the additional weight above, stole more and more window space. The steel frame, on the other hand, transferred the weight to a few points of support; the problem was so radically solved that the masonry or clay walls could be built from the top story downward if desired; the lowest story (where light was most desired) could be encased with all-glass between the slender steel piers. Here, indeed, was a revolutionary difference out of materials — and sign that the third great determining method of building in the world's history had arrived.

The second distinctively modern material soon came to aid the fabricators of steel frames: concrete. This was not strictly a new building material — the Romans had used it to a limited degree — but only after 1875 did it assume importance. By 1900 it was displacing a great deal of masonry and wooden building. For the floors of steel-frame structures, for instance, it offered fire-proof construction at low cost. It was merely necessary to construct temporary rough wooden " forms," lay in iron bars, and pour wet concrete to the desired thickness; when the concrete dried the forms could be knocked off and one had in effect a solid stone floor (with a metal heart). Reinforced concrete, or ferro-concrete, found many independent uses, outside connection with the steel frame: entire buildings of nearly twenty stories have been constructed of the material, and poured-concrete unit houses are a favorite form of experiment with Modernist architects. Although it is difficult to rid ourselves of the feeling that important " monumental " buildings must be at least faced with stone, no one who has understood the economy, logic, and adaptability of poured concrete can doubt that a different architecture, large and small, monumental and intimate, will arise out of its potentialities. Its emergence as a determining factor has been less spectacular than that of steel; but already it finds greater world currency and a wider variety of uses.[1]

The use of glass, set in metal, has greatly increased, and measurably aids in trapping sunlight; and there is a very special branch of Modernist effort concerned with the decorative values of glass construction. In the same way, sheet-metal brings its own values, decorative and sanitary and constructive. But after all, it is steel framing and concrete pouring that seem destined to shape the larger forms of the immediate future world architecture.

How a few artist-engineers leapt to meet the challenge of a new principle and new materials, constitutes the story of the chapters that follow; it is meet that in the last pages of this present chapter, of historical background, we return to those who spent their lives hiding the new steel core under surface trimmings borrowed from the past. But let us pause to note that Louis Sullivan flung his challenge to the timid, the cultured, and the hypocritical architects as early as 1892, speaking out with a passion and scorn that made him an outcast from the American profession, at the same time establishing him in Europe as a prophet and god of the younger revolting generations. All he asked for, in the final analysis, was *honesty*. He wanted honesty as to both use and materials. Even in the middle nineties he was designing a few skyscrapers in which the exterior walls were frankly a sheath over a frame, not pretending to be masonry piles; and he declared the function, and invented whatever ornament he added. And he kept up his running fire of attack on the Eclectics who went on pasting pilasters and colonnades along the false masonry fronts, who hung useless galvanized iron cornices over the top edges, who so carefully disguised the inward character of the structure.

The Eclectics simply overlooked the significance of the new inventions.

---

[1] The use of Portland cement, which is mixed with sand and gravel to produce concrete, grew in the United States as follows:

1870 ........................ less than 10,000 barrels
1900 ........................ approximately 10,000,000 barrels
1928 ........................ 176,000,000 barrels

They did not recognize that a great change in surface design must come ultimately by virtue of the steel frame or other new material or method — at present, those were matters for the engineer, purely structural matters, and " art " didn't have anything to do with structure.

Nineteenth century architecture in America had begun as Classic revival, had indulged in indiscriminate borrowing — Victorian, Gothic, Chinese, and what not — solidified itself for a time in Romanesque, turned Renaissance, and went out in dual Roman and Beaux-Arts French, the while two or three Neo-Mediævalists shrieked the virtues of the Gothic. Toward the end of the century, quieter counsels prevailed over what had long been a battlefield of the styles; and thenceforth it was decreed that *any* style with a respectable historic lineage might be adopted for any particular job, and the architect remain within the fold of the orthodox and the elect. It was so much better thus — a man need no longer raise a standard on one side or another, strike and defend; instead he had all the past to choose from, respectably. Eclecticism was born, became a new, inclusive God.

Let us see just what this leaning on the past meant — for a whole quarter-century after the steel frame came into use. All decorative façades hung on the steel skeleton were borrowed, all were absolutely unrelated to the life of the time, to industrialism, to democracy. The planning might be true to purpose, the engineering efficient, even daring and soul-stirring; but the architect added façades that lied, that confessed lack of spirit, lack of originality, impotence. The *art* in these buildings was as superficial as that in the old-time painted stage scenery: a veneer, a make-believe, an illusion, a representation. In average work, an almost unbelievable fashion of uselessly heavy, " monumental " masonry was established, with illogical pictorial decoration in stone, weighty false cornices, deep-set windows, etc., etc.

In the outstanding monuments, there was caught occasionally some reflection of nobility or effective proportioning or decorative richness, out of other times. In our " great " American buildings of the decades on either side of 1900 — the Boston Public Library, the Pennsylvania Station, the Columbia University Library, the West Point buildings, St. Thomas' on Fifth Avenue, the Yale and Princeton college halls, as well as the early renowned, historic skyscrapers — there are fine surface qualities. Sometimes these go even deeper. But false premises lie under the design of all. Sometimes the outer shell is entirely a disguise, the true building within existing and functioning perfectly behind the pleasant mask; in other cases, the true functioning of the building-organism has been crippled, distorted, in order that architects might erect the stylistically correct façade, with the limited area of windows, the relation of column and cornice, the hollow buttresses, etc., established traditionally by Gothic practice, or Italian Renaissance, or Roman.

All these monuments of the Eclectic age have a common, and not inconsiderable, virtue: they remind one of architecture. The designers in these particular cases chose well; the buildings *reflect* the strong works of eras when some human drive came to architectural expression. Here are echoes of the fine solidity of a Florentine fortress-palace, the nobility of the Pantheon, the gigantic lift of the baths erected by the Emperor Caracalla, the fragmentary grandeur of early Gothic churches. Nor would I want to undermine your enjoyment of these structures; only let us remember that they *are* reminders and echoes, not the real architectural thing. I find pleasing that vague memory of nobility when I am crossing 116th Street, find a momentary repose in gazing across Copley Square, feel a breath of old dreams on Fifth Avenue approaching 53rd Street. These are pleasant museum bits; but there is no living beauty, only vague images transported out of other times.

The architects transferred for our passing enjoyment certain outward forms, because they could not, in the materials, methods, and idiom of their own time, express the fundamental aspirations and powers that had made the originals soul-stirring and "beautiful." These nineteenth century architects were borrowers, servants of other men's minds, imitative professionals. That they were resourceful in their adaptation —

some people call it their picking-and-stealing — that they were im- peccably trained to maintain correctness, that they had taste, goes without saying. But in the light of the creative new spirit abroad in the world, they were timid, impotent, slave-minded.

Lest we be thought too critical of our own country, let us note that American architecture of the Eclectic era was world-typical. Even as the Classic revival a hundred years ago had brought as intelligent adapta- tion in the United States as in London or Berlin or Munich or Paris, the culminating nineteenth century Eclectic-materialistic architecture af- forded us a sprinkling of monuments comparable to — perhaps more brilliant than — those erected in our " mother countries " across the Atlantic. Railway stations and hotels and universities and country houses were being set out with a lavish hand that gave our architects opportunity to surpass their fellow Eclectics overseas; and in the bor- rowed envelopes most used one may study on this side of the Atlantic the finest " modern Roman," " modern Collegiate Gothic," and " modern Renaissance villa " existent anywhere. Indeed, long years ago Platt in New York and Polk in California were building Italian houses more lovely than any Italian designer could produce; Cram and Goodhue were doing Gothic and Spanish churches more creatively adapted than any being done in France or Spain; and McKim and White were erecting monu- ments that cry shame to any erected in Rome within man's memory.

We might profitably pursue this thought about Rome. There are critics who point out that in its most imperialistic decades, the United States swung naturally to the so-appropriate Roman-Imperial architec- ture. (The Philippines experience and the slight personal experience of the World War have since given Imperialism, except the trade sort, a final set-back in the American group-mind — let Europe and South America believe it or not.) There was the exact duplication in triumphal arch and commemorative tomb, the same spirit behind the showy up-flung railway stations, exposition halls, and libraries, all with their masonry overlays of Roman motives. Need I add that of all the great architec- tural styles, the Roman is vulgarest, dullest, spiritually emptiest?

Benjamin W. Morris
*Architect*

A. H. Scott &
J. A. W. Grant

Jarvis Hunt

Nicolas Wassilieff

Bourgeois, Dunlap &
Morgan

James Gamble Rogers

C. H. Bebb &
C. F. Gould

Frank Fort

Bliss & Faville

Giuseppe Boni

H. Hornbostel &
E. F. Wood

A. Fellheimer &
S. Wagner

Eclectic skyscraper practice, as revealed by the " Honorable Mention " designs in the competition for the Chicago Tribune Tower, 1922; wherein one may detect the business building disguised under " motives " from Greek and Roman temples, French, Flemish and English cathedrals, Florentine towers, Venetian palaces, Egyptian obelisks, etc. [By courtesy of The Chicago Tribune]

But the point we are pursuing at the moment is that Eclecticism made architecture tame and unoriginal *throughout* the European-American world. If you would take London instead of New York as an example, you would find less of brilliant adaptation, though more of passable and uniformly cautious orthodoxy. The fact is that London, centre of the dominating imperialistic advance for two centuries and more, is the dullest empire-capital that ever existed. The architectural aspect of the city is drab beyond comparison. The few "monuments" that intrigue one's passing interest — the Houses of Parliament, Wren's churches, parts of Westminster Abbey, Regent Street, the Cenotaph, the Bank — are wholly unrelated in placing, style, spirit, or conception; not one an original British style, hardly two claiming nodding acquaintance as the same sort of Renaissance, the same sort of re-hash. For the rest, London is tamely self-effacing. Few of the strident monstrosities that occasionally happen in Chicago or Brussels or Berlin; but monotonous weakness, bespeaking a total stagnation of the creative faculties. London is occasionally rhetorical in the matter of architecture, but never convincing, never stirring, hardly living. The wastefulness of this moribund building is merely more restrained, the air is more respectfully servile, than elsewhere; it is a different phase of Eclecticism. France suffered less from heterogeneousness than other countries in this era, a thread known as French Renaissance becoming merely weaker and more florid in " Beaux-Arts " — but you may walk from the Classic Madeleine to the Pantheon and see on the way Roman arches, Renaissance railway stations, Baroque churches, Byzantine theatres, Gothic houses. All Europe — and wherever European nations colonized and " brought art " to the natives — is trailed over with this confession of architectural relapse, of spiritual bankruptcy.

That is the architectural background to our study of Modernism: the immediate background to our glimpse of a new world-order and of an appropriate and honest art of building. That is the architectural *status quo* which ninety-nine hundredths of the architects will try to maintain, to the exclusion of the types of building that grow out of the uses and materials of today. That is the mirror, showing how the true art of architecture was betrayed. Again let us remember: as men think, as they plan their lives, as they do, so they practise their arts — weakly, hypocritically, boastfully, materialistically, if those are the ways of the age. As pride, conquest, imperialism, based on social division between weak and strong, on exploitation and civilized savagery, were keywords of the age, so you may see those qualities memorialized, showily, alongside the weaknesses, on your streets, in your proudest public squares, and in your colleges.

Not that there were no *transitional* examples between Eclectic practice and a clean-cut, honest Modernism. No one can draw a line and say, " Here Eclecticism ends, and here the new world architecture begins." The architects might at first torture concrete into a semblance of roughcast stone, or line it out to suggest piled blocks; and they might grain the painting of metal doors to make them look like wood — these were minor ridiculous sacrifices to the sacredness of the past. And very certainly they did at first, in dressing the skyscraper, build heavily at the base of the building in an effort to suggest that the masonry supported the weight — denying that the load of stone sheath was carried on a metal frame to isolated points of support; they wanted to preserve certain " picturesque " effects of projecting and indented stone courses and of deep-set windows and portals.

But these most illogical of their practices gradually fell away before the ruthless logic of the engineers, before the reasonable demand of owners who wanted economy and who wanted in the lower stories more light than the heavy masonry wall would permit — and before the pursuing mockery and scorn of the little band of architectural rebels led by Louis Sullivan. In the skyscraper the "masonry look" was reluctantly given up. The idea of pasting pilasters and false colonnades and networks of studied arches, pediments, false cornices, decorated entablatures, etc., etc., over the *entire* façade, was eased out of architecture in favor of a different sort of dishonesty which seemed to have at least a catch-hold on architectural precedent. In short, the Eclectics came to that standard mode in which the high building was treated after the manner of a Classic column: base more or less glorified; shaft plain; cap a real flowering of ornament, leading up to a cornice. The tall building was thus divided into three parts, the long middle one lost to the architect with the decorative itch, but the top and bottom parts offering display space for echoes of past architectural glories. But before going into that phase — which is to give place in turn to the Neo-Gothic — let us turn to a few actual examples of early Eclectic skyscraper design. Of the great monuments of the first twenty years, one may note the famous Flatiron Building and the *World* Building in New York as suffering from over-devotion to " the masonry look." Today the huge cornice on the Flatiron Building is alone enough to damn it in all logical eyes. The *World* Building illustrates the attempt to make the stone-work at the base *look* heavy enough to seem organic, as if it were a self-sufficient stone wall of huge building blocks — instead of what it is, a hanging protective screen on a steel frame. You meet the resulting deep window embrasures and cavernous portals, copied from Florentine palaces or Greek temples or Romanesque churches, in a hundred early skyscrapers of New York and Chicago. The same inordinate and unpleasant heaviness marks the *Times* Building — though a section of eight stories somehow escaped into near-modern simplicity — and here one may mark the more direct stealing of motives, particularly in the flowering into Giotto's Tower. It is rather, however, in the Metropolitan Tower that the skyscraper is tortured into a single borrowed stylistic envelope: a St. Mark's Campanile punched full of window-holes. Oftener the disguise was more freely worked out, with mere resting on Classic " elements " or Beaux-Arts idioms: the medium-height Italian palace skyscrapers, or the Singer tower with the Beaux-Arts " bulge."

Since, so far, we have examined the whole question of Eclectic skyscraper-design from the æsthetic point of view — seeking the logic or illogic of trying to make a building *look* something it isn't — let us examine now the economic aspect. As a matter of fact, not one of those manipulated buildings escaped sacrifices to the architects' " additions for beauty's sake," in wastefulness of material and labor, and in loss of light (as those of us who at one time or another have had offices, for instance, on the arcade floors of the Metropolitan Tower — the thirty-first, I think, was mine — can testify). The pyramidal top on the Bankers' Trust Building, so long a feature of the downtown New York sky-line, embraced six full stories of blind enclosure, without windows. The Mausoleum in Halicarnassos had no windows, and the top twelve stories of this twentieth century monument were planned as a " creatively adapted " replica of the Tomb — and therefore six floors of space were given over to mausoleum darkness.

This Bankers' Trust Building is in the mode, already mentioned, based on the divisions of a Classic column unit. At this time the orthodox architects were saying to themselves, " We will forget the back and sides of the building, and study the front façade in divisions; we will treat that in the proportions proper to a column with a capital, set on a base." And so there came that nearest approach to a standardized skyscraper: the building with the first four or five stories unified in a designed but not too ornamental " base "; a section of naked honest building for twenty stories or so above, corresponding to the shaft; then a flowering in a sort of classic temple or Renaissance arcade laid over the top stories, for capital. This is the formula of the orthodox men still; driven from considering the whole building as masonry, they pretended that the whole hanging façade was a composition to be divided according to the " laws " of one masonry unit, the column.

The worse examples are with us in a hundred versions, weak and unattractive. (Some photographers, with radical tendencies, seeking truth, have taken malicious pleasure in slighting the carefully studied fronts and picturing the undesigned backs of these buildings, where the engineer's soaring lines and unashamed masses have risen unembarrassed by stylistic overlays; and up to a few years ago, some of us found these records more exciting than those so carefully embalmed by the architects in their trade magazines.)   The better examples, however, gave us our least offensive false skyscrapers, occasionally studied *on all four sides*. Among the type examples are the mentioned Bankers' Trust Building, wherein twenty stories of undisguised offices rise between a double base, bearing engaged columns, and a capital of the temple type, with free-standing columns and cornice; and the Municipal Building in New York, with a complete Roman triumphal arch embedded in the false colonnade of the base, sixteen honest stories, and a band of (badly spaced) columns and pilasters at the top.   It happens that both these buildings have " show " elements erected above the natural roof: the one the useless pyramid roof referred to, the other a French-pastry sort of agglomeration of temples, minarets, etc.   Such afterthoughts are no more trivial and ridiculous in the sound architectural view than was the whole logic of treating a new structural problem in terms of alien ornament and under the theory of ancient building methods, stone on stone.

It is obvious, however, that the sacrifices of light and view, in these three-division buildings, were generally less than where the masking ornamental architecture had been drawn over the entire front.

There was one type of historic ornament that had none of the uglier disadvantages so obvious in Greek, Roman, and Renaissance when applied to the high thin façade.   Gothic, the Neo-Mediævalists pointed out, not only emphasized the soaring line; it had been developed in every detail for structures supported by isolated piers.   Indeed, the mediæval cathedral was the only building in history that showed the slightest analogy to the modern skyscraper: ergo, this was the only decorative idiom that could be logically (?) applied on the front of a thirty- or forty-story building.   Admit the basic premise of the Eclectics, that there are no new styles, and we must agree absolutely with these Neo-Gothicists.   And certainly the Gothic skyscrapers, whether viewed individually or as units in the Modern City, please the eye as do no other business buildings out of that pre-Modern age.   Here if anywhere the Eclectic architects scored

The Woolworth Building, New York. Cass Gilbert, architect. [Photo by courtesy of the Atlantic Terra Cotta Company, manufacturers of the terra cotta used in the exterior]

a real triumph.   Here is the final reach of the apostles of the past in their effort to hold the machine building of the present to traditional forms. And it is all summed up in the Woolworth Building.

This is the end of history and the beginning of a new time.   This is a frankly stylistic envelope taken *in toto* from the past, encasing a steel frame.   We have gone now beyond the period when the architect made pretense that the masonry of the lower stories carried the wall-weight above; the walls are frankly light sheaths of terra cotta, with only shallow window-reveals.   This is obviously a pier-and-screen system of construction, with weight distributed to a few points of support, through vertical shafts.

And we seldom fail to be stirred by the " lift " of the building.   The bulk and the conception of the thing are stupendous.   The fundamentals of proportioning and massing are creatively handled, there is surface unity, there is form.   From a distance, moreover, where detailed ornament becomes too intricate for the eye to catch, there is no conflict between functional lines and borrowed garment.   There, indeed, lies the secret of the architect's success: he chose a style that does not actively belie the structural method, and he set away the more questionable elements to such a height that they blend into shadow and cross-line unobtrusively. In short, failing of creative ability to originate an envelope to match the engineering and proportioning, the designer chose a style originally invented for a similarly vertical method of construction, repressed detail too idiomatic, and cunningly interwove ornamental pattern and engineering fabric.   The moment one comes too close for the blurring, then the lying of the ornament becomes apparent: there are even gargoyles at the twenty-seventh story and flying buttresses at the forty-second, and whole rows of offices suffer for light where the main decorative overhang is.   To this extent there is compromise — perhaps dishonesty — for the sake of the " picturesque."

Here, then, is where Eclecticism came closest to an acceptable achievement, by the happy circumstances of a past style of ornament being fitted in accent to a new type of structure, and through the architect's under-

An early view of the Woolworth Building, from the rear. [By courtesy of *The Architectural Record*, New York]

standing of the limits and uses of surface ornament. But nothing that we can say or do will ever alter the fact that the reason any architect today borrows a stylistic envelope from the past is because he is not original enough to create the one truly appropriate to the new era. There is an element of dishonesty in his approach, in his thinking.

And in the end, reviewing history, and then recalling the examples of the new world architecture that most please us, it should be clear to us that honesty is at the heart of the matter. If we have not integrity and direct dealing, we shall have nothing but further evasions and compromises. There is no use talking about a new art unless one begins where all creative design must begin, with the capabilities of the medium. If your purpose is to make concrete seem like something it isn't, or to make a metal frame support something copied from the days before steel fabrication, then go ahead with your activities but don't call it architecture. Architecture is the art of building beautifully; and beauty has nothing to do with shams, with disguise, with overlaid cleverness, with transfers.

During all the quarter-century preceding the Woolworth Building, there had been a sort of uneasiness in the writings — toward the last, the apologies — of the Eclectics. It was as if there were a sort of continuous vague thunder on the horizon; the orthodox, if they stopped to localize it, probably looked to wherever Louis Sullivan was sitting in his prophetic chair. Or perhaps it was a music they heard: the hum and drone of machines — and they knew in their hearts that their architecture had no relationship to that music.

The architecture of the past, of thirty centuries, had known nothing of the machine; but somehow, intuitively, the architect of the late nineteenth and early twentieth century must have foreseen that machine-age thinking would lie at the heart of building design in the time to come — must have known, even while too servile to acknowledge it.

The old and the new vertical architecture: a view in Cologne.  Museum by Adolf Abel (right)

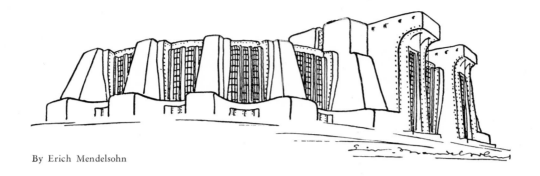

By Erich Mendelsohn

# CHAPTER III

## FACE TO FACE WITH THE MACHINE

NEITHER any hint contained in inventions up to this time, nor the wildest imaginings, can paint for us a complete picture of the life of man as it will be lived fifty years from now, after another half-century of the increasingly swift process of mechanization. We are loath, indeed, to admit how far the first hundred years of steam power applied to transport and industry, and of electricity in home and office and factory, have dislocated old modes of living and venerable ways of thinking. Even as we switch on the electric light, or ride in the automobile, or dispatch a radiogram to Egypt, we say that the old fundamental facts of life are the same, that nothing can change human nature very much. But if we stop to consider, as compared with a hundred years ago, how many people in any given community now are *clean* — tubbed daily or twice weekly — and would be outraged if asked to live without running water and automatic plumbing; how many people in our town take it for granted that education will be offered to their children, as a matter of course, education in a pretty broad and humanizing sense; how many families have motor cars, in which they may at any moment be whisked away to visit friends, or off on a tour that will bring renewed contact with nature, with other communities, even with other peoples; or how many eager pleasure-seekers are " going to the shows " (10,000,000 daily in the United States alone) : stopping to consider these things, we should

73

perceive that no other period in mankind's history has known so extraordinary a dislocation of values and the opening of so many roads to the fuller life and wider experience. For those desirable things, cleanliness, education, travel, and enjoyment of the arts (however crude), which are new gains to the masses, used to be the prize to a few, pathetically few, of the people of the earth; and it is the mechanical revolution that has directly or indirectly made them accessible to the larger half of mankind.

We may, for one or another of many reasons, close our eyes to the seriousness of this revolution, deny its far-reaching implications — though the surface change in *living* is an indication of a radical revolution also in the way of world thinking. We may blink the truth because we want to see the church of our fathers — once a bedrock to us, too — kept in authority; or because we have found *our* economic situation pretty soft (and so we just lazily resist any change); or because we were taught that a certain removed thing is art, and that industry and the machine are inimical to it — and we would rather mechanization slowed up and let us fuss more with the " beautiful things of life." Or for any one of a dozen other reasons we claim that old ways are the best — even though whenever we sit down and analyse our place as compared with that of our grandparents, or for an instant dare to glance at the blinding possibilities of the future, we know that life is on a toboggan, with the dæmon (or demon) of machine-inventiveness at the wheel.

If we face this thing honestly, we know, among other facts, that the tidy little world which the thinking class had painted as the ideal one (when there were only two classes) is a myth: the larger fixed earth is found to be not fixed, nor more than a speck floating in a universe of multitudinous worlds; and the smaller man-made securities, the contrived refuges, the places of luxurious withdrawal — " every man's home his castle " — are violated by new machines that look in from overhead, new forces that pierce walls and invade hidden space, and laws that prohibit shutting off too much of God's territory from God's peoples.

On the one hand the petty limits of the earth have become a reality as compared with a larger space-world so extensive that no one can guess its boundaries; on the other hand, on the earth, in the achievements of science, the things we " know " change form, disappear, give place to other wonders. Even the scientists, who claimed for long to test every-thing by absolute material standards, come now before us hinting at forces that will negate all materiality, that will turn living into even now unguessed paths. The machine-contrivers have been utilizing ele-ments that we but half understand (how much do we truly basically know about electricity?), and we may look to the imminent conquest of forces hardly glimpsed as yet in our exploration of the mysteries of space-time.

Old conceptions die away. Old mechanical contraptions wear out. Newer, more powerful, simpler ones come into being. There will ul-timately be machine-developed energy to solve all men's work problems, with no more labor than is involved in passing control. The elements themselves will be tamed, weather tempered, transportation become effortless, cleanliness universal, the works of the intellect and of the artistic faculties will be transported instantaneously to all. Living will be speeded, concentrated, regulated, as never before.

There is no turning back. There is no hindering the swiftness of humanity's advance toward that time. No one can foresee the organiza-tion that will turn all this to the good of the human soul, when the old pivots on which individual life has turned — labor, making a living, money, protective nationalistic governments — are scrapped. We only know that increasingly now the problem of nobly utilizing leisure time becomes all-important. We are past the possibility of challenging the machine, of curbing it, of attempting escape from it. We must live in a way that crowds into a week what used to be the experiences of a year, that makes a half-hour's work of what used to occupy our grandparents for a day. We must move by machinery, communicate by it — live by it.

The sin would be to let the machine control us: we must ride above it, control it. We must make it so easy, so efficient, so noiseless, that we rise beyond it to enjoy those serenities, those spiritual contacts, those pleasures of quietness, that enriched life (for a few) before the machine era. If the speed and the concentrated power and the extensive drive of it seem at first to create a chaos, we shall save ourselves by pushing that chaos underfoot, rising by mental effort — into regions where we create new religions and more glorious arts. And appropriately we shall find those arts related to the machine foundation underfoot.

Face to face with the machine. It challenges us. We stand up courageous and confident in its presence. But the architects have faltered. And indeed, anyone who now conceives architecture without reference to this factor, who considers architecture still as primarily a matter of styles, falters; nay, worse, seeks to forbid the tides, to bind time to the past. If architecture is to continue to be an index of man's living, a fixation of his thoughts, his doings, and his dreams, instead of a barrier raised between some sheltered inner self and his way of living, then it must move forward in step with machine-organized society.

We who have caught glimpses of the new world-organization of society, who have a vision of living in the new time, we know for a certainty that mankind cannot live the new sanitary, open-minded, art-enriched life with Victorian furniture or in ornamental-wasteful houses or the old inefficient office or work building. We know that the machine element is an inevitable factor, whatever aspect of building we consider. That is why we ask the architect to conceive the building first as a machine, not as a decorative shelter. We demand at last that he answer directly, daringly, without evasion, when brought face to face with the challenge of mechanized living.

*The building as machine.* The conception cuts across all lines of traditional thinking, of imitative design, of swagger, of commemorative architectural rhetoric, as the automobile and the radio cut across the path of him who thinks to withdraw today into a mediæval seclusion,

Where machine and building meet. View in the Klingenberg factories, Berlin, Germany. Klingenberg & Issel,
architects.

a literary-precious aloofness. The constructive engineer, the sanitary engineer, the electric engineer, long ago pushed into the house and the trade building with their efficient heating, plumbing, lighting, and mechanical service equipment. Only the architect resisted the tide, built his outer sheath faithfully inefficient, decorated and stylistically involved. Now that larger conception pushes forward: house, office building, factory, theatre, school, library, even church, all as *machines*. Architect must be *architect-engineer*.

Let us suppose an architect forgets all he has been taught at the schools; puts out of mind all the " civilized " styles, the traditional way of disposing façades, panelling walls, decorating ceilings, disguising radiators, etc., etc. We won't perplex him at first with those wholly new problems that grow out of the uses of today, where he can't find any precedent, even at the back of his mind or in the largest library — hangars, garages, broadcasting stations, quarter-mile-long train sheds, moving-picture theatres. Rather let him take up anew the oldest of all problems, house design, the providing of shelter for a man and his family. Won't he, sooner or later, have to conceive the building as a mechanism existing and functioning for absolutely defined purposes: to provide fresh air, tempered shelter from heat and cold, means for cooking and for serving food, lighting, means for cleansing, and for whisking away sewage and waste: involving piping for hot and cold water, wiring, lights, power sockets, central heating with arms in all directions, plumbing, drains?

These needs constitute a new problem in the world. The first central heating plant was installed in a home in the mid-nineteenth century. Edison invented the incandescent light only in 1879. Running water came into general use in dwellings hardly more than a generation back. Electric refrigeration grew to common use only within five years. House design has changed from a collection-of-rooms problem in 1850 to a problem of disposing the elements of a living organism, with a network of ducts: flowing water, electricity, heat, etc., and with a dozen other fixed mechanical units set in at exactly determined positions. This functioning organism is the beginning of the new " home " architecture.

When you are still clinging to the idea that it is the ornament on a building that spells Art, you are likely to find the machine-starkness too insistent. What decorative elements there are, seem to grow out of the practical fittings introduced for efficiency: there is no applied beauty. But we are warranted in asking the architect: would you ask for that if you were approaching the building as free-mindedly as you approach a motor car, an airplane, or a railway coach? You wouldn't think your automobile any more beautiful if ornament were applied to the hood or

The builders of machines are teaching the architects. A portion of the S. S. *Leviathan*.
[Drawing by courtesy of the United States Lines]

the doors. The very extraordinary beauty of your Chrysler or Nash or Cord is due to the honest decorativeness out of materials, efficient disposal of parts, massing, stream lines, with added warmth through color and the flash of metals. It is perhaps the all-pervasiveness of motor cars characterized by sheer, appropriate, and organic beauty that makes so many of us today irritated with art carrying a great load of ornament. With so much of honest æsthetic fare always with us, we find the stuffier modes distasteful. Once we recognize the truth that a dwelling or a school or a club-house might be as efficient, bright, and inviting as an automobile, then civilized architecture, wasteful, based on arrangements

of ornament, sickens us.  We wonder why no inventors arose to meet the
need for the dwelling-machine, as they arose to meet the need for the
fountain-pen, the airplane, and the linotype machine.

The " radicals," as a matter of fact, have been assiduous in calling
the historic architects' attention to the finely architectonic beauty in
motor cars, airplanes, and steamships; exhorting that they find inspiration in these other answers to the machine-age challenge — if their own
lore taught them not any inventiveness or courage.  And does not a car

An automobile: The Chrysler Imperial

like this make us hungry for a house of like virtues?  Note the perfect
precision expressed in every outward detail, the strength, the economy,
the sweet-running effortlessness reflected in surface simplicity of line
and silhouette.  Here a harmony of the new living is externalized, a sense
of perfect functioning brought out in terms of visual beauty — and not
a stroke of *ornament* anywhere apparent.  Here is a clean athletic
transportation-machine for the modern clean athletic body — and we
should have houses to match.

The " building inventor " of the mechanical age will ask what can
be made of the materials that go into the perfect disposal of living space
and service mechanism: what of massing, proportioning, what of the
rhythms of family living, what of the porches and terraces and shelters needful to the open life?  And he will forget all the stylistic
rigmarole of his forefathers, refuse to complicate his problem with

an effort to squeeze the mechanism into a predetermined ornamental envelope.

There was one architect-engineer who guessed as much way back in the nineties. It was machine-logical thinking that led Louis Sullivan to enunciate the first law of the Modernists, a dictum inscribed today on the walls of all the progressive architectural schools of Europe: *Form must follow function*. Sullivan — whose story we mustn't anticipate here, because it will form the main thread of the next chapter — clothed a few of the earliest steel-frame structures in honestly architectural expressiveness thirty years ago, and throughout the following quarter-century of Eclectic falsity continued to damn out heartily all attempts to hide or soften the new — machine-age — method of building. Truthfulness to use and truthfulness to materials: nothing more revolutionary could have been preached in those days, and nothing more prophetic of the scientific spirit of today. It meant for the architect no more false buttresses — you might as reasonably paint buttresses on your motor car for " looks," for all the use they served — no more false cornices, no more encrusted pilasters and cartouches, no more concrete shaped to simulate stone. And beyond all that was the basic implication of each type of building growing organically on a plan determined by the intended use. Let us drape no more columned temples over our banks, no more gabled monasteries over our college halls — really educational factories needing more light and air than the small leaded windows will let in — and no more French palaces or Roman imperial baths over our railway stations; instead a clean expression of mechanization.

One of the most active crusaders among the Modernists, the French-Swiss Le Corbusier, summed it up, as regards the house, thus: " We no longer have the money to build historical souvenirs. At the same time, we have to wash. Our engineers provide for these things and they will be our builders."

Le Corbusier goes beyond architecture as commonly understood and demands that whole new cities be constructed exactly like machines. He, and one or two Germans, and some of our American designers, during a decade past, have been drawing intriguing and imaginative plans to meet the needs of the combined subterranean, terrestrial, and aërial living and transport, as exampled in the drawing by Hugh Ferriss, opposite.

New needs. New ways of meeting old needs grown complex and exacting. The clean life, the open life, the universal life. The house engineered for comfort and service and freedom. Old chores automatically discharged. The immemorial house drudgery of women mechanically reduced to a fraction of the old burdensomeness. The business building elaborated, soaring, integrated for multiple service. Everything tending to larger concentration: department stores, workers' apartments, mass-production factories. The organism growing, man's creative powers stretching to meet ever more complex challenges. These are problems of today, of a new age; not to be solved by mulling over ornamental modes and studied stylistic façades and " systems " out of the past. To be solved only by getting back to the materials of building, to the mathematical bases of design, to creative thinking and the intuitive feel for beauty. Here are space and walls to be dealt with, and flat planes and scientifically determined openings; steel frames and electric elevators and the mechanics of heating, ventilation, and sewerage. All demanding the bold mass, the hard line, the brilliant metallic surface, the precise veining, the sweet harmony of smooth-running machines.

Now mechanization is supposed in some quarters to degrade and brutalize architecture, just as once it was widely considered a force for evil in the crafts-life of the world. The mechanization of industry was bitterly fought over. You and I, we who are more enlightened, who see an epic spirit in the rise of the machine, must check our enthusiasm, must realize that there is opinion against opinion, that nowhere else are we so opposed by a great body of learned men, as here in this matter of faith in inspiration and beauty growing directly out of machinery.

Anyway, ever since the inception of the industrial-mechanical revolu-

An imaginative drawing, by Hugh Ferriss, of a future city, with special reference to automobile traffic ways and airplane shelves. [From *The Metropolis of Tomorrow*, by Hugh Ferriss, by courtesy of the publisher, Ives Washburn]

tion, there has been confusion: the epic strain has been mixed with mean strains; the fine cleanliness of machine design and the chaste action of machinery have been mixed with dirtiness. Greed has confounded imagination. And because men who cared about art could not overlook the dirt and the evil intent of the factory-owning class and the meanness of the factory workers' lives, there has been almost uninterrupted antagonism between industrialism and orthodox architecture. From the unfortunate and shortsighted denunciations by Ruskin on to the scornful attacks by Ralph Adams Cram — both men whom we admire for independence and passion and sincerity — there has been an almost continuous stream of protest and condemnation and opposition, against the encroachments of industrial manufacture, industrial life, and industrialized building into the realm that should be reserved for practitioners of " the beautiful." Never guessing that there is a characteristic beauty growing out of mechanization, failing to realize that they were striving to perpetuate sorts of art that can only be lovely anachronisms in the new world — in any free world — these apostles saw only the dirt strewn over the earth by early industrialism, saw man becoming enslaved in a new feudalism by the lords who owned the machine-tools of labor, saw art flickering low. And the later antagonists felt thus even though, at the moment, Sullivan or Berlage might be preaching capture of the machine by the artist, instead of weak surrender; Van de Velde might be applying mass-production ideas to furniture design, while Hoffmann and his associates created an industrial plant infused with the handicrafts spirit, in the *Wiener Werkstætte;* and even though Frank Lloyd Wright might be initiating an actual new industrial architecture, appropriately clean-cut and monumental, and not without elements of nobility.

We may pause to note two specific ways in which the " artistic " architects had reacted when faced with the problem of designing a mill or a power-house — and this was where they first met the challenge. Either, convinced that everything connected with the machine is ugly anyway, they put up mere sheds, undesigned beyond useful shelter (perhaps they washed their hands of the whole affair, suggesting that a carpenter would be as satisfactory as an architect — thus opening the way for the entry of the engineer a bit later); or else they designed the shelter on a purely utilitarian basis, and then "ornamented" it — with perhaps a portico off an Italian palace, or a Tudor battlement, or a Beaux-Arts cartouche over the doorway. Of course those decorated factories and mills were infinitely worse than the drab carpentered structures. There was not only the lack of architectural beauty to distress the honest eye, but the transference of utterly inappropriate museum bits to salvage insincerely a thing not believed in. In the *fin-de-siècle* factories of the well-meaning Beaux-Arts men, of the Eclectics, there was always a faint suggestion of perversion — of sugar tastefully sprinkled on beefsteak.

The "plain" factories of the nineteenth century are by far the better half of a dispiriting exhibition. We meet the paradoxical fact that under the conditions of architectural belief then prevailing, under the reign of stylistic snobbery, the architect who felt himself defeated by industrialism, who gave up in disgust and impotence, muttering " oh, well, we'll put a roof over it, and let it go at that," did a better job than the conscientious one who studied long and painstakingly over the problem of bringing art to industrial building. For not one of the fancy styles then in vogue could be stretched over the gaunt factory frame without violence to the style, and a certain ridiculous pretense of fashion and culture in the building. We return to that fundamental principle: decorativeness is worse than profitless if it does not grow out of structure, if it is ornament idly added to the outside.

It was really the irresponsibility of larger human society, if early industrialism left cities that are like scars on the face of civilization. The machine, instead of being made the servant of a new freedom, was allowed to enslave man. It was machinery geared to business greed that dirtied the earth. There is, indeed, much of brutality and meanness and drabness in the story of the opening up of the mines, the coming of the steam engine, and the extension of the factory system of manufacture. The

unrestricted soft-coal period of industry left us cities in which the architecture is not only drab and uninspired, but actually coated over with the
grime of chimney-soot and wheel-ground dust.　The memory of nineteenth century Pittsburghs will long give color to mean and sordid pictures
of " the machine age " painted by those who never saw beyond the *waste*
aspects of fire tamed, electricity harnessed, and water put to work.

I am somehow reminded just here of the pathetic " independent " English women whom one meets in such numbers on the Riviera and in other
Continental " playgrounds ": utterly out of step with the times, striving
vainly to perpetuate the tradition of caste, of the gentlewoman, bereft of
loveliness, living meagrely on the income of a few shares of stock in a
coal-mine or a spinning-mill.　Beyond them one may read the story of
evil nineteenth century industrialism: the many toiling cruelly that a
few might keep up a show of leisurely culture, of gentility.　The relics
of that sort of industrialism must go: there is something unhealthy, un-
clean, unjust, about it — that grates in this machine-logical age.

But let us get back to those " authorities " who still oppose all machine-
living: let us pause to consider a protest by A. Kingsley Porter, as set down
in his book of essays *Beyond Architecture,* published as recently as 1918:

" He who takes the pains to look, will soon perceive that our life is
surrounded by ugliness as has been the life perhaps of no other civilized
people in any age.

" Architecture gives us a clue to one of the underlying reasons for the
degeneracy of the modern artistic intellect.　We Americans once possessed
a good architecture.　The buildings of the Colonial period, and especially
those erected at the end of the eighteenth and the beginning of the nineteenth century were often full of charm and dignity. . .　Then good
architecture came to a sudden end in America about the year 1850.　The
cause is not difficult to find.　It was the machine which crushed out handwork, it was the machine which killed beauty.　The Neo-Grecque house,
of good proportions and dignified detail, gave place in turn to the Victorian or wholly evil dwelling, adorned with lathe work, turned balus-

trades, little cupulas, scroll gables, incredible gingerbread of every description.

" The machine killed architecture in America, not only because it killed handwork and because it substituted quantity for quality, but also in a more subtle way. It changed the ideal, the nerves, the entire nature of our people. It is an eternal truth that to think highly one must live simply. Our people ceased to live simply. Life became ever more complex, ever more agitated. Prosperity entered at the front door, and thoughtfulness, poetry, and repose were forced out at the back."

In this passage there is one point of truth that we may easily agree with — though we find the general indictment based on a limited view and a typical vague longing for the long-ago and far-away. That point is the terrible achievements in architectural ornament accomplished on the lathe and scroll-saw. What duplications of slick-turned balusters, scroll foliage in wood, and ginger-bread ornament came out of a few simple machines in the Victorian era, a hundred houses in your town will testify. A cheap thing in itself is not necessarily bad; the evil creeps in when the cheap imitates the expensive, when mechanical duplication floods us with lifeless approximations of things valuable specifically for a hand-made feel and for an appropriateness in a special position. The jig-saw scroll in a place where a sensitive hand-carved detail might reinforce the decorative beauty, turns us sick at heart; and in a simple house a balustrade of turned wooden members simulating the fat stone ones at Versailles or in Firenze, that too sickens us by its pretense and inappropriateness. But perhaps what the commentators should point out to us is not that the machine was guilty of manufacturing these fakes; but that a simple balustrade made of precise machine-squared members would have been in place, perfectly fitting and genuinely pleasing. It is the machine misused by the greedy and untrained manufacturer, for pandering to thoughtless desire for the showy and the fashionable, that is at fault. The machines of the local planing-mill added to bad Victorian building its last touches of vulgarity, in contorted wooden scrolls and alarming spiked edgings; but to argue the failure of the machine as a factor in life, from that, is illogical, misleading, and wholly incompetent.

But there is, even today, I think, the feeling among the majority of practising architects, that if only they could get back to the days when the machine and steel and concrete had not complicated both life and architecture, they would be able to design palaces and opera houses and cathedrals that would rival those of the past. The hands of dead men have guided their education; and it is with dead men that they are fitted to compete.

THE challenge of the times can be met by the consumer in any one of three differing ways. First the job of housing industry and of building appropriately for the other needs of humanity can be turned over to those " leading " architects — willy-nilly. Second, humanity can see through the falsity and anachronism of the architects' compromise, can throw out the architects and turn over the job of building to engineers; and then at least the work will be honestly done, the house or school will function smoothly — and some say there is a " beauty " in that. Or third, new artist-creators may appear, to meet the challenge directly, with honesty, daring, *and imagination*; artists greater than either architect or engineer, detecting a spiritual as well as a mechanical-material challenge, visioning forms as different from those coded by the older architects as the business building is different from cathedral or palace.

In the first case, of course, if the world or a country turns the problem over to the safe and tried architects for solution, the new impulse passes off as a revival of a style, or at best there is something approaching a Renaissance. The new architecture that would meet the need in terms of today fails to be born.

In the second contingency, engineers build skyscrapers, bridges, hangars, that stir our imagination by their boldness, cleanness, and fitness to use. But that is all. The finely engineered structure is a welcome relief from the ornamentally disguised sorts. The engineer, however, finding in his hands the " artistic " problem of the deposed architect, falters the

The hangars for dirigibles at Orly, France, designed by H. Freyssinet

moment he tries to improve the "looks" by any known formula. That quality, that added value, that feeling for creative form, belongs to another — alone to the born artist-creator, the architect-engineer.

There is a saying among young German architectural students: "Study the American engineer; suspect the American architect." If challenged, they will add, "Of course Sullivan and Wright are exceptions." But they know that in general practice it was the engineer who first translated the epic spirit of steam and oil and electricity into at least the heavy beginnings of an architectural language. They look to the American grain elevators, silos, power plants, and automobile factories as stirring examples of direct thinking and creative handling of new materials in response to new needs. Even in France, where there is less disposition to grant pioneer leadership to America (or any other non-French country) one finds Le Corbusier writing this: [1]

---

[1] From Le Corbusier's *Towards a New Architecture*, translated by Frederick Etchells. New York 1927.

" The *architects* of today, lost in the sterile backwaters of their plans, their foliage, their pilasters and their lead roofs, have never acquired the conception of primary masses.  They were never taught that at the schools.

" *Not in pursuit of an architectural idea, but simply guided by the results of calculation (derived from the principles which govern our universe) and the conception of A LIVING ORGANISM, the ENGINEERS of today make use of the primary elements and, by co-ordinating them in accordance with the rules, provoke in us architectural emotions and thus make the work of man ring in unison with universal order.*

" *Thus we have the American grain elevators and factories, the magnificent FIRST FRUITS of the new age.  THE AMERICAN ENGINEERS OVERWHELM WITH THEIR CALCULATIONS OUR EXPIRING ARCHITECTURE."*

The achievement of these early engineers was, of course, the moulding of concrete and glass into industrial buildings that, by utter absence of ornament and elaboration, proclaimed sufficient solidity, trapping of light, and efficient shelter.  In addition, there is often a feel for elementary geometrical design, for proportion and sculptural mass and precise adjustment.  Occasionally the elevators stand up with the stirring " lift " of Greek columns, while the concrete-and-glass factories, with accented floor lines and great grilled window spaces, spread out in restful and precise horizontal patterns.  Still it is only when the inspired architect-engineer, rather than the engineer feeling toward architecture, re-enters the story, that one finds structures that give back any appreciable measure of that vague but all-important quality termed " architectural form." Some of the engineered grain stores and elevators, in particular, come amazingly near to the completed architectural unity, with proportioning, mass, balance, repetition of compelling line, etc., all seemingly drawn up into one appeal.  But it is when the architect again comes in that a human quality and controlled emotional appeal enter.  The engineered building, for all its fine reasonableness in its place, for all its overwhelming

Silos near Stockholm. E. Sandahl, architect. [By courtesy of the
Swedish State Railways Information Bureau, New York]

powerfulness and declared logic, lacks usually the overtone of creative
manipulation that would make us go back again and again to enjoy it
æsthetically.

This reservation need not lead us to overlook the importance of the
interim in architectural history during which the engineer ruled. And
there are rare engineered monuments not to be forgotten. In bridges,
which somehow often escaped the blighting architectural hand, the engineers provided stirring examples of daring and structural honesty; and
for a time the factories and train-sheds had a distinct vogue just because

they were directly designed to purpose — and no discrimination exerted
to discover whether they deserved ranking above commonplace shelters.
The story was the same in all countries: the conservatives insisting on
holding the façades — whatever the purpose — to old forms, to traditional modes.   And everywhere an engineer or two daring to raise his head
in defiance, sometimes leaving monuments more or less stirring to all eyes
even down to today: the fine Brooklyn Bridge, the now distinctly awk-
ward-looking but daring Eiffel Tower, some of the machinery halls for
the great expositions, the Rhine Bridge at Cologne, the hangar at Orly.

But to such a stirring challenge as that offered by the new needs and
the new materials, and by the glimpse of mechanized life ahead, a giant
mind might dream other answers.   A truly original mind, a mind not
blinded by self-interest, might vision architectural feats as glorious and
unprecedented as those long ago accomplished by the builders of the
Parthenon, of the Gothic cathedrals, as those Michelangelo crystallized, or
Brunelleschi.   In this connexion, it is pertinent to note that the names of
two American architects are now known round the world, whereas no
engineer is singled out from the mass for immortalization.   The reason
is that Sullivan and Wright were imaginative artists first of all: deserving
in the fullest sense the title " architect-engineers."   In guessing the greatness of the revolution which we in our lifetime have witnessed, they recognized that there was an *architectural* equivalent for mechanical efficiency,
for the conquest of power.   Their imaginations were stirred by the reach
into the heavens for electricity, the reach into the earth for new metals
and oils and structural materials, by the taming of raging fires and falling
waters till they serve man by sustaining life — but they had the vision
of the *beauty* that might be crystallized out of dreaming over those
accomplishments.

It is a building designed by Wright that we shall take as first specific
example of creative architectural treatment in response to the machine
challenge.   It happens that the Larkin Building, put up from Wright's
plans in 1903, served as a pioneer landmark on the way to a recognized

The Rhine Bridge at Cologne

modern architecture, having been pictured in many a European book on the subject, as well as serving American critics as a touchstone.

It is not exclusively a manufacturing plant: it houses as well the great mail-order business of the firm. Thus it is not quite as stark, as metal-heavy, as a " straight factory " might be. But it was perhaps the first building to compass the power feeling, the ruthless directness, the drive of industrialism, and at the same time achieve importance as an architectural entity. That there is a dignity here, an inherent nobility of expression, none will question. And it is just this severe majesty that the Moderns aim for as a legitimate reflection of the spirit of machine-age manufacture and trade. The architectural form, breathing power and solidity, arises out of calculations as precise, out of creative processes as direct and logical and imaginative as those that resulted in the existence of modern industrial machinery. For the fineness and the " drive " of this building are those of great simplicity and noble proportioning.

You may object that after all there is relief here for the heaviness and

The Larkin Building, Buffalo, New York, Frank Lloyd Wright, architect.   [1903]

Interior office view in the Larkin Building. Brick construction with metal
fittings. By Frank Lloyd Wright. [1903]

sombreness, in the sculptured bits topping the two pylons; but if you will
cover (as I have just done) these decorative bits in the picture of the
building, you will find that the sense of noble form remains unimpaired:
that the essential structure speaks as eloquently, as pleasingly to the eye
as when the " ornamental " touches are seen. The massing, the repeated
uprights, the sense of independent creativeness (with not an indication
anywhere that the architect had known earlier styles of architecture existed), and the honesty are the essential elements. The decorative bits are
secondary, reinforcing what is already accomplished in larger terms, from
deeper planes. Here is the precision not of grace and delicacy but of
concentrated power: here are metal-sheer surfaces, hard edges, clean lines,
and calculated volumes, brought into rhythmic expression.

In view of the hardness and sense of power that have come into architecture, much that has been canonized in the books on nineteenth and
early twentieth century architecture is going to look soft, trivial, and
spineless to coming generations. The lacy foliation and the clay-

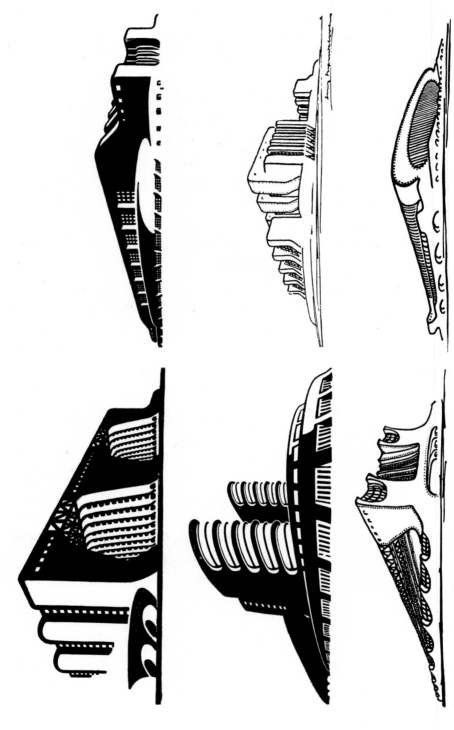

Sketches for industrial buildings, by Erich Mendelsohn. At left, hangars, a factory for optical goods, and a vehicle factory; at right, an aerodrome, chemical works, and a railway terminal. [By courtesy of the architect and of the editors of *Wasmuth's Monatshefte für Baukunst*, Berlin.] See also sketch at the chapter head.

modelling cartouches and wreathes that the French introduced as a sort of universal pastiche, found its way into all the Western countries, not least damagingly into the Americas; and not even buildings close to the machine life escaped — as witness the operatic front on America's most noted railroad station, Grand Central Terminal in New York. Imagine a Grand Central Station in the Larkin Building spirit. Instead, we have something soft, sweet, profuse, shallow — a betrayal of the epic railroad spirit: an attempt to hide industrialism, not to interpret or express it. The spaces enclosed are epic, and no one can fail to be impressed by the mighty engineering reach — but the mask is weak, pathetic.

Perhaps it is just as well to jump immediately to acquaintanceship with the architect who most rationally and most intensively — in projects and pictures, at least — made buildings expressive of the "feel" of the machine. Erich Mendelsohn, conceiving new characteristic building forms out of concrete, metal, and glass, surprised the world, just after the war, with a series of sketches of hangars, factories, and railway stations without precedent and intriguingly powerful. It will be noted, in the several sketches reproduced, how expressiveness of the intended use of the building is combined with an expressiveness of materials. Here there is no question about the originality, vitality, and machine-massiveness of the designs. Nothing could be further from echoing a lingering past, from stylistic tag-ends and souvenirs. Rather here young Germany, the after-the-war generation, spoke out clear and strong, and with the assurance of power. These designs begin with utter simplicity and structural truth, and carry on with creative shaping. They are only projects, and none of the ones shown has been worked out in actuality, but they have helped to determine architectural-engineering thought over a decade past.

Something of the powerfulness, the heavy simplicity, is shown, however, in this photograph of the interior of a factory. One gains a hint here of the really majestic and stupendous feats that will be accomplished with reinforced concrete, out of the great monolithic members, once we

Interior of a German hat factory.    Erich Mendelsohn, architect

rid ourselves of the idea that this is a " cheap " material, once we capitalize to the full its fundamental capabilities, its extraordinary reach.

Among the nakedest examples of the new industrial building is the extensive plant of the Siemens Factory in Berlin.    I imagine it affords one of the best available tests of the spectator's power to forget his training in polite architecture, to appreciate the concentrated machine-age hardness and cleanliness and power.    In talking about a coming new architecture with groups of friends, I have found that this picture turned a number away — " forbidding," " bare," " stark " — but that others, particularly the young, found in it an austere and lithe attractiveness. It has " lift," like the skyscrapers, but with an appropriate industrial metallic simplicity.

Not that all architecture will come to the heaviness appropriate to grain elevator, mill, and factory.    But no better immediate corrective to Beaux-Arts softness could be imagined.    As the realization spreads that

Part of the " factory city " of the Siemens Company, near Berlin.  Hans Hertlein, architect.
[By courtesy of *Wasmuth's Monatshefte für Baukunst*, Berlin]

the world is in for an age of mechanized life, an era when primary human welfare depends on industry and further development of mechanical power, the basic conception of what constitutes beauty changes.  Part of the new architectural beauty will be definitely heavy, massive, and stark, where industry is to be directly housed; and we may foresee that all of it will have gained spine and solidity and depth.  The zoning of

United States Appraiser's Stores, New York. Ely Jacques Kahn, architect. [Photo by Tebbs-Knell, New York]

cities, so that factories and art galleries and houses won't elbow one another, all losing character in attempting a common sort of style, is an indication that strictly industrial building is coming into its own; for though factories are the thing legislated *against*, the architect for a segregated type of building soon begins to express the character of that type in distinctive idioms, and pleasing ones.

Speaking of spine as the most obvious thing that all architecture is gaining out of the honest building engineered to use, we may note that the

Municipal bath-house at Hilversum, Holland.   Willem Dudok, architect.   [By courtesy *l'Architecte,* Paris]

part of the Larkin Building around the corner from what we saw in our two photographs, is made up, in the long panel between the heavy corner pylons, of successive piers rising through four tiers of windows.   That is an idiom that can be seen on hundreds of later factories, mills, and business buildings, including this German one; precisely because the logical architectural mind recognizes that here is decorative effect gained honestly out of structural skeleton.   It is an accenting, in tall buildings, of the rhythmic upright members — quite as legitimate as spreading successive free-standing columns in the ages when columns still carried the weight above — with a counter-play of half-accented floor and window lines between.   It is, of course, the factory counterpart of the pier-and-grill method of design which we shall meet during our study of the skyscraper.   It was not necessarily original with Wright — you will remember that his teacher, Sullivan, applied it to office buildings in the nineties; but, so far as I have been able to find, in neither America nor Europe was

Shipping house of an industrial plant in Cologne.  Emil Fahrenkamp, architect

The Schocken department stores, Stuttgart, Germany. [By courtesy of *Architecture*, New York]

it utilized in industrial structures before the Larkin Building so successfully demonstrated the logic of it.

Beyond the simplification, structural strength, and powerful proportioning of the factory buildings, it has been the quality of machine-room *tidiness* that has most distinguished the new manifestations. From the extreme of that confusion and dirtiness which "æsthetic" artists once visualized as inseparable from industrialism, a few architects have travelled all the way to that other extreme of tidiness and polished-metal spic-and-span-ness which by rights characterizes machinery (for we all know that a really dirty mechanical contrivance goes but half-efficiently if at all).

It is not so surprising, perhaps, that a bath-house should have clean implications; though I think the example on page 101, by Willem Dudok, is quite extraordinary for the way in which that quality is carried into the building design. (You will find that the same " feel " is incorporated into the notable school building by Dudok shown in a later chapter, but with more " relief.") More standard examples of the tidiness of modern industrial buildings are to be seen in the pictures of the exteriors of the Appraisers' Stores Building in New York, and the precisely designed

The Bauhaus, Dessau, Germany.   Walter Gropius, architect

Rheinstahl shipping-house by Emil Fahrenkamp.   Of all the buildings I have inspected, however, I think I felt the cleanliness, the flatness, and the freedom from complicated detail best expressed in the Bauhaus at Dessau. In this combined technical school, crafts-shop and producing factory, I sensed a precise cleanliness due to the economical and rational use of concrete, glass, and metal.   That the thing is carried out decoratively as well as for functional efficiency, one may see by the photograph.   But for further study of the æsthetic values — for this is a famous example wherever "Rationalist" architecture is talked — we shall wait till we come to the chapter on "Work-Places."   Just now our interest is less in the details of structure and the varying methods of achieving decorativeness than in establishing a relationship between the new architecture as known and the emergence of the machine as a dominant factor in human living; in the traces of machine heaviness, hardness, and cleanliness in building design.

But while we have been insistent upon these qualities as common to the early typically modern answers to the machine challenge, let us not be dogmatic about carrying them *unrelieved* throughout twentieth cen-

American concrete construction, "without benefit of architect." [By courtesy of Wasmuth's *Monatshefte für Baukunst*]

tury building.  Let us remember that we are still in the pioneer days, when a certain austerity, a severe discipline, becomes us, as preparation for the fuller life to come.  Even now we know that color is to enter generously as an enrichment; and that some architects are discovering ornamental modes that seem to reinforce, not weaken, the structural appeal.  And to those observers who find in the square, box-like forms and the flat roofs so common to Modernist experiment an unwarranted starkness and monotony, one may point out that the new materials *can* be moulded more easily than the old to round and oblique forms.  The grain elevators and silos are evidence that concrete will serve some of the same purposes of majestic repetition of cylinder forms that the world has so admired in the Greek stone columns: and serve them so cheaply that the corn country is full of examples.  Many a traveller from Europe has picked out these "common" structures for comment while overlooking our swankier banks and libraries.  And as for the flat roofs, one may acknowledge that there are many places where material, climatic, and æsthetic considerations demand that even modernly simple and organic buildings have sloping roofs — and that the finest architecture in the residential suburbs of German cities has that feature. After all, we need be no more exacting, make no more formulas, than in the designing of the machine itself; we wouldn't insist that the inventor use only square bits of metal in any part of his machinery. But the fact remains that the flat surface and the long clean line *characterize* machinery; and no inventor breaks up a surface or complicates a reach if unnecessary. There is a hint in that.

I sometimes think that those who worry about the forbidding aspect of Modernist architecture are of the same breed as those who feel that an arch is in itself more artistic than a squared opening; or that putting Greek columns on the front of a building puts it *ipso facto* into line with the Greek architecture of the past. We are today finding our suitable forms, and it happens that machine-like lines and square angles and simple walls are fundamental to them; whereas some people are still thinking that the cake can't be so good without an outside coating of the pink-and-white sugar trimmings that they learned to dote on when they were children.

PERHAPS as a last stimulus to our thinking about a *machine-conscious* architecture, we may profitably glance at certain phases of railroad building: they seem to sum up the achievements of the engineers, the failure of many architects to meet the challenge of mechanics, and the emergence of a few artists, architect-engineers, who saw a different world coming and built for it.

Standing on a viaduct over railroad tracks, looking along the gleaming rails where the rock-filled roadbed cuts its ruthless line through hill and marsh and plain and valley, for perhaps a straightaway of miles, I experience a realization of man's mechanical achievement such as comes at no other moment. We may feel a sense of exhilaration in motoring, and find æsthetic delight in the expressiveness of the automobile; and the lift

The spirit of the railroad. [Drawing by courtesy of the New York Central Lines]

of the airplane as it soars from the ground, frees itself of roads and tracks and earthly obstacles, is thrilling. But the very complications of railroad engineering, and the ways in which it challenges architecture, make it exciting to the mind looking for signs of man's advance toward machine-age building. There is a hint here, if anywhere, of what mechanized life is coming to. The interfabrication of rails, roadbed, signals, crossings, stations, etc., is a sort of network of contrived building that foreshadows a machine-articulated world.

Setting aside the epic spirit that was behind the throwing of railways across the most difficult continents, we may come with disappointment up against the fact that nowhere have engineer-architects designed an entire railway system with imaginative regard for expressive values. Most often they let us down in their station buildings. An express train glides magically over plains and fills and bridged chasms, through tunnels and

The Badischer station at Basel, Switzerland.   Karl Moser, architect

along smoothed ledges on canyon-rims, thrilling the mind with difficulties gloriously overcome and lulling the senses with the hum of wheels — and then pulls up at a station designed in the image of Versailles or Athens or Seville.   From the pretty cottage stations of New England and the castle-stations of the Western mountains to Grand Central Terminal and the Pennsylvania Station in New York City, we feel a sense of betrayal.

Railway station at Bussum, Holland. H. G. J. Schelling, architect. [From *Nieuwe Bouwkunst in Nederland*, by Aug. M. J. Sevenhuijsen]

We may find the spirit of the railroad, of the machine, of the freeing of mankind by mechanics, elsewhere along the line; but, in general, station builders have successfully masked it. Not completely, of course. When it comes to the actual train-sheds of the larger terminals, the grandeur and economy and the cleanliness are sometimes there. Even the Pennsylvania Terminal, so slavishly Roman and wasteful elsewhere, has one glorious and honest hall.

But as if to prove that almost at one moment an impulse to think directly was felt in widely separated places, architects in Finland, Holland, southern Germany, and Switzerland designed within a very few years a series of railroad buildings organically sound and wholly appropriate to the industrial age. Where formerly the architects not only had failed to declare the function — even hushed it up, blanketed it, denied it — these men told what their buildings housed, gloried in the expression of railroad mechanics, at the same time shaping the design to the uses of a city portal.

It was Eliel Saarinen, later to have an extraordinary influence on sky-

Two views of the railway terminal at Stuttgart, Germany. Paul Bonatz and F. E. Scholer, architects.
[By courtesy of the German Tourist Information Office, New York]

scraper design in America, who planned the great central station at Helsingfors; and the followers of Berlage in Holland brought railway-terminal design into keeping with the rational treatment of schools, apartments, and factories.  But we may best find illuminating illustrations in the Central Station at Stuttgart, by Paul Bonatz and F. E. Scholer, and in the "Badischer" Station at Basel, by the Swiss-German Moser.

The Stuttgart terminal is characteristic in these points: function is so expressed that the building immediately suggests railroad station (not opera house or Roman baths) to the casual observer's mind, masses are machine-heavy, lines are machine-clean, proportioning masterly.  There is no ornament wasted here, and yet — despite an overcoldness in such great masses of grey stone — there is pleasing decorative value.  Critics have pointed out that the architects returned to Romanesque instead of Renaissance or Roman forms, hinting that this is simply another sort of Eclecticism.  We may note, however, that the designers of the Stuttgart Station have overlooked every *ornamental* feature of the Romanesque style: the deep-cut, multiple-arched doorways and the sculpture-enriched windows.  Remembering too that one of the designers, Paul Bonatz, is a veteran among Germany's progressive architects, we have reason to believe that this is no mere shift to an old mode for the sake of coming within a style.  The whole thing bespeaks honesty and clear-thinking too audibly for that.  The station happens not to be indebted to new twentieth century materials.  It is a masonry structure through and through, even the tower being laid up without metal skeleton.  (There is, of course, no more reason to use concrete or steel, in a region where stone and labor are cheap and just as suited to the purpose, for the sake of being "modern," than there is for killing off all the horses in the world because automobile travel and transport are usually quicker and more economical.)

The station at Basel catches the clean, heavy railroad look but with an admixture of something out of the older Teutonic building.  The general form is simple, solid, and neat in proportions, but the larger elements, central hall, tower, and office building, are shaped with a vague

Detail of the railway terminal at Helsingfors.   Eliel Saarinen, architect

reference to solid German tradition.   Note, however, how reticently the very few ornamental bits are touched in, without breaking up the main massing.

As an example of a smaller, more intimate station, designed directly to purpose, unornamented but exhibiting a definite sense of stylization, there is the building at Bussum, Holland, by H. G. J. Schelling.   Could one ask for anything more simple and more pleasing as a modern city gateway — less masked by the old pretense and show?   And as a further step toward rationalization, toward a stylization based on railroad-mindedness, on the feel of steam and electric transport, let me turn to certain of those " radicals " who have preferred to forget entirely the practice of the past, who have designed terminals to fit conceptions of complete machine-age cities.   How near these two " projects " for stations come to foreshadowing the future, whether their studied abstract-

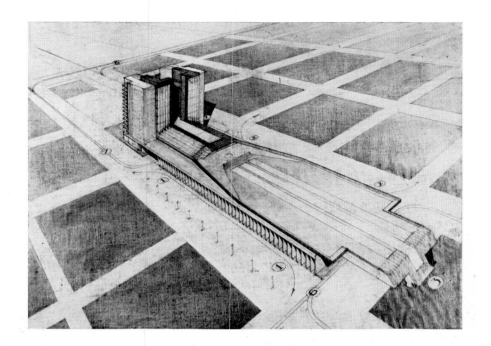

Designs by Richard J. Neutra for a typical machine-age railway terminal: being part of the architect's plans for " an abstraction of a modern American metropolis."

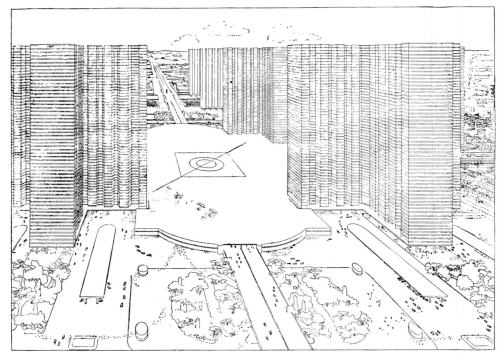

Design by Le Corbusier for a combined subway, surface and elevated (airport) terminal at the center of a skyscraper city. [From *Urbanisme,* by Le Corbusier, by courtesy of Payson & Clarke, publishers of the English translation]

ness of design, their heavy leaning upon the geometry of machine design, is a warrant that railroad architecture will be more than ever based on steel rail, concrete culvert, electric-engine and steel-car sheerness, neither I nor anyone else can rightly predict.   But these are logical, if extreme, answers to the challenge we have been studying.   They illustrate one more phase of the creativeness of a few architects who stood up face to face with the machine.

Since we have emphasized and re-emphasized the economic and functional elements underlying architectural composition in the new age, it would be wrong to close the chapter without returning to the affirmation that architecture is more than *mere* utilitarian building.   The machine may do its work and be sloppy about it, dirty and ungainly in looks; but at the same time airplanes, steamships, automobiles, and refrigerators afford some of the most satisfying æsthetic experiences commonly available in the world today. An element beyond practical efficiency has entered in. Some seekers for ultimate truth say that if the machine is perfectly fitted for its use, the æsthetic value grows out of that. Others feel a creative, inventive shaping above the achievement of highest efficiency. At the moment we need not pause over the alternatives. We know that mankind is happier with the beautiful machine than with a sloppy one; that many of his treasured recreational and spiritual moments in life come from the experience of that overvalue. We may affirm, then, that the *merely* engineered house is not good enough, will not be good enough in the new world-society. The architect must go on with us into the new world structure. He must be engineer first; no longer at heart a decorator. But to him we must look for that glory out of buildings that speaks to us thrillingly through so many of the " Monuments " of the past — and somehow through the machines of today.

Believing, too unsuspectingly, what we are taught at school, by the inheritors of nineteenth century taste, that the picture on the wall is art, or the photographic statue in the town square, but not the things we use, we too readily feel some antagonism between the idea of the machine and the idea of beauty. That is because we were taught by only the reminders or the perversions of art. Remember that beauty as recognized had run down from a thing strong, deep, and creative to a thing superficial and diverting, even frivolous, in the latest phases of civilization. The weak, imitative buildings that we reviewed, the nineteenth century monuments, are a record of the architects' reach for beauty in so far as nineteenth century life and organized taste permitted. Perhaps that age could only stand beauty at second hand, in echoes. In the same era sculpture lost the last vestiges of its profoundness, massiveness, and strength; became light, decorative, pretty, suave; painting became anecdotal and photographic, with great technical dexterity but no deeper conviction, was often opulent but never richly living. Art weakened,

The railway station at Helsingfors, Finland: one of the earliest instances of escape from palatial and
operatic motives in station design.    Eliel Saarinen, architect.

was a surface attainment.    In all the arts, beauty — if you accept that
as a name for what is satisfying in art — became fluffy, slick, or wastefully
showy.    Naturally this does not agree with machinery.    If you are a
devotee of culture of that materialistically strong but spiritually spent
century, you will continue to find the machine disturbing.

But in the end it is the machine that will hold its ground.    Nor will
you ever make the machine — dynamo or automobile or house — " artistic " in the civilized, luxurious sense, with surface ornament.    The revolution in living is too complete for that.    Instead, a new art is growing
up directly out of the materials, the masses, and the directions of
the mechanism, out of scientific economy, out of man's feel for
æsthetic " rightness."    When you have thrown away your nineteenth

The Army Supply Base Building, Brooklyn, New York.   Cass Gilbert, architect

century sort, sickened of its false glamour and wasteful opulence, you may turn around and find a gloriously clean, austere, and liberated art rising up out of the machines themselves. That is where lie a new strength, a clarity, a fundamental purpose, and a new profound vitality for art.

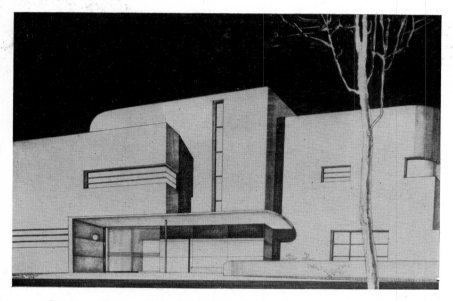

Country residence at White Marsh, Pennsylvania. Howe & Lescaze, architects

By J. R. Miller & T. L. Pflueger

# CHAPTER IV

## *PIONEERS : STRIPPED ARCHITECTURE*

THE CHURCH SPIRE, rising from its cluster of houses, dominating its village, pointing eternally and symbolically to the heavens, used to be called, poetically, the Finger of God. There are hundreds of old world villages still where one may see — and enjoy — the huddled group of dwellings with the church uplifted above them, the spire or campanile carrying upward the eye and the imagination. But one need not go closer to know that automobiles are tearing through the too-narrow streets of those villages, that poles carrying telephone, telegraph, and electric wires mar their simplicity; and perhaps out on the edge of the settlement a factory rises gaunt, its brick stack and its steel water-tower rivalling the church in height. And if the community be a " progressive " one, soon a business building or a multiple apartment will rise to overshadow the church, to dispute domination with God. These idyllic villages, symbolic of the old quiet life, of the trust in a distant Divinity, born of local circumscribed existence, of living on the flat plane of the earth and in simple ways — those villages and that life are doomed.

What figure the poet might employ to describe the skyscraper, dwarfing the church, outpointing the cathedral spire, I do not know. There is an epic implication in man's defiance of the laws of gravity, and beauty in the naked lift of uprising steel and concrete. But the purpose of the skyscraper is not poetic. Perhaps Commercialism is a new God, only too powerful and too appealing, to Whom men are building today their largest, costliest, and most laudatory structures. In this service they are building higher and ever higher, concentrating more and more activity into less of ground space, stealing light and air from their neighbors, piously recording in their structures the Exploitation that is right-hand attribute of Commercialism.

At any rate, the skycraper is the typical building of the twentieth century. New York City, to be sure, is erecting, slowly, a belated mediæval cathedral; but each year consumed laboriously in that archæological task sees the rise of scores of business buildings larger, more honest in methods of construction and in purpose (for the cathedral in coming times, as now, can be little more than a show place, a piece of insincerity), and more expressive of contemporary living. Business rules the world today, and as long as business can best be served where many offices are concentrated in one small area, in buildings designed as machines for the efficient discharge of buying, selling, trading, banking, law disputes, gambling, and exploitation, business architecture will be supreme.

Cities may prohibit the high building, may legislate against competitive grasp at upper space and sunlight, but they then limit their participation in the scramble for markets, cripple themselves as efficient trading-centres: put a handicap upon their business men in the race for world trade. Twenty floors of offices in one stack, with electric-elevator communication between, are immeasurably more efficient than those floors would be if spread side by side over ten acres; the stacking-up eliminates

The 50-story Irving Trust Company-One Wall Street Building,
New York. Voorhees, Gmelin & Walker, architects. [From a
copyrighted drawing by Chester B. Price, by courtesy of the
Irving Trust Company]

travel, facilitates exchange — though the concentration complicates out-side street traffic at " the rush hours."

Not until the basis of all living changes, until we get away from com-petitive fortune-making and from nationalistic government designed primarily to protect and increase hoarded wealth, shall we find other than the business building the chief structure in our cities. To be sure, supremacy in world trade, bringing a flow of wealth and a margin be-yond business needs, may — as just now in our own land — permit vast enterprise in other types of building, seemingly more concerned with the living of the good life: libraries, universities, country clubs, stadiums, art galleries, theatres. But up to this time the trade structure remains the keystone of our architectural achievement. And the new world aspect of this structure is shadowed by old evil purposes.

The skyscraper, then, is the building that symbolizes the times, the peak of human trade-progress, that reflects the thinking of the ruling business man. Let us not too easily look down instead of up, in our effort to place this species, this type; contrasting him unfavorably as an unproductive middleman, as distinguished from the productive hand-laborer and artisan, or the intellectually laboring " professionals." After all, he is the one who has made the historic progress out of barbarism into civilization, and through all the stages of that era to this final one when trade decides empires, opens continents, overshadows churches. For it was barter that led to meeting-places between tribes, to towns, cities; and increasingly it was trade enterprise that " civilized " all the dark places of the earth, that shaped the form of governments, that pushed the flags of Western Europe around the globe in conquering glory. The business-man-trader is the organizer of society. We are agreed that there is a fundamental flaw in his method of organization — not on a world-plan or for the basic protection of all — so that the fruits of world-wealth and culture are spread on a table precariously balanced and likely to collapse in any decade; but the business man did it. And his is

The skyscraper city as seen from the air, about 1922.  [From a photo copyright by Underwood & Underwood]

the art that is with us; materially, his is the first great architecture of the machine age.

We are beginning our more intensive study of the history of the " modern " building, then, with the emergence of this doubly characteristic thing, the one achievement born of the dual spirit of the age, out of capitalistic feudalism and out of the reach forward of mechanics.  The churches and chateau-palaces and theatres that were the glory of architecture in the past — that we Americans go to Europe to see — have no contemporary counterparts.  Nor is the skyscraper only *symbolically* typical of today: nowhere else is architecture so perfectly expressive of the wholly new materials.  Without those materials the structures could not be designed so precisely to a new use; the individual building could not be so exactly and so wastelessly a machine for purposes of the scientific-management, mechanistic age.  There were no precedents for the forms of 200-feet-high honeycomb buildings; new massive foundations and new engineering were called for.   What effort was made to confine the sky-scraper to old architectural elements broke down within thirty years. We have now seen it rise straight, naked, and inescapable.

You will remember that the Eclectic architects masked the building effectively during their reign of a quarter-century after the invention of steel framing (before that invention the true skyscraper was impossible).   Their masking first had taken the form of façades making believe that the masonry of the lower stories carried the load of roof, floors, and walls above, resulting in heavy Romanesque and Florentine stone effects, with deep inset windows and portals, ponderously dishonest; but later they divided the façade after the proportions of a single classic column-unit, decorating orthodoxly the top and bottom sections, but leaving the main shaft of the building simple and sensible.   Many a daring American engineering feat of those early days was, so to speak, sunk without trace under oceans of Roman pilasters and columns or Gothic traceries.   The mask might be story on story of identical superimposed pilasters and incipient cornices, or piled-up arches (the windows of two or three stories peeping out timidly under each arch), or perhaps an adaptation of some historic monument, like the Metropolitan Tower enveloped in a semblance of St. Mark's Campanile, or an honest shaft-like building set on a triumphal Roman arch and capped with a Greek temple.   But even while the architect was thus hiding the real structure, the engineer was technically perfecting the new method of building, was fabricating his steel frame economically and honestly, was fitting to it the new network of veins, nerves, digestive and waste organs: the plumbing, the wiring, the heating system, the elevators, etc.   The structural engineer made the *interior* of the building safe, convenient, and simple; even though a huge hollow metal or real stone cornice might hang over the top edge outside, cutting off light and endangering lives below, while a hundred Palladian window-frames complicated the simple upward lines.

We have seen, too, how this engineer was lauded for his work by that small group known as the Intelligentsia.  For a few people saw through to the wonder of the functioning machine behind the architect's disguise, guessed that here was one of the stupendous achievements of the dawning new age.  They saw the outward sign of it in the rear elevations, the neglected sides that had escaped the architect's attention; there the unbroken height and the confessed bulk were often fine, with thrilling hard, clean lines, logical materials piled up in new combinations, and newly huge areas of wall.  Buildings like that bespoke power, heroism, and adventure.

But the engineer alone could not go beyond the honest handling of materials, fitness to purpose, and precision.  Without having two lifetimes — a second one to spend in study and dreaming as an artist, — he could not accomplish those finer, subtler expressions of beauty connoted in the word " architecture."  Exact calculation is the basis of engineering.  There is a complementary element of inspiration or " feeling " where the artist works.

This truth comes back to us when we praise the engineers' buildings. We remember a little uneasily a certain starkness that might pleasingly be modified — without losing vigor or solidity or precision, and a somewhat inhuman lack of color and " relief."  There is wanting the finer adjustment, the counterpoint, the enrichment.  We remember uneasily too that the engineer gave us the stoves with riveted-on flourishes and the iron ornaments on the Eiffel Tower.

GENIUS cuts through all distinctions — between architect and engineer, between frame and enrichment, between nakedness and beauty.  Louis Sullivan was the genius who pierced through the cloud of architectural pretension and " culture," who experienced the vision of a new art of building.  He was the creative architect who, after studying through all the formulas and fashions of the architectural schools, saw the need to go back and make himself engineer first.  He created richly, recorded his beliefs and discoveries, was all but inundated for three decades under the recurring floods of Eclectic cultural building — but now comes into full recognition, almost suddenly, in a brief five years, as prophet and first practitioner of the new world architecture.

Louis Henri Sullivan was as American as American can be: that is, he was born in Boston of a full Irish father and a mother half-German, half French-Swiss; experienced both country and city life in his childhood and youth; studied at common schools, then specialized at a technical college, and exposed himself to a finishing-off process in Europe; and spent his mature life in the Middle West. A lover of nature and of music and of solitude, a believer in the creative power of man, a dreamer, distrusting intellect exercised without intuitional and imaginative guidance, perceiving critic of academic culture and relating it truly to its parent feudal civilization — he combined many of the attributes of natural philosopher and mystic with those of the active, overworked architect.

We may be sure that Louis Sullivan knew thoroughly the art of architectural design as practised before and in his time; and it happened that his life work spanned the period from before steel framing to the fullness of the Eclectic practice in the early twentieth century. He studied at the Massachusetts Institute of Technology, in that early day already under the guidance of a leading Boston architect with a French assistant fresh from the Beaux-Arts School, and he stuck it out for a full school year; though much earlier he had become unfitted for the absorption of routine education: "His history book told him that certain buildings were to be revered, but the buildings themselves did not tell him so, for he saw them with a fresh eye, an eye unprepared for sophistries, and a mind empty of dishonesty."[1] At "Tech" he learned about the orders and other idols and historical scraps; and he fled to experience with practical architects, in Philadelphia. Still, he thought it might be the Institute of Technology that was at fault, and he determined to go to the fountain-head of sacred architectural knowledge, the *École des Beaux-Arts* itself, in Paris. Again

[1] This and the following brief quotations are from *The Autobiography of an Idea,* by Louis H. Sullivan, New York 1926. This book, without any illustrations of architecture, must be placed first on any reading list of works on the new world architecture. It goes beyond practice to philosophy and spiritual causes.

The German Pavilion at the Seville Exposition, 1929, by Mies van der Rohe. [By courtesy of Frederick Kiesler]

he mastered the basic teaching of a school, but found it, in spite of brilliancy and cleverness, " a method, a state of mind, that was local and specific, not universal " — and " not the reality he sought." Here, indeed, at the end of his second brief experience of architectural schools as they are, he chose consciously the way that he foresaw would be lonely and difficult.

Returned to America, he went to Chicago, then emerging from boomtown into big-city status, and crying out for builders of imagination. While he worked as assistant in one after another of the larger offices, he passionately studied engineering — and gradually developed his own theory of building design. He "found himself drifting toward the engineering point of view, or state of mind, as he began to discern that the engineers were the only men who could face a problem squarely; who knew a problem when they saw it. Their minds were trained to deal with real things . . . while the architectural mind lacked this directness, this simplicity, this singleness of purpose." In 1881 Louis Sullivan became partner to an older and highly successful architect, and from that year forward the name "Adler and Sullivan" entered prominently into the record of architecture in the Middle West.

And so this straight-thinking, imaginative architect-engineer was in a position of influence and authority when the steel-frame building was "invented." Characteristically Sullivan credits the use of steel as much to the salesmen of the steel companies as to the several Chicago architects who had built competitively higher and higher buildings, in their search for a solution of the problem of tall structures without excessive masonry thickness at the base. But we may be sure that it was Louis Sullivan — who had already arrived at his basic principle, that form must follow function — who alone was ready to meet the "skyscraper" challenge wholly honestly; who was able to foresee the revolutionary change that the steel frame would ultimately entail in the world's building; who would at once build honestly structural skyscrapers and flay the academic men who came to recognize the problem but preferred masks and evasions to honest statement. And yet history will tell us that those orthodox, slave-minded architects obscured the message and the work of Louis Sullivan for a full thirty years.

Before returning to the skyscraper as Sullivan designed it — though I am putting in here a picture of one of his structures — I will complete the brief account of his life, with a particular note of the way in which respectable Compromise drowned out his plea for Truth, his insurgency. It would seem that youthful America, pushing up to a place of importance among the nations, the home of mechanical invention, the boasted land of freedom, would have allowed expression to this creative spirit, would have called its own his inventive genius and his freedom of mind. But the architectural professionals of these United States, not understanding what blessing was theirs in having no stylistic past to enslave them — uneasy perhaps without chains — had assumed the burden of Europe's past, particularly that of France, after the manner of the unoriginal mind taking refuge in borrowed culture. They decreed among themselves that nothing would be sanctioned as artistic that did not reflect Athens or

The Prudential Building, Buffalo, New York.   Louis H. Sullivan, architect.   1896.   [From Claude Bragdon's *Architecture and Democracy*,
by courtesy of Alfred A. Knopf]

Rome or Paris or London as pictured in a Beaux-Arts mirror.   The Columbian Exposition of 1893 — curiously enough a Chicago affair — gave
the Eastern academicians the opportunity to scotch this snake of the
West.   Through the influence of Daniel H. Burnham — a great business-
architect up to a certain point, but then an expedient policy-man and
toadier — the Eastern architects were brought out, in the spirit of bringing culture to the West.   "The Dream City," a marvellous object lesson

to millions of Americans, took on a classic aspect, belied America and Chicago and Columbus, but showed out a great beauty to be gained from foresight and wise planning — along with the glamorous pull of warmed-over European " art."

It happens that for many visitors, particularly Europeans, seeking a glimpse of the true America, the one building contributed by Sullivan to the World's Fair was the most enchanting, and certainly the most honestly appealing structure in the group. There was no skyscraper problem here; but true to his own principles of form following function, Sullivan made the Transportation Building frankly declare what it was: a temporary stucco structure, a colorful screen raised for a season; he gloried in the shallow ornament and brilliant color appropriate to an ephemeral building and occasion — and he made " the Golden Portal " a lasting memory among artists who visited the Exposition. At the same time he doubtless sowed seeds that grew and came to blossom in Europe years later. But the Transportation Building, as it was the only colored structure in the famed White City, was also the exception in ways that carry deeper significance: for the Exposition otherwise was a triumph for academicism and timid orthodoxy.

Let us pause a bit longer over this occasion, for nowise else can we obtain so clear a view of the American scene at a moment just after a new and epoch-making mode of building had been born. The latest and best-accredited historian of American architecture, Thomas E. Tallmadge, who wobbles between rigorous faith in Eclecticism and " sympathy " for the Moderns — and who thus does spread out the whole picture, however distortedly, in his *The Story of Architecture in America* — includes the following lines in his rhapsodic chapter on the Exposition. (The italics are mine — added without malice, merely to show out the contrast between the creative mind we have been studying and the standard architectural mind.)

" When we were children and our stock of conversation had run low, we always filled the void by saying, ' Let's talk about the World's Fair.'

The " Golden Portal " of the Transportation Building, World's Columbian Exposition. [1893]

We are still talking about the World's Fair, and the lapse of thirty-three years has not dimmed nor has custom staled its infinite variety. . .

" The Exposition as completed, with its banners fluttering in the breeze, its fountains splashing in the sunshine, its lagoons troubled by the courses of the launches and gondolas which crashed into a million fragments the fairy visions reflected on their breasts, its emerald lawns jewelled with flowers and birds, and its tremendous and many palaces with their regal equipment of terraces, bridges, and esplanades all bathed in sunshine against the azure setting of the lake, furnished a spectacle unequalled in the history of the world for the magnificence of its beauty. Imperial Rome in the third century might have approached but surely did not surpass it. Such was the conviction of my boyhood, and thirty-three years of increasing sophistication, which have included most of the architectural spectacles of the generation, have not dimmed the splendor of that picture nor changed in my mind the schoolboy's verdict.

"Only the great buildings need be mentioned. Architecturally, the palm went to Atwood with his Palace of Fine Arts, the only building on the grounds built with any claim to permanence, and now after a generation of neglect and ruin happily in the course of restoration. *It is pure Greek Classic,* in the Ionic order except for its low dome, and even that looks as though it had been dropped into position on its beautiful shoulders by the hands of Callicrates himself. The south portico is especially interesting. *Atwood borrowed it complete from a Prix de Rome design of the time,* and when Besnard, its creator, saw his drawing in its consummation he remarked that he had had no idea how great an architect he was! . . .

"The Administration Building by Hunt was the next in popular esteem, and it majestically and regally occupied its post of honor at the end of the great court and opposite the golden figure of the Republic. Technically, I think it suffered in comparison with its two beautiful companions, the Agricultural Building by McKim, Mead and White, and Machinery Hall by Peabody and Stearns. *The first was pure Roman.* . .

"The note struck by Peabody in Machinery Hall has echoed the longest. It has reappeared in expositions again and again when the other sweeter strains have long since died away. . . The style, I should say, *was French in disposition,* particularly in its colonnades which remind one of the Place de la Concorde and Perrault's east end of the Louvre, *and Spanish in decoration.* The twin towers, the domes over the corner pavilions, the silhouette — the entire ensemble had a dash and vim that fire the blood even in faded photographs or blurred memories. It was an admirable building.

"The great Manufactures and Liberal Arts Building, the largest building in the world, was dignified and satisfactory, its corner and central pavilions being *adaptations of the well-worn triumphal arch motive.* . . The Fisheries was not intended to be a building of great importance, but it ended by being one of the outstanding successes of the Fair. *It was the swan song of the Romanesque, a song so full of charm, of humor, of pathos, . . ."* etc., etc.

There one has indeed the make-up of that " infinite variety " which Mr. Tallmadge finds un-stale after thirty-three years: " pure Greek Classic," " pure Roman," French, Spanish, Romanesque (the Gothicists alone seem to have fared ill at this feast of the Eclectics). In short, the Exposition that might have been a great object-lesson in creative design became the stick with which the Eastern architects whipped wavering American taste into respectable conformance with French Eclecticism. And there came the great tragedy of Louis Sullivan's life; at the same time a greater tragedy for American building. Even the skyscraper was to be, for thirty years thenceforward, squeezed into the stylistic envelopes sanctioned by the World's Fair architects, masked behind Classic façades, with doorways hidden through those same well-worn triumphal arches. We can only guess what were Sullivan's thoughts and feelings during the months of the building and opening and closing of the Exposition; but years later he wrote: " These crowds were astonished. They beheld what was for them an amazing revelation of the architectural art, of which previously they in comparison had known nothing. To them it was a veritable Apocalypse, a message inspired from on high. Upon it their imagination shaped new ideals. They went away spreading again over the land, returning to their homes, each one of them carrying in the soul the shadow of the white cloud, each of them permeated by the most subtle and slow acting of poisons; an imperceptible miasm within the white shadow of a higher culture. A vast multitude, exposed, unprepared, they had not had time nor occasion to become immune to forms of sophistication not their own, to a higher and more dexterously insidious plausibility. Thus they departed joyously, carriers of contagion, unaware that what they had beheld and believed to be truth was to prove, in historic fact, an appalling calamity. For what they saw was not what they believed they saw, but an imposition of the spurious upon their eyesight, a naked exhibitionism of charlatanry in the higher feudal and domineering culture, enjoined with expert salesmanship of the materials of decay. Adventitiously, to make the stage setting complete, it happened by way of apparent but unreal contrast that the structure representing the United States Government was of an incredible vulgarity . . .

" Thus architecture died in the land of the free and the home of the brave — in a land declaring its fervid democracy, its inventiveness, its resourcefulness, its unique daring, enterprise, and progress. Thus did the virus of a culture, snobbish and alien to the land, perform its work of disintegration; and thus ever works the pallid academic mind, denying the real, exalting the fictitious and the false, incapable of adjusting itself to the flow of living things, to the reality and the pathos of man's follies, to the valiant hope that ever causes him to aspire, and again to aspire; that never lifts a hand to aid because it cannot; that turns its back upon man because that is its tradition; a culture lost in ghostly misalliance with abstractions, when what the world needs is courage, common sense, and human sympathy, and a moral standard that is plain, valid, and livable.

" The damage wrought by the World's Fair will last for half a century from its date, if not longer. It has penetrated deep into the constitution of the American mind, effecting there lesions significant of dementia."

Louis Sullivan continued to work for decades after that; but with decreasing " success," once the high tide of Eclecticism flowed over the country. His " large commissions " were fewer; and ultimately he came to the truth that his pen would have more weight than his buildings in leading a younger generation out of the miasmic fogs of the higher and alien " culture." It is true that some of his pupils did carry on continuously and clear-sightedly; and one is by all odds the greatest living architect today, but not at all concerned in the field of the steel-frame building, and therefore to be discussed as the outlaw-genius of another chapter. At present, concerned with the skyscraper, we may disengage the Sullivan buildings of the nineties from the surrounding welter of

The Wainwright Building, St. Louis, Missouri. Louis H. Sullivan, architect. 1890. [From *Missouri's Contribution to American Architecture*, ed.
by J. A. Bryan]

learned architectural miscegenation, and see why historians of the future
will link up the Western-American steel-frame building of 1895 with
world building of 1925–1930 — with very little attention to manifestations of the period between.   (Though Tallmadge, missing any spiritual
or material affinity between the early work and Saarinen's *Chicago
Tribune* Tower design or the New York Telephone Building, both of
which he lauds roundly at the close of his book, entitles his chapter on
radicalism of the nineties " Louis Sullivan and the Lost Cause.")

On page 129 is a photograph of the Prudential Building in Buffalo,

designed by Sullivan and erected in 1896.  Over-leaf is a picture of the
Wainright Building in St. Louis, of an earlier period.  In these two
examples one may note how the basic idea of form following function is externalized.  In the first place, there is no attempt to make these
out masonry structures; from top to base windows dominate: the walls
are mere screens of glass and protecting clay or stone hung on the metal
frames.  There is frank declaration that the weight is carried in pillars
to a few points of support.  The upward structural lines are stressed,
affording, in Sullivan's own words, " the sense of vertical continuity."
We should note also that there is surface ornament; though Sullivan insisted that decorative features should never obscure, deny, or weaken
structural truths, he was the first master of original ornament among
American architects.  He created his own idioms, independent of the
historic styles; and it is no accident that today the two Americans who
are most original and most influential in this field are old students of his.
Even in his skyscrapers of 1896, so simple and so directly expressive and
so business-like, ornamental enrichment had its place.

Here indeed was the direct, simple thinking of the American engineer
coupled with the vision and the imagination of the eternal architect.
Here was expressed that creative power of man so passionately believed
in by Louis Sullivan as source of all that counts on earth; here were the
first emerging monuments of that Democracy that he so idealized, so
illumined.  Here are mass, weight, power, loftiness, and a sort of geometric harmony.  Here is honest plastic construction, enriched by the
artist's sense of rhythmic beauty.

Now I am very little a patriot in the usual sense; and a blind nationalism seems to me the ultimate cause of the greater evils that afflict mankind today.  But I cannot help finding in Louis Sullivan an affinity with
certain other Americans who could never have developed on any other
soil, and a rough directness or drive that is of and by these United States.
What we call the honesty of Lincoln is assuredly in these early Sullivan-
esque buildings, along with something of the homeliness and the aspiring

The Shelton Hotel, New York. Arthur Loomis Harmon, architect. [1923]

faith and the flint-like purposefulness of that artist-president — and there are no less the tenderness and the great humanity to be detected in Sullivan's writings. Sullivan was of that line which began with Lincoln and Whitman, and which had its latest exemplar in that artist who also revolutionized an art, as prophet and practitioner, throughout the world — Isadora Duncan.

In all these there was the straight thinking that cut through all expediencies and cultures and polite conventions, to the creative beautiful thing; the same elemental youthfulness; the same intuitional, emotional power; the same wider love. It is along that hard, direct, emotional line that American genius up to this time has moved; not along more civilized, traditional, and intellectual channels. We have had our more polished poets, our prettier dancers, our more ornamental statesmen, and assuredly a great lot of tamer architects. But it is through Lincoln, Whitman, Sullivan, Isadora, that the old pioneer American spirit has moved, down to — possibly — the dawn of the world revolution of tomorrow. If you will read Lincoln's hard-cut, rhythmic speeches, Whitman's " Song of the Open Road," " Pioneers! O Pioneers! " and " Song of the Redwood Tree " (or the prose " Democratic Vistas "), the chapters " Face to Face " and " Retrospect " in Sullivan's *The Autobiography of an Idea,* and Isadora Duncan's essays entitled " The Dance of the Future " and " I See America Dancing," you will find, I think, the same unmistakable, granite spirit informing all, the same note of affirmation — and, in all except Lincoln, the same note of protest against the civilization that is. If you ask me why I believe that these writers breathe the real America, when they are so much the exceptional artists and so much the critics of existing America, I can answer only that the deeper part of me responds to them as seers and prophets, that I believe with them that much of the outward show of life and culture in these United States is tawdry, false, pretentious, borrowed, not true to the essential living of the American people. They are the ones who carry over the spirit of the American pioneers, the promise of youthful, courageous America, to the dawn of the new world-organism. And of them all, Sullivan has spoken out most passionately for the integrity and creative power of man's soul as the beginning of all beauty, of Democracy, of a new world-order.

Let us note, then, above all, the honesty, simplicity, the integral purposefulness of these old buildings by Louis Sullivan. They were done in a time when almost universally other architects were disguising the true structure within, denying the metal skeleton, offering amiable excuses for buildings. Perhaps in the ultimate view the most important

The Bush Terminal Office Building, New York.  Helmle & Corbett, architects.  [1918]

thing that Sullivan did was to *get back to architecture,* when all others were playing with ornamental building-faces.  In the age of emerging capital-imperialism, those other building-faces were being sculptured with an unwonted grandeur and flourish and opulence.  But whether they were stamped with the Classic idiom of McKim and his group, or the French boudoir accent of Carrère and Hastings or Warren and Wetmore, or the almost-American patois of Burnham, they were all conceived as masks, as disguises for the true structure.

Let us take up the story again a quarter-century after Sullivan's buildings of 1895.

By this time a few architects have discovered that one orthodox style out of the past has a real surface affinity with the steel-frame skyscraper.  Gothic ornament, because created for a type of building similarly resting on isolated supports (in place of masonry wall), is appropriately a thing of vertical accents and up-pointing.  It fits perfectly into the current masking business — and who is to cavil at a possible spiritual antagonism between ecclesiastical architecture and business-machine, when even bishops and professors can comfort the kings of finance by phrases like " the Cathedrals of Commerce " ?

The Woolworth Building is the masterpiece of the style; but in spite of the very fine impression it makes when one sees it from a distance — the ornament blurring into the impressive masses — I could not bring myself to picture and describe it here where " stripped architecture " is basically my subject.  I have instead set it back into the chapter on history, where it stands as the culmination of what the Eclectics were able to accomplish, in the last phase of history before the sudden deluge of stripped architecture in the years 1925–1929.

But in order that we may remember that there was, among the reigning academic architects, a timid evolutionary progress toward simplification, a process of cutting off superfluities, a gradual rationalization of the skyscraper problem, we may pause over one or two later examples wherein

"Proportioned boxes": an early example of experiment in frank
confession of the shallowness of the outer sheath-walls on the steel
frame. Top stories of a New York skyscraper by Ely Jacques Kahn.
[Photo by Sigurd Fischer]

the finely engineered and thoughtfully massed structure almost completely escaped the old historic envelope, if not quite. The Bush Terminal Office Building in New York, with its four-fifths honesty and
well-imagined proportioning, is a fair example: a satisfying and in its day
(1918) an exceptionally daring piece of design, despite its one-fifth
Gothic ornament, confessing unoriginality on the architect's part. At
the time of its erection, the building seemed unusually simple, massive,
and sheer; and it is interesting to note that today, when our eyes have
become accustomed to the block-like forms of later designers, the one

The American Radiator Building, New York. Raymond
M. Hood, architect. [1924]

part of the Bush Terminal Building which seems weakened and anti-
climactic is that area where the architect's love of Gothic tracery led him
into intricately broken surfaces and "picturesque" detail. There were
signs here, however, of the breakdown of Eclecticism, and of a return to
the principles set forth by Sullivan.

Top stories of a New York skyscraper, with emphasis on the "box forms," as contrasted with the more usual vertical-accent designing. Ely Jacques Kahn, architect.

The American Radiator Company Building in New York, erected in 1923, still carried traces of devotion to old world picturesque effects, but marked another step out of wasteful decorativeness. The main shaft of the building came clear, without disguise, and declared the shallow sheath of clay over the metal frame; and the total structure indicated creative attention to proportioning under the new zoning law "set-back" regulations. By this time the old attempt to break the building into sections horizontally, by incipient cornices or bands of ornament or pillared stories had completely come to an end. The building was original, too, in the attempt to use color creatively: the body was made black, the finials gold — an experiment not wholly successful, but refreshing in the midst of too-tame surroundings.

But at this time there were events stirring that marked even more clearly the beginning of a new architectural era in New York. In 1923 there rose up a building, the Hotel Shelton, which so subordinated ornamental modes to manipulated bulk and the play of clean machine-sharp lines that no one could thenceforward doubt that the skyscraper problem was to be solved by a return to consideration of fundamental structural — and specifically steel-age — principles, and not by study in the realm of the orders and styles. At the same time a man not claiming to be practising architect, but certainly an inspired artist and direct thinker, began to publish drawings of " fundamental forms " — and probably Hugh Ferriss deserves more credit than any architect since Sullivan for stirring the imaginations of designers, students, and public. Many a building of 1928–29 looks like a fulfillment of a Ferriss " idealistic " sketch of four or five years earlier. At about the same time a number of younger architects, not before known as out-of-the-routine men, began to poke the heads of their stripped creations up through the old welter of Classic adaptation, wasteful masking and mere hat-box architecture. By 1925 New York architecture was indubitably " going hard," divesting itself of historical souvenirs, creatively playing with the problems of steel framing, sculptural composition, and expression of machine-age life. There have been conspicuous examples of building under the Eclectic banner in the years since, that compelled attention by their immense size, or showiness, or successful reflection of ancient glories; but for better or for worse the stripped architecture men have won the skyscraper field.

The most dramatic event of the transitional years, however, occurred in Chicago, original home of the skyscraper. In 1922–23 the *Chicago Tribune* held a competition, offering prizes sufficiently large to attract from all parts of the world plans for a tower office building and home for the activities of the newspaper. The designs submitted afford in themselves a comprehensive view of the chaotic striving going on wherever architects are passionately absorbed in modern problems or are well

" An Imaginary City ": drawing by Hugh Ferriss. [From the copyright drawing, by courtesy of *Vanity Fair*, New York]

First prize design in the *Chicago Tribune* competition.
John Mead Howells and Raymond M. Hood, associate
architects.

paid. France and England were hardly heard from, at least not in accents
that counted; but Germany (with thirty-seven entries) and Holland
sent designs of the most varied (but largely ultra-Modernistic) sorts.
It was the relative ranking of first and second prize plans, however, that
rocked the none-too-stable architectural world. First prize was awarded
to a design by New York architects, for a building Gothic-gowned but

Second prize design in the *Chicago Tribune* competition.
Eliel Saarinen, architect.

highly attractive in its method of half-hiding naked beauty under a decorative cloak; and construction was immediately begun on this last flower of the Eclectic plant. Second prize, in contrast, was awarded to a design by Eliel Saarinen, a Finnish architect of Modern tendencies. His logical, powerful, nakedly impressive structure was the very flowering of Louis Sullivan's teachings.

Andrew Rebori    H. F. Mertens (Holland)    Ralph T. Walker and
McKenzie, Voorhees &
Gmelin

Stahler & Hörn (Germany)    George F. Schreiber    Bertram G. Goodhue

Six progressive designs in the *Chicago Tribune* competition. For contrast, see the group of Eclectic designs on page 63. [By courtesy of the *Chicago Tribune*]

The New York Telephone Building. Voorhees, Gmelin & Walker, architects. [Photo by Sigurd Fischer] Another of the fine series of Telephone company structures is illustrated in the chapter headpiece: the San Francisco Telephone Building, by J. R. Miller and T. L. Pflueger.

Of course nothing could be done to change the award; a jury of business men had chosen according to their understanding, their training, their environment. But a chorus of protest went up all over the land — and showed that the spirit of truth and progress and courage had not died, had only slept in those decades since 1896. Even Louis Sullivan,

The 56-story Chanin Building, New York. Sloan & Robertson, architects.

now sixty-seven years old, rose out of the obscurity that had overtaken him, and wrote an article on the competition so logical, so merciless, so true, that architects throughout the land were compelled to listen. With unerring analysis Sullivan showed out the fault that lay at the heart of the Gothic first-prize design: the piers that rose up, ostensibly accenting the steel frame, through more than a score of stories, turned out in the end to be supports for a false ornamental masonry crown. What started out by seeming a near-logical metal-frame structure ended with this bit of absurd pretense. Saarinen's design, on the other hand, exhibited that " vertical continuity," that loftiness, that flowering of formal beauty out of function, which Sullivan had so long fought for, toward which he

Western Union Telegraph Building, New York. Voorhees, Gmelin & Walker, architects. The surface material is brick in graduated shades of red.

had taken the first practical steps thirty years earlier; and Sullivan hailed this as a fulfillment — as the complete miracle come true.

And Saarinen's design, and the acclaim that it evoked, in 1923, seem in retrospect like the beginning of a deluge. It was as if a dam had broken, and the waters of logic and truth flowed over the land. Perhaps a thousand new skyscrapers have been built since, and at least three-

The Richfield Building, Los Angeles, California: latest, and most successful, of the "black and gold" skyscrapers. Morgan, Walls & Clements, architects.

fourths of them have frankly stated in their outer garb the sort of bodies confined within — not with Saarinen's genius, but with his honesty. If masterpieces are still few and far between, we still may marvel that so suddenly the talk about the Eclectic architects was cut off, and talk substituted about Arthur Loomis Harmon and his Shelton Hotel, about Ely Jacques Kahn and his block-built mercantile buildings, and about the

At right, a study of " fundamental forms " for skyscrapers, by Hugh Ferriss. At left, study for a
financial office building for Los Angeles, California, by Morgan, Walls & Clements; indicating how
a standardized vertical-accent type of skyscraper design has developed throughout the country,
along the lines suggested by the pioneering of Sullivan, Ferriss and Saarinen.

cliff-like New York Telephone Building and its associated architects and engineers. From New York to San Francisco, from Detroit to Dallas and El Paso, the new stark skyscraper arose naked and with at least a rough beauty.

There are so many photographs which ought to be included just here, by way of illustrating the various methods of solving "the skyscraper problem" with integrity and expressive "drive" and "lift," that I despair of getting them all into a book designed to be of modest dimensions and to cover briefly all the world's new types of building. Examples showing the effect of the New York zoning law, however, demand special notice; because in response to the demand for certain "set-backs" at certain heights, there is an indication how at last the architect is stirred to creativeness by a new need. He has been quick to grasp the possibilities of proportional massing, and the opportunity for play of light and shade, in these jutting crags and receding terraces. Nor do the obligatory horizontal breaks seem to shatter the upward continuity, the sense of lofty aspiration, as did those other horizontal interpolations, cornices and pillared stories and friezes, that the Eclectics used to introduce when they still thought the problem was to disguise the height.

It is notable how seldom a sloping roof appears in any of the outstanding new buildings. The immense New York Life Insurance Building has just been all but ruined by one, and the monumental Fisher Building in Detroit is similarly softened, anti-climaxed. The boldness of the block forms is so much an asset, so clearly an appropriate machine-like element, that the sloping roof can only serve to weaken the effect — if not to make the whole as ridiculous as a naked man under a hat. Ultimately we shall come to use our flat roofs and our terraces far more than we are doing, no doubt; when the drift toward the open life becomes a directed current.

In this book I shall consistently avoid going into technical matters, believing that my readers are interested first to see the subject of the new world architecture laid out in its broad outlines, and then just enough

The News Building, New York City. The most striking example of the "utter simplification" movement. John Mead Howells and Raymond M. Hood, associate architects.

Drawing for skyscraper at Broadway and 39th Street,
New York.   Ely Jacques Kahn, architect.

analysis given to fix the chief types and principles and structural features
in mind.   The pictures will serve to inform the discerning eye about
many a technical method, and to emphasize the commoner idioms of
expression.   In this direction I may, however, go so far as to repeat those
conditioning, basic principles: the steel-frame building is essentially a
skeleton with a thin protective sheath of glass, metal, and baked clay or
other wall material hung from it; and thus it is only common honesty
if the exterior proclaims its shallowness (without deep-set windows);
the heavy structural pieces are the uprights, and it is those that the main
lines of the sheath will emphasize or " express "; and any ornament added

Detail of top of Telephone Building, Syracuse, New York.
Voorhees, Gmelin & Walker, architects. A pleasing (if somewhat
soft) decorative finial for the long vertical pylons.

out of the architect's inventiveness and reach after enrichment will be
more harmful than satisfying if it fails to accent structure and to emphasize proportioning, if it cuts across structural lines, or weakens mass, or
serves to disguise any inner truth.

As an outgrowth of these principles we see two common " systems "
of design emerging. One is the so-called " pier-and-grill " type: the
essential upright supports are expressed in a series of strong piers rising
the height of the main façade, and between these soaring posts the space
is filled with a grill of glass and slender supports, with the cross-floor
girders slightly set back and subordinated, to give the upright lines fullest
structural validity. Or else there is a constant play of heavy pier and
only less accented floor-line, corresponding to the post and girder of the

Design for the Philadelphia Saving Fund
Society Building in Philadelphia, by Howe &
Lescaze.

steel-work.  The development of this idiom, from Sullivan's Prudential
Building down through Saarinen's design and to the New York Telephone
Building and other latest structures, is made clear by the illustrations.
The other treatment that has become idiomatic is that box-like one which
arises out of the conception of cubes, without outward emphasis on the
support-lines.  The reasoning here is that if it has become common
knowledge that the façade is merely a hanging screen on a metal frame,
there is no need to treat the composition as other than a box side, with

Drawing for building at Broadway and 41st Street, New York. Ely Jacques Kahn, architect. Note the emphasis on vertical lines, as compared with the earlier work of the same architect on pages 141 and 143.

window openings left in a palpably thin shell of clay; and what decorative effect is to be obtained will grow out of the proportioning of the boxes and perhaps some shallow ornament.

But usually the two systems are more or less combined. And there is almost unanimous agreement that outward emphasis of the main steel piers is logical, and that here will enter the element of enrichment: that a definite skyscraper "style" will grow out of what the architects do with the externalized lines expressing strength and lift. (No, dear reader, I am not *against* style in architecture — as you may have apprehended from certain vigorous statements about stylistic stealing and historical style-mongering. It is only that I believe that a style should be at the *end* of the development of any given type of building, of experiment with new material and function, and not a starting point.)

THE story of the skyscraper and of steel-frame buildings as fabricated belongs so largely to the United States that one might fairly close the chapter without considering the rest of the world. If you have, even within the year, had occasion to call on a lawyer, an exporter, or even an engineer, in Paris or in London, you will recall the monumental stairs you climbed, the dark hallways and the wastefully spacious offices, with marble-manteled fireplaces, and ornamental plaster ceiling decorations. And somehow these seemed out of key with " doing business " — after you had known our American compact little cubicle-offices, fairly shining with light and cleanliness, reached by electric elevators, steam-heated, with telephones, typewriters, etc., etc., within easy reach. You may have had the same experience of being ushered into offices that still reeked of the stuffiness of Victorian living-rooms, in Berlin or Munich or Leipzig; and if so you may be unprepared for the statement — easily proved — that such skyscrapers as Germany has are, on the average, superior to the American. That is, they are just about as efficient, considered as business-machines, and more satisfying in the æsthetic aspect. In the larger view, the reason is to be found in the fact that for every fine modern skyscraper

A business building in Leipzig, Germany. The new simplicity slightly relieved by ornament. German Bestelmeyer, architect.

in New York or Chicago or Detroit, there are a dozen bad ones hanging over from the days of experiment and fumbling or from the reign of the Eclectics; whereas the Germans built with the benefit of American experience behind them (and with an ear to Sullivan's writings, and in complete ignorance of the high historic learning of McKim, Warren, White and other academicians). The Germans are gluttons for logic and scientific analysis and solidity; when they got around to the building of office skyscrapers, their architects knew the theory, history, and logic of the form as not one out of five American practising architects does. Indeed, German books and magazines were spotted with experi-

Angle and façade of the *Chile-haus*, Hamburg, Germany. Fritz Hoeger, architect. [Photos by courtesy of Walter Steilberg]

A typical German skyscraper, in Cologne. Jacob Koerfer, architect. [1925]

mental, tentative, "ideal" and proposed *hochhäuser,* and even whole skyscraper-city designs, over a period of fifteen years; and so when the German puts up a high building, it is no matter of a quick solution of an unforeseen need.

It is reported that Raymond Hood was still making studies of the top portion of the American Radiator Building in New York when the masons finished encasing the first seventeen stories; and Claude Bragdon tells of an instance where owners had engineers go ahead with the steel structure and invited architects to submit designs while the frame was being erected. These are, of course, extreme cases, but none the less suggestive of a difference between American and German approach. (And oh!

Part of the Crafts Building, Hamburg, Germany.　Fritz
Schumacher, architect.　[1913]

don't the Germans sigh for the opportunities that American architects
have wasted!)

So it is no matter for surprise that the very few skyscrapers in Germany are marked by a sense of design, by a finish, and by logical expression, that may well be studied by the rest of the world.　There is indication, too, that in most cases due attention has been given to surroundings.
These are usually isolated towers rising out of traditionally determined
street-ensembles, and the contrast of modernity must not be too abrupt.
It is in the field of this tempered radicalism that I have chosen the first
of my German illustrations, a *hochhaus* — fairly *hoch*, at least — in Leipzig.　And a clean, simple, modern thing it is, in spite of the touches of
mediæval ornament designed to put the structure into keeping with an
ancient city's main square.　The industrial-mercantile building in Co-

The Wertheim Department Store, Berlin. Alfred Messel, architect. [1904]

logne is even more in the spirit of contemporary German architecture. No country has gone back more whole-heartedly to stripped architecture, to fundamental functional planning and machine-clean lines and machine-heavy massing.

With so little of analysis we may leave the German skyscrapers: the country is at the beginning of its experience of them, despite a dozen examples of outstanding merit — and no distinguishable *type* has emerged. But in another field of business building, the department store, the German architects have led the world for a quarter century. In general, it may be said that, in the æsthetic aspect, the British and American stores have been bad examples of masking; while France combined some interesting iron engineering with soft and cloying French decorative art

Office and show-room building in Düsseldorf, Germany.  Peter Behrens, architect.  1912.  [From *Die Baukunst der Neuesten Zeit*, by Gustav Adolf Platz]

— pretty good in an exceptional case or two, but generally horrible.  As long ago as 1904 Alfred Messel designed the still notable Wertheim Stores in Berlin, combining some clear-cut modern structural conceptions with some traditional aspects of clean German building.  Indeed, we may mark this as part of a general development of Modern architecture in Central Europe, that expressed itself in homes and schools and theatres as well as stores, during the first two decades of the new century: deriving directly from the insurgency of Otto Wagner in Vienna, and most influenced, perhaps, by Joseph M. Olbrich, who came to Germany from association with Wagner.

Olbrich, Messel, and Peter Behrens and one or two others standardized a sort of store and office building that might be recognized anywhere as Teutonic — and yet universal in its grasp of essential honesty and modern cleanliness of mass and line.  Without having studied out the chronology,

The clean-cut pre-war commercial architecture in Germany.
A small hotel and restaurant building in Berlin. Bruno Paul,
architect. 1912. [From *Die Baukunst der Neuesten Zeit*, by
Gustav Adolf Platz]

beyond knowing that the Wertheim Stores by Messel were done in 1904
and the Tietz Department Store in Düsseldorf erected by Olbrich in
1908, I do know that structures recognizably related to these are to be
seen in almost any town in Germany.    Usually very pleasing they are,
too, even today when we are more critical of unnecessary roofs or gables
or window-traceries.    Even so early the Germans were using freely a
variation of the pier-and-grill idiom.

    While Germany lacked any such pioneer leader as Berlage of Holland
or Sullivan of Chicago, there was a more marked trend toward rationalization and considered severity in that country than in any other before

the war — not a revolutionary change, but the most satisfying progress toward utter simplification. The two pictures here, of the office and show-room building in Düsseldorf by Peter Behrens, and the Zollernhof Restaurant Building in Berlin by Bruno Paul, are typical.

We are not now, of course, considering the steel-frame building primarily. And while we are on the subject of other materials creatively manipulated, a word should be said of the achievements of Fritz Schumacher in building with brick. One of his earlier structures is the Crafts Building in Hamburg, erected in 1913. It is not unrelated to the work of Olbrich, Messel, and Behrens that we have been considering. In later years Schumacher has gained extraordinary effects out of brick composition, with due regard to the structural principles of the Moderns.

But today the German department stores that make any pretense to fashionable Modernism revel in a very different sort of designing. *Horizontality* is the thing that has carried all else away. Where the upright pier-and-grill with a Teutonic accent and roof once filled all towns with variations and echoes, now every department-store architect from Cologne to Breslau is duplicating the horizontal-banded fronts brought to prominence by Erich Mendelsohn. I think there are fewer near-masterpieces as yet than in the elder style; but you may judge from the photographs herewith how fit this new treatment is to the department-store needs, with almost continuous bands of windows for each floor, with contrasting ribbons of masonry between. Here is a pier-and-grill building laid down on its side with the piers running horizontally! Which merely means that construction of comparatively low buildings in combined masonry, metal, and glass has become so elastic that any arrangement of windows and wall space is possible, and any accent of line or massing — everything permissible, indeed, except the overlaying of the actual structural materials with good historical unrelated ornament or bad Modernistic ornament.

But *stripped* architecture is the chapter subject, and the hero is the pioneer, the American Sullivan: the prophet who foresaw the beauty of the

The Herpich Store Building, Berlin; an outstanding example of the
new and popular "banded front" type of design.   Erich Mendelsohn, architect.   [1924]

rugged crag-like towers of our teeming cities.   He foresaw no less the
lawlessness and the devastation that false skyscraper architecture has en-
tailed.   He wrote[2] of "the pious, hypocritical virtues of our so-called
architecture — the nice, good, mealy-mouthed, suave, dexterous, diplo-
matic architecture."   Then, going back to look for the causes, he spoke
thus of the early skyscrapers of lower Broadway: "This is not American

[2] In his early magazine articles, quoted here from excerpts reprinted in Claude Bragdon's *Architecture
and Democracy*, New York 1918.

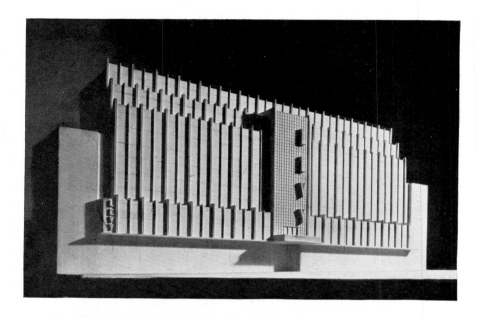

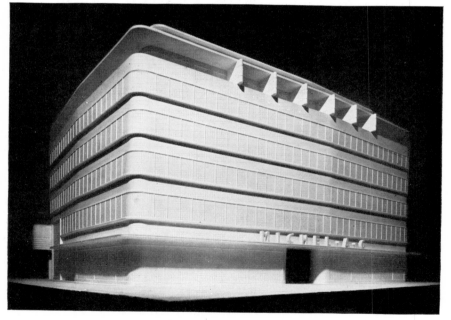

Two models for department stores, showing contrast between design based on emphasized horizontals and one with accented verticals. The design above by Emil Fahrenkamp; the one below by Professor Fahrenkamp and George Schäfer.

The Telschow Cafe, Berlin. Luckhardt Brothers and Alfons Anker, architects. [By courtesy of the German Tourist Information Office, New York]

civilization; it is the rottenness of Gomorrah. This is not Democracy — it is savagery. It shows the glutton hunt for the Dollar with no thought for aught else under the sun or over the earth. It is decadence of the spirit in its most revolting form; it is rottenness of the heart and corruption of the mind. . . These buildings are not architecture but outlawry, and their authors criminal in the true sense of the word. And such is the architecture of lower New York — hopeless, degraded, putrid in its pessimistic denial of our art and of our growing civilization."

But Louis Sullivan lived on to see the time when American business life and American orthodox architecture did not always "master and confine" the artist building commercial towers; when men not unlike that ideal sketched in his *Autobiography* — " a righteous man, sound of head, clean of heart, a truthful man too natural to lie or to evade " — came out of the ruck to affirm in metal and stone the power of the human spirit and the greatness of simple truth.   It is not a bad place in our story, perhaps, when we are so deep in essential Modernism, to stop long enough to witness Louis Sullivan discovering a giant of the architectural past, finding inspiration and confirmation in Michelangelo:

" Here he came face to face with his first great Adventurer.   The first mighty man of Courage.   The first man with a Great Voice.   The first whose speech was Elemental.   The first whose will would not be denied. The first to cry YEA! in thunder tones.   The first mighty Craftsman. The man, the man of super-power, the glorified man, of whom he had dreamed in his childhood, of whom he prophesied in his childhood, as he watched his big strong men build stone walls, hew down trees, drive huge horses — his mighty men, his heroes, his demi-gods. . .

" Now was he in that veritable dreamed-of Presence.   Here was that great and glorious personality.   Here was power as he had seen it in the mountains, here was power as he had seen it in the prairies, in the open sky, in the great lake stretching like a floor toward the horizon, here was the power of the forest primeval.   Here was the power of the open — of the free spirit of man striding abroad in the open.   Here was the living presence of a man who had *done things in the beneficence of power.*"

As we gaze today at some of the latest skyscrapers, built directly on the pioneering of Louis Sullivan, we may well feel that his vision of a later manifestation of that Power in the human hand and the human imagination, of that Elemental creativeness, is being fulfilled.   Indubitably, many, many of these American skyscrapers are *powerful.*   Is it too much to believe that soon many examples will fulfil the wider implication of that other phrase of Sullivan's — used in praise of a work of engineering: " beautiful in power " ?

# CHAPTER V

## *PIONEERS: THE SEARCH FOR A STYLE*

THE LIFE worth living is rich with beauty.

Now it is true that the quality of beauty is more openly prized while generally neglected than any other manufacturable commodity. A few, a very few, men, called artists, devote their lives to the contriving of it, for the sake of their fellows; others have made a religion of it — and perhaps they have travelled their paths through the world more satisfied than those who have deified goodness or truth or obedience or other abstractions. Workmen, craftsmen, without ever formulating their allegiance in words or philosophies, have lived contented lives because they continually sensed overtones of beauty breathing from their finished practical work. That sort of direct hand contriving grows less in contemporary specialized industry. And indeed mankind's direct pursuit of the beautiful seems sadly relaxed. Yet we know in our hearts that this is the thing we want more than any other gift from the gods.

In contrived as in natural (or cultivated) beauty, one may mark two general sorts: an inner, fundamental, characteristic sort, and an outer shallower, sensuous sort. In the example of natural beauty that is most with us, that of woman, we are accustomed to say that surface prettiness is bootless without soul shining through (though we do indeed value " just " surface loveliness, grace, and style, more than we usually confess) ; and that is a warrant that there is such a thing as spiritual beauty, expressing itself under a woman's prettiness — in character, a fine-fibredness and a show of proportion in meeting life. In the truly and deeply beautiful woman the outward and physical loveliness and cultivated " style " are appropriate to — seem like a reflection of — the character, the inner light, a steady burning flame of spirituality, steadfastness, and nobility.

In the realm of art one soon becomes confused if one does not make a similar distinction between a surface sensuous appeal and a deeper characteristic one. (We all should approach art, of course, as directly and intuitively as possible, without thinking out too many distinctions and divisions; but living as we do in a time of transition, of changing values, and being inheritors in our youth of the distorted nineteenth century traditions and limitations, we have to seek out some primary guide-posts.) And it is indeed possible to mark a perfect parallel, to perceive a difference, between art that is of a surface sort, charming, melodious, decorative, and a deeper sort that is characterized by that quality of rhythmic form which is as unexplainable as spiritual beauty in the person — and as fundamentally necessary to permanently satisfying art.

The application of this idea to the building art affords a basic distinction. What we crave in the end is a beauty organic throughout the structure, informing every element from the inside outward: an honesty of purpose, of materials, reinforced by proportioning, by contrapuntal organization, by a breathing rhythm of loveliness. It is in this all-

pervasive beauty, of the spirit and the structure as well as the outer garments, that the strange thing called " architectural form " resides: the
essential, satisfying, ultimate " character." But — although it is not
the basic thing — the outward allure, the style, is seldom absent from the
total appeal. And one whole group of Modernists has come at the new
architecture from a search for a stylistic garment. They have now pretty
generally absorbed the back-to-honest-structure principles which we
have been so concerned with in chapters past, so that they offer us today
a style appropriate to an inner sincerity and a clean-engineered frame;
but their story is that of artists who were animated at first by a conception
of a new outward loveliness that a building might have. Along the way,
during the early decades of the twentieth century, they gave the world
its most seductive, if not most lasting, examples of the new building art.
After the emergence of the early skyscraper, historically theirs was the
first great conquest in the name of the new world architecture. They
have made the term " Viennese Secession " almost a synonym for elegant
grace — particularly in the field of interior decoration.

Of course the structural Modernists, as soon as they begin to think of
" enrichment " for their stripped and honest structures, turn — unless
they be doubly creative geniuses like Frank Lloyd Wright — to these
Viennese " decorators " for sympathetic aid, and almost insensibly the
Vienna " touch " is added to the composite structure that is taking shape
as typically new. The French Modernists, as a matter of fact, have fat-
tened themselves a bit over-assiduously on the Blue-Danube seductive
grace, until Paris passes on to the Americas and to England and points
more remote a hall-marked French decorative mode that is really sweetened and popularized Viennese.

Still, the story of the seekers for a style cannot be told in terms of the
Austrians alone — though there is no name to put beside that of Joseph
Hoffmann, unless among his own compatriots. Back in the last decade
of the nineteenth century there was an architect-decorator who hailed
from — of all places under the sun — Scotland, who invented a light

half-Gallic, half-Oriental ornamental mode for tea houses and similar not-too-serious architectural problems. Charles R. Mackintosh and his few fellow spirits seem to have left no considerable trace of that grace and inventiveness in the schools of architectural design in the British Isles; but somehow his influence carried across Europe to Vienna — perhaps only by the vague chance of a few magazine articles and an exhibition of drawings — and his name is known there as that of a pioneer and a source. It is easy to see from the illustration here that his talent touched on that stream which gave the world Aubrey Beardsleyism and other *fin-de-siècle* decorative developments — a bit too sophisticated and attenuated to seem other than affected, since it came not at the end of a long course of elegant and gracefully decadent design, but as a sudden interruption to a current stodgy mode.

But despite the insistence upon its own " differentness," as evidenced here in the leading of the upper windows and in the light brackets, there is an extraordinary reach forward toward the Viennese sort of thing. The consolidation of upper windows, door, and show-window into two decorative units set into the unadorned wall; the edging of the building with the simple checked border-lines, the emphasis on the black horizontals, the smart squareness throughout: these are idioms of much later work. If we went beyond this one front, we would find other points that would seem to link Mackintosh with Olbrich and Klimt and Hoffmann. And indeed here is almost a lone figure standing out as a creator among imitators, a decorator who foreshadowed the development of a national school of ornament — in another nation — and handed on an impetus that flows still in the broadened current of world decorative effort.

One guesses that Mackintosh had admired to good purpose the arts of the Japanese — you will find a flavor of that so-decorative architecture in the Viennese as in the work of Sullivan and of Wright, though one can seldom detect whether there has been conscious adaptation or only a new beginning, with Japanese delicacy of touch and Japanese horizon-

Front of a tea-house in Glasgow, designed by Charles R. Mackintosh; before 1905

tal accent, and Japanese love of fine wood for its own sake. But more illuminatingly here, one might guess further that Mackintosh arrived at the sort of designing illustrated in the Willow Tea House after practice in the mode known as *Art Nouveau*. There is a nervous agility in his outlines that suggests that so-restless mode.

Now *Art Nouveau* was a curse that fell on the world of architectural decoration about 1900. It was doubly a curse because its inventors claimed for it the title they did, " The New Art." In its spectacular failure it more or less automatically damned everything that brought novelty, either bad or good, into building for many years after, in the minds of many liberal people who might otherwise have recognized progress in the work of Sullivan or Berlage or Hoffmann. " Oh, yes, we've tried the New Art," was the burden of their remarks, and they turned a cold shoulder to innovators ever after.

Of course *l'Art Nouveau* was bound to die quickly and completely, as every attempt to found a style on a formula is certain to do. It had no concern with structure, with materials, with use. It was wholly a surface revolution — a conception of a new sort of mask. Its only law was *Use curved instead of straight lines.* Nothing could be more unarchitectural, nothing further from machine-age thinking. But for a number of years *l'Art Nouveau* was a sensation. Sometimes it was called " The Belgian Style "; and there were many variations, a host of varieties. But invariably the proof of the style was in the curved line. No upright, even though it should in all logic express strength and support, escaped being tortured into a curve; no building-front could ever be straight-walled — a bulge was more " artistic." (That bulge, refined somewhat but unmistakable, persists in an extraordinary portion of French decorative building to this day.)

Well, as I started by saying, Mackintosh did not escape entirely the influence of the *Art Nouveau* restless twisting and turning. Just when one begins to think that there are spine and vigor in his stylistic creations, one comes up against a stencilled bit or a bracket or a carved wooden panel with that peculiarly disturbing bulbousness and sinuousness. It may have been this that led the English to snuff out " the Scotch style " till hardly a flavor of it is to be found in current British architectural decoration today; though perhaps it was less a matter of its being confused with *l'Art Nouveau,* which had to be destroyed at any cost, than a question of its inability to stand up against traditional English reserve and love of the old ways. One may read in the documents of those days the blighting criticism of new elements coming in: " As a people we rather pride ourselves on the resolute suppression of any florid display of feeling," wrote Reginald Blomfield. At any rate, Mackintosh went down to eclipse with the really florid offenders. The more's the pity, for at his best he lent a real distinction and grace to the buildings he touched; and upon his

Entrance detail of the *Werkbund* Exposition Theatre, Cologne, Germany, 1914.
Henri Van de Velde, architect.

achievements and those of Margaret Macdonald Mackintosh and Frances and Herbert McNair, the British might have founded a true decorative school.

Other promising architects, particularly in Germany and France, who might have been up among the leaders of the new world architecture if they had not mistaken a decorative formula for a Heaven-sent law, have more justly seen their names go down to oblivion by reason of the *Art Nouveau* curve. It is difficult today to understand why so many talented men flocked to the *Art Nouveau* standard, failed to see the superficiality of the creed, when any student can note that it has nothing to do with *building*, only with decoration. But aside from the horrors of *ornamentation* that the disciples inflicted on the world, there was even twisting of true architectural members, columns, beams, as well as infinite repetition of the swelling motive, the bulbous bulge, in stair-rails, base-boards, brackets, etc. Of course furniture-designers saw the value of novelty in the mode, and for long they avoided like a plague any straight line in chair or table legs or chandelier or sideboard top. Even the cross-bars in leaded-glass windows or doors must be artistically curved. I am adding no illustrations of the "style." Only too likely there is a reflection of it in the design of your chiffonier, or in the stencilling on the walls of the restaurant where you lunch, or in the stair-rail in your front hall.

There is one artist, however, who was victim of the *Art Nouveau* fever and yet wrote his name large on the emerging Modernism of the early twentieth century. In decorative detail, Henri Van de Velde never outgrew the fallacy of the curved line. Again and again he shows himself a strange mixture of the straight-seeing, craftsman-like, modern engineer-architect and the *Art Nouveau* æsthete. The hard quality is softened, the straight and precise edge gives way to a flourish, squareness and strength spread into bulginess. Van de Velde was Belgian-born, and worked for a number of years in Paris, but found the only real welcome for his work and ideas in Germany. He designed a number of buildings that are considered among the monuments of early Modernism in Germany, among them the Museum at Hagen-in-Westphalia, and the Werkbund Exposition Theatre in Cologne (now torn down). The famous Champs-Elysées Theatre in Paris, long heralded as a chief monument to French inventiveness, was in reality built almost without change from Van de Velde's designs, though unfortunately all French commentators drop his name in favor of the French architects who " adapted " his plans for nationalistic reasons. (Perhaps the most convincing argument for believing it Van de Velde's, is that it remains even to this day the finest theatre in France.) At any rate Van de Velde greatly influenced Germany, both by his actual buildings and through the printed page; influenced the younger generation toward simple forms and toward a craftsman-like decorativeness tinged with the decadent curve. In summary, he did some quite fine things, but took the edge off his own achievement by forcing a preconceived surface style.

With Mackintosh and Van de Velde out of the way, the rest of the story

House in the suburbs of Vienna.  Otto Wagner, architect

is Vienna's.  There are those who will go back to detect sources in the
earlier English school of craftsmen, in William Morris, Walter Crane, and
even John Ruskin, as well as in the Belgians of the *Art Nouveau* cult.
But these and other influences had flowed into the general world-current,
without crystallizing into a style or even a tendency with universal implications.  The main root of the " Secession " thing rather goes back to a
solider Viennese predecessor of the Secessionists, a fellow-pioneer of Sullivan and Berlage, of the last decades of the nineteenth century.  Otto
Wagner even published a book entitled *Moderne Architektur* as early as
1895; and his buildings exhibited a tendency toward structural simplification and rationalization together with thrusts toward a flatter,
smarter decorative idiom.  He left as few personal monuments as did
Sullivan or Berlage, but he came nearer to founding an immediate world
school of stylists.  His name deserves to live on permanently with theirs:

Viennese stylization: corner of the Stoclet mansion in Brussels.  Joseph Hoffmann,
architect.  1905.  [By courtesy of *l'Architecte,* Paris]

as pioneer, prophet, master-artist.  He joyously and effectively chased the
pedants out of his Viennese field.

The Secession people were all for flatness and smartness.  They soon
ruled out the Van de Velde curved motives because they wanted the long
unbroken line and the clean, un-swelled surface.  They harked back
rather to the attenuated forms of Mackintosh.  But no Scotchman could

ever have caught fastidious grace, a sensuous elegance, as the Viennese now caught it.  The spirit of the City of the Danube was crystallized. It did not flower in its purest form until Hoffmann consolidated the gains of all who had gone before him; he is the present master.  But from the original Secession group on, there was progressive capturing of the elements (and tricks) that go to make up surface smartness, colorful elegance, lush stylization.  No one had ever before brought out of his magic hat so many rooms " with just the right touch "; no one since the regal days at Versailles had so charmingly feminized architecture; no one (saving the Orientals — who, be it noted, had sent wave after wave of influence over Vienna) had so richly colored buildings without breaking up wall sense.

Of course the earlier practitioners were living in the height of the Eclectic period, when respectable Academy architects were all piling up Classic or Baroque or Renaissance structures with the old decorative motives intact.  There were no simple broad surfaces on which to immortalize the new style.  And it was difficult at first to design buildings with such surfaces: even if one stripped off Renaissance ornament, still there were laws about window-spacing and cornices and what not that made it difficult to bring clear the flat spaces and long lines necessary to showing out the fundamental contrast of rich-spot-against-simple-background. It was long before they learned to consolidate openings, to concentrate details here and gain the broad effect there, to afford themselves opportunity for the long vista and repeated straight edges.  In colorfulness they were daring from the start — though the passion for richness did not blind them to the fact that a certain delicacy was to be the very index of their stylization.

Joseph Maria Olbrich designed the Secession Building erected in Vienna in 1899.  Even today one may admire the boldness with which it was executed.  But one may measure too, by comparing it with Hoffmann's work, the growth in refinement, in stylishness, in richness of decorative idiom, in the thirty years since.  Of the early group there were, besides

Corner of the Tietz Department Store, Düsseldorf, Germany.  [1908]  Joseph Maria Olbrich, architect. [By courtesy of the Ernst Wasmuth Verlag, Berlin]

Wagner and Olbrich, Kolo Moser and Joseph Urban and the painter Gustav Klimt (who was the lushest decorator in a school that made a fetish of rich exoticism).

After Wagner, Olbrich was the leader of the early group, by token of fecundity and enthusiasm and evangelistic zeal.  Meier-Graefe once wrote of him: "Liebermann's celebrated saying that fancy is a makeshift is approximately true of architecture.  Olbrich's success was so great that his projects never had time to cool; they reeked of wash and paper even when they became bricks and mortar.  This made him popular; and little Olbrichs multiplied like the illegitimate children of foreign potentates."  This is perhaps a little severe, as one may verify by looking at the least washy of Olbrich's buildings; but even so progressive a structure as the Tietz Department Store in Düsseldorf, attractive as it is with its repeated clean vertical piers, savors somewhat of the study, is man-

Court of the German Pavilion at the Exposition in St. Louis, Missouri, 1904.  Joseph Maria Olbrich, architect.  [By courtesy of the Ernst Wasmuth Verlag, Berlin]

nered rather than self-forgettingly stylish.   Perhaps leaving Vienna, to take up permanent residence in Germany, took Olbrich out of the atmosphere of the searchers after style, made him more a cosmopolitan searcher after structural qualities first; and by the same token he took something of Vienna abroad, to be absorbed in Germany and Switzerland.   And he even designed the German pavilion for the St. Louis Exposition of 1904, which may have stimulated a few Americans to search out information about Austrian-German radicalism.

But in this chapter Olbrich is most important as a mid-figure between Wagner and Joseph Hoffmann.   The latter remains today the leader of the Viennese group, and his buildings illustrate what is finest in the achievement of the Secession designers.   They are smartly simple, alluringly enriched with color and pattern, chic, modish.

In Brussels — yes, he carried his Vienna challenge right into the heart of the enemy's territory, where the Belgian Style of bulgy architecture had originated — there is a house (though " a palace " better describes it) which is the *chef-d'œuvre* of Hoffmann's early work.  The home of M. Stoclet is at once Hoffmann at his smartest and Hoffmann in his most mannered manner.  No one can overlook the Stoclet mansion as a monument of the new building; but it is so unusual, approaches so close to being a *tour de force,* that one hesitates to urge it as representative.  From the pictures you may understand how distinguished it is, how striking, how elegant.  (One can visualize our 1930-model bright lithe motor cars gliding through its bridged drive to the carriage yard with absolute appropriateness, though the smooth metallic walls must have made the decorated carriages of a quarter-century ago, when the mansion was built, seem strangely out-of-date.)  And from the pictures, too, you may understand how perfect a sense of *sustained* stylization it breathes.  But without going into it, you cannot know how perfect it is, considered as a modern palace-dwelling.

Granted that one cares to live in a palace, here is luxury ideally wedded to simplicity; color without stuffiness; elegance and ease; fresh air and floods of light and yet intimacy for napping or reading or talking; and everywhere enrichment for the eye; and mechanical efficiency.  This was an achievement that foreshadowed much that came to general acceptance among radicals during the following twenty years (except with those like Le Corbusier and the *Bauhaus* group, who demand functional justification for *every* detail.)  Here are plain surfaces and emphasized structural features; and declared use of materials for their decorative value — the interior is rich with straight-edge marbles chosen for their warmth of color and their veining, and with tiling, mosaics, inlaid wood floors, and metal railings (but carved-wood ornamentation of the usual sort is notably absent).  The designing of the furniture, incidentally, was considered " part of the architect's job "; it all came from the hands of Hoffmann and of his fellow artists of the *Wiener Werkstaette.*

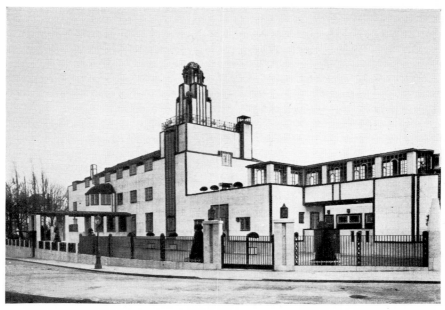

Above, the Stoclet mansion, Brussels, as seen from the street. Below, the dining room — the most "decorated" of the rooms. Joseph Hoffmann, architect. [Photos by courtesy of *l'Architecte,* Paris]

Pergola and detail of rear, Stoclet mansion.   Joseph Hoffmann, architect

One may note here, even in the photographs of the exterior, many distinctive idioms of the Secession mode: especially the accenting of the
square forms by a black beading along the edges — *that* you will see often
in Vienna — and the gathering of as many details as possible into a few
involved compositions played against the simplest of white surfaces.

But the palatial thing is so small a part of Modernist achievement, and
of Hoffmann's, that we may better turn to the study of those common-

The Austrian Pavilion at the *Werkbund* Exposition, Cologne, 1914.   Joseph Hoffmann, architect.

est of buildings, exposition halls.   Annual fairs and occasional expositions are much more usual to the life of European cities than of American; and in Germany particularly the temporary buildings are an exercise-ground for the progressive architects.   We shall see in a moment that many a German architect displayed his talent (and his debt to Wagner and Olbrich and Hoffmann) in exhibition rooms and *Fest* Halls.   But first let us note that Vienna led the way in spreading smart and alluring temporary

Interior corridor of the Austrian Pavilion at the Decorative Arts Exposition, Paris, 1925. Joseph Hoffmann, architect. [See exterior photo at head of chapter]

buildings through the exposition cities of Austria and Germany, and even of France and Italy.   Meier-Graefe in his compendious history of modern art (1908) notes that " in 1900, when Austria appeared at the Paris Exhibition, she was already the only country acknowledged to possess a modern style."   The buildings by Olbrich at Dresden a few years later are still remembered in German architectural histories.   In 1911 Hoffmann designed his exceedingly simple and fragilely lovely Austrian Pavilion for the Exposition at Rome, and in 1914 his memorable Austrian Building at the Cologne *Werkbund* Exposition.   And in 1925, at Paris, when most of the French architects were building Gallicized versions of earlier Viennese stylization, Hoffmann erected a different sort of modish pavilion, original along fresh lines, though less restrained and less thoroughly architectonic than the Cologne pavilion.   It showed Vienna to be still in the vanguard of those cultivating a new style, with a grasp of refinements and adjustments not yet understood by more recent converts to Modernism.

The buildings at the Paris Exposition must have convinced many observers that there is no short cut to sustained loveliness. The Viennese had worked in their style for a quarter-century when the exposition was held; in that time they had developed not only a mode, but artists and craftsmen in all the lines of decorative art related to architecture. The Austrian building, though breathing more of elaboration than is usual with Hoffmann, with even a flavor of decadent baroque, was of a piece; whereas many another country exhibited architecture that was one thing, decoration that was another, and furniture and fittings that were something else again.[1]

The earlier Cologne Austrian Building carried a certain monumental impressiveness along with its new decorativeness. The photographs indicate the style of the structure, its fine simplicity-in-richness, its solid dignity. But for Hoffmann's " smarter " qualities, for style in its more striking and colorful aspects, it is necessary to know the interiors of his buildings; and unfortunately illustrations in black-and-white do scant justice to the charm of his interior dressings. The exposition buildings often showed *tours de force* in room decoration; though usually they were given up to halls and galleries without any relationship to "living" quarters. It is rather in homes like the Skywa House or the Knips Villa in Vienna that one may see the marble stair-hall, the wood-panelled recep-

[1] The reasons for the non-participation of the United States in the Exposition of Decorative and Industrial Arts are worth recounting as instructive if distressing. The French organizers made a rule that only *new* buildings and exhibits would be admitted: that is, architecture outside the historic styles, and creative craft-work. The story goes that the invitation to the American government was answered by a declaration that we would be pleased to send over some excellent reproductions of Colonial furniture and silverware, of old this and authentic that — presumably in a Neo-Classic Pavilion by an American Beaux-Arts architect. The answer was that only *creative* designs were desired; and the matter was instantly dropped. Apparently the government and its architectural advisers had never heard of Frank Lloyd Wright, nor of native creative craftsmen whose names any Arts and Crafts Society could have provided; nor did it occur to anyone that some of the most exciting industrial craftsmanship and decorative art of today is to be found in automobile fittings, electric refrigerators, cash registers, and the like. Wright, of course, creator of decorative styles, was one of the two men in all the world best fitted to give what the Frenchmen wanted.

But perhaps it is a mercy, considering the government's conservatism (or is it innocence?), that the invitation was declined: if the commission had gone to a " recognized " architect or to a timid " progressive," we might have been as badly served as, for instance, were Italy, England, and — I had almost said, France. An *order* for a Modern work is a dangerous thing.

Corner of exhibition room of the *Wiener
Werkstaette* branch in New York. Joseph
Urban, architect.

tion-rooms, the tiled bath, and the more frankly " decorated " sleeping-
rooms, each with its own appropriate grace or " air " or elegance.   Here
one may note the typical simplification of surfaces and preservation of
long lines; the avoidance of mouldings or borders or elaborated door-
frames and window-frames; the accenting of the larger masses by contrasted edging; the playing of concentratedly rich bits against proportioned whites; the generous use of colorful all-over pattern.   The magic,
of course, lies in the perfect adjustment, the exact proportioning, the
sophisticated understanding of the colors, the contrasts, the harmonies.

Of all this Joseph Hoffmann has proved himself master beyond all his
contemporaries; but perhaps the praise should be accorded to the Vienna
group rather than to its leader.   Karl Witzmann's name should be remembered.   There is Oskar Strnad who also had to do with the Cologne
Pavilion and who now practices internationally; and Jan Kotera and
Joseph Frank.   Joseph Urban was once a foremost practitioner of the
*Wiener Werkstaette* group, and brought to America a fine talent for the
Viennese stylized thing.   For many years after his arrival he was absorbed
in the problems of modern stage decoration — he did pioneer service in the
revolutionizing of American stage-setting, beside the native workers,

Corner of bedroom designed by Joseph Hoffmann

Robert Edmond Jones, Sam Hume, Lee Simonson and Norman-Bel Geddes; but after the war he established a branch of the *Werkstaette* in New York, in rooms breathing the true fastidious loveliness, and later turned back to his old profession, architecture. But we shall meet him in the chapter on theatres, churches, and such.

If the Viennese carried the gospel of style out into the rest of the world, through the buildings of its own designers at expositions in distant lands, and through a few architects who, like Olbrich and Urban, studied and worked with the home group for a while, and then went elsewhere, it was Germany that profited most by the process. A group of Munich architects and artists particularly carried on the impetus; so successfully that the Bavarian capital is more notable than any more northern city for a clean-cut sort of craftsmanship and for stylish decorative art, though

The "Iron Monument" at the Leipzig Exposition, 1913: early decorative use of metal and glass. Bruno Taut and Franz Hoffmann, architects.

officially conservative regarding architectural exteriors. (Berlin and Hamburg and Cologne have more in common with American and Dutch endeavor.) Max Klinger was close to the Viennese workers; the *Jugend* group was at least congenial in spirit — and one may guess that the "Munich poster style" was a sharpening and flattening of the Viennese manner of colorful contrast rather than a wholly independent development. In architecture, one sees the influence in Max Littmann's charming "Art Theatre" in the Munich Fair Grounds; but Peter Behrens, who spent his most formative years in Munich, was rather the one who all but ran away with the mode.

In the end Behrens has become far more than a borrower or an adapter — he is almost the foremost *structural* Modernist in Germany today. But back in the decade 1900–1910 he played with the typical idioms of

The Munich Art Theatre. Max Littmann, architect. [1908]

simplified walls, flat all-over pattern, accented square forms — and smartness. He even attempted, in some temporary exposition buildings, to apply a posteresque decorativeness to the exterior walls. And photographs from Oldenburg (1905) and Dresden (1906) indicate that the applied colored compositions must have had a real loveliness as well as catchiness — though perhaps a bit " light " for permanent architectural living-with. I find even today that some of the German Modernists who (I feel) should believe in color as one of the new, or revived, glories of architecture, are skeptical, " having seen it tried," they say; and I suspect that applied decorative patterns on the outsides of buildings are what they visualize. I keep, of course, my own faith that there is a colorfulness that may be wholly appropriate to structure. And in a certain class of buildings, including exposition galleries, even this light sort of applied garment of surface pattern and color may be architecturally right. (Re-

The Coonley house, Riverside, Illinois.  Frank Lloyd Wright, architect.  [1908]

member that throughout this chapter we are exploring primarily the lesser beauty of style, sensuous charm, and elegance, rather than the deeper contrapuntal values of structural proportion, character, and architectonic " form.")

Peter Behrens' lasting claim to fame, however, is in a long series of more permanent buildings, particularly factories; and even in a later exposition pavilion, at Berne in 1916, he proved his versatility by abandoning applied line, color, or pattern, and gaining the entire effectiveness out of proportioning, accenting of structural lines, and capitalization of the inherent virtues of wood.

Even outside the Teutonic countries, the story of the expositions is inextricably tangled with that of an emerging new world architecture. In Paris, where it is considered that expositions are seasonal things, like hats, and that the buildings may therefore be millinered and draped rather than architecturally designed, there is the Eiffel Tower of the 1889 occasion to foreshadow later metal-frame building modes. In America, where paste imitations of real monumental buildings are oftener the exposition thing, there remains, nevertheless, the memory of enchanting color at San Francisco in 1915, to remind us of something architects must in fairness to us, the public, recapture in more lasting manifestations. But it is in Germany that the expositions have been frankly trying grounds for new modes of building, for new structural stunts, for decorative fancies, for sketches of an architectural tomorrow.

Not only have there been innumerable examples of the Viennese Secession style at the German shows, from those already mentioned down to the International Press Exposition at Cologne in 1928, but not infrequently Central European cities have established permanent Fair Grounds, with a quota of lasting fire-proof exhibition halls, and most of these are typically of the new architecture. Throughout Germany the two main currents are meeting: the structural-honesty, back-to-essentials current, and the decorative one from Austria. Without reviewing the score or so important expositions, I may note that many of the outstanding Modernists in Germany have found opportunity in them — sometimes their first opening of a big sort. The 1914 *Werkbundausstellung* in Cologne alone brought together Hoffmann (assisted by Strnad and others of the Vienna group), Van de Velde, Behrens, Bruno Taut, and Walter Gropius. Other Fairs have brought to notice Wilhelm Kreis, Max Berg, Adolf Abel, Hans Poelzig and Heinrich Tessenow. I am adding one more illustration of the sort of achievement in stylization fostered on these occasions: the Iron Pavilion at the Leipzig Exposition of 1913, by Bruno Taut and Franz Hoffmann (page 194).

OUTSIDE the achievements that may be grouped as of, or influenced by, Vienna, there is only one stylistic phenomenon that is outstanding: Frank Lloyd Wright. Seven years ago, during my first week upon the European continent, a Dutch architect was showing me radical architecture in Amsterdam and thereabouts. We rounded a corner and came face to face with a building that brought me up short.

" Ah, yes," the Dutchman said, noting my immediate interest, " that is what we call the American style."

" Shades of Frank Lloyd Wright! " I murmured. The building had the long emphasized horizontals, the low roofs, the grouped windows, the bit of patterned surface at just the right place, that spelled early Wright.

" Not American, but Wright," I said. And I explained that in the United States not one reputable architect in ten would know Wright's name, unless as a heretic and wild man. To be sure, this mode of accented-horizontals in building had been caricatured in suburbs all over the country. But as for being typical *American* — what a laugh that would have afforded at any meeting of the American Society of Beaux-Arts Architects in the year 1922! [2]

[2] I think I am not unduly critical here. In that very year 1922, it happens, the Education Committee of the American Institute of Architects compiled a book on architecture, designed particularly for university students and for popular cultural reading, and it was duly published in 1923. It does not even mention Wright's name — despite the long list of notable contemporary American structures and designers. Even today the only volume in English on Wright's work is foreign-published, consisting of seven consecutive issues of the sumptuous Dutch periodical *Wendingen*, brought together with a title-page reading, " The Life Work of the American Architect Frank Lloyd Wright with Contributions

Three early examples of house design by Frank Lloyd Wright; illustrating his
revolt against the current high and spiky forms — and his feeling for style.

Details from the Barnsdall house (California Art Club) and the Barnsdall cottage, Olive Hill, Los Angeles, California. Illustrating, in contrast to the preceding plate, how the architect created new stylistic idioms out of new materials and new methods of building, and to accord with different climatic conditions. Frank Lloyd Wright, architect. [By courtesy of the publishers of *Wendingen*]

Nevertheless, my companion proved to me that even then Wright meant American architecture to the Dutch students of the subject; that he had wielded an enormous influence (chiefly through two books of his plans, and of photographs of his buildings, published in Germany in 1910 and 1911). And indeed I saw many proofs in the following weeks that Wright had come and had conquered; and even now I occasionally stumble upon a building in Germany or Switzerland — or even England — which indicates that some belated student of those early books has learned to spread Wright's horizontals effectively, to touch in his ornament firmly and precisely. (Let me add that the Dutch and the Germans later took what was proper that they should from both Sullivan and Wright: new ideas about structure and materials, a revolutionary conception of space as the basic element in architecture, and — not a ready-made style so much as the faith that a style could be created directly out of the methods of modern building.)

Wright had created a style before 1900. It may have been partially invented by Louis Sullivan but Wright perfected it — and produced more lovely examples of it than any who followed. In some ways it was far more distinctive, certainly more individual, than the Viennese Secession development. It was so personal that you can mark every echo of it even today — whereas Secession modishness has flowed into, and been lost in, much modern German building.

But Wright is not a man to be limited to a style, even if he did create it himself. Even while he was perfecting that earliest mode in dwellings, he was designing a factory (1903) that was destined as much as any one building in the world to establish a new and imposing industrial architecture. And when his early house style had crystallized, had become recognizable in Oak Park or Amsterdam or Darmstadt, Wright was off creating

---

by Frank Lloyd Wright, an Introduction by Architect H. Th. Wijdeveld and Many Articles by Famous European Architects and American Writers; Publisher: C. A. Mees, Santpoort, Holland, 1925." As warrant of the esteem in which Wright is held among the great practitioners of modern architecture in Europe, one may note that the chapters include tributes and analyses by H. P. Berlage, J. J. P. Oud, Robert Mallet-Stevens, and Erich Mendelsohn.

Architect's drawing for the Barnsdall cottage, Olive Hill, Los Angeles, California.  Frank Lloyd Wright, architect.

a different outer garment, quite unlike the old, and certainly unrelated to any other known to the Western world.   (Just a flavor, perhaps, of the Orient, there was.)   Then, suddenly, a third distinctive mode of stylization came out of a theory of use of a new material.   One feels, indeed, that Wright's fecund genius would give rise to as many styles as there are types of use, types of site, or sorts of building material, and each creative, each colorful, each pleasing, each appropriate.

Only time can tell how far his great imaginative genius will affect the course of American or world architecture; but it is evident that certain phases of his work are the most original and most stimulating individual

Details of houses built by Frank Lloyd Wright in California, illustrating the decorative values possible in the use of his recently invented cast-concrete-block system of construction.

Decorative cast-concrete slabs used in contrast with sheer re-enforced concrete walls, as seen in two California houses designed by Lloyd Wright, son of Frank Lloyd Wright, inventor of the method. [Photos by Will Connell]

contribution to the advance of the new architecture up to this time; and it augurs well that no one of his styles is of a sort to be put on or off; each belongs to a type of construction, or to climatic conditions, or to a conception of what a dwelling is for (mediæval-minded people find his open, horizontal-spirit houses intolerable); and yet all have universal potentialities broader than idiom or place or use, that made it possible to echo him everywhere.

I despair of describing the qualities and differences in the several phases of Wright's work, and I am to a certain extent substituting illustrations for analysis here. The earlier photographs, of the houses in the Chicago neighborhood, are, of course, illustrative of the mode that has been copied from California to Amsterdam and Budapest, the horizontal-accent, low-roof type. A second individual trend crystallized, in a conspicuous way, first in the Barnsdall residence (and in designs for the theatre and cottages originally planned for a surrounding " development "). It is heavier in aspect — as is appropriate in concrete and stucco construction — but at the same time lightened by a very distinctive, and at times almost jewel-like ornament. There are no sloping roofs, and there is greater gain from massing of the squarer elements, from proportioning of the main sculptural masses. If I may put it so rawly, the earlier dwelling-houses had proved Wright's genius in gaining decorative values, even brilliancy and smartness, out of elements that sprawled out — a prairie wideness had to do with it, perhaps; whereas now the values grew rather from the piling-up of forms. In some ways the later mode is broader, nearer universal in its possibilities. The earlier style never seemed destined to cover more than houses and country-clubs and informal shelters like studios and kindergartens and inns.

The third well-defined style is more closely related to the second than either is to the first. It grew out of Wright's own invented method of building with pre-cast concrete slabs. His designs in the mode are frankly and obviously compositions built up with articulated slabs: the structural feature is emphasized and the ornament is integral to the slab-casting.

Ruhlmann Pavilion at the Decorative Arts Exposition, Paris, 1925.   P. Patout, architect.   [This and the following three photos by courtesy of *l'Architecte*, Paris]

All-over pattern becomes a matter of such ease, and color is so easily built in (not added), that these latest buildings are more richly dressed than the designer's earlier works.   Again Wright has created an expression that is unmistakable, distinctive, outstanding.

If I were treating all of Wright's contributions to modern architecture in these few pages, it would be inexcusable to entitle the chapter " The Search for a Style "; for Wright begins with structure, has a passionate appreciation of the beauties of building materials in their own right, and damns loudly the proponents of any style for its own sake, divorced from needs and methods.   But the fact remains that on the basis of honest facing of the space problem, the use problem, the materials and mechanics problem, he has created the most striking, the most brilliant outward architectural investitures, known to these modern times.   This is the loveliness that grows out of a sense of style but at the same time reflects

Garden façade of the Ruhlmann Pavilion.   P. Patout, architect

inner character.   This is machine-age engineered building plus an appropriate loveliness of finish.

Hoffmann, too, might well be exempted from the limiting implications of the chapter title; but in other hands the Secession stylization has often lent itself to the flaunting of a mere attractive decorative garment.   And the only further development that we shall explore, the only one that has become known to the rest of the world, the French, seems to me to suffer sensibly from superficiality and catchiness.

What I have in mind is the sort of thing that was paraded most conspicuously at the Exposition of Decorative Arts in 1925.   I want particularly to guard against including Le Corbusier, Perret, and Mallet-Stevens in any general criticism of the French decorative style: the former two are sincerely anxious to get back to structure and to machine-age austerity; the latter has a distinctive mode, too personal to be French, and more related in feeling to American and German phases.

Rotunda interior of the Nancy Pavilion at the Exposition of Decorative Arts, Paris, 1925. Le Bourgeois and Bourgon, architects.

(Auguste Perret's theatre was outside the spirit of the Exposition and of French decorative architecture — he has been frankly critical of both.)

What I mean by the French style is the seductively millinered building: the exteriors that have the Viennese smartness but softened and rounded and sweetened; and the interiors that are fastidiously elegant and rich — but oh! so feminine. From many photographs of the French buildings at the Exposition spread before me, I throw aside those which are obviously " stunts " of fashion experts, window dressers, and stage costumers who imagined that they were for the moment architects: the gates of honor, the grand staircase, and the show-pavilions of the department-store deco-

Façade of the Nancy Pavilion.  Le Bourgeois and Bourgon, architects

rators, " Primavera," " Pomone," Louvre, and Lafayette.  And I come finally to the Ruhlmann pavilion as the best of the typically Parisian things.  Note the accented square edges, the flat surfaces, the concentrated ornament, the freshness — all details that we have remarked as elements of modern stylization among the Viennese; but the "air" of it is French, isn't it?  Somehow the round pillars, the rounding of the central motive, the disrelation of structure and effect, are different from what Hoffmann or Behrens would have done.  Nor is the massing as simple and elemental as they would have wanted it.  But chiefly it is a lighter, more graceful quality that characterizes the garment — pretty and seductive but spineless.  The garden façade is severer and withal more interesting, but hardly more architectural.  You might look back to verify that the Vienna pavilions are structurally sound, architecturally fine, first, and then graceful (and the one in Paris even a bit playful).

Here is a second example of the French Modernism, the Pavilion of Nancy at the 1925 Exposition.  There are features of solidity and concentration that are considerably better, and the interior of the rotunda achieves an effect both novel and intriguing (if wholly unrelated to the exterior); but the hardly sincere treatment of the main portal gives the

Apartment in New York. Howe & Lescaze, architects. [Photo by Sigurd Fischer.] Indicating that " Modernism " need not mean coldness.

Functionalist simplification at its best in modern French interior decoration: a dining room by Djo-Bourgeois.

façade away. And it is this lack of depth that so often disturbs me when I look at examples of modern French interior decoration. Modish, alluring, swanky, lush; they lack structure, character, outlook. I am the more insistent upon the fault — despite many a pleasant hour in the rooms at the Decorative Arts Salons in Paris — because lately some of our American architects have been industriously importing these soft French interiors, without inquiring into their soundness or their appropriateness; just as they used to import Renaissance panelled or Louis XVI boudoirs. Let us beware of the too effeminate thing, the assumed prettiness, the sensuous loveliness without innate architectonic virtue. By a curious conjunction of circumstances, some of the French ocean steamships have been fitted with dining-halls and suites in this lush and sweetened manner: those same steamships that in the logic and cleanliness and efficiency of their outward

Modern interior decoration in America, in its simplest and its most elaborate aspects. At left, the richly dressed dance and dining hall at the Central Park Casino, New York, by Joseph Urban; at right, reception room of a broker's office, Los Angeles, California, by J. R. Davidson. [By courtesy of *The Architectural Record*]

Swedish Pavilion at the Decorative Arts Exposition, Paris, 1925.  Carl Bergsten, architect.  [By courtesy
of *l'Architecte,* Paris]

decks and windows and machinery gave stimulus to the functionalist and
anti-decorative Modernists.

As a last word about the Paris Exposition (since it was consciously designed to bring together world manifestations of new styles), I may
remark the distinctive achievements of the Swedes, the Danes, and the
Poles.  The simple and attractive exterior of the Swedish Pavilion, with
its high pillared porch, not wholly " unhistoric," was matched with interior rooms equally clean-lined but more colorful; and the Danish building, perhaps over-severe outwardly, was filled with some most daringly
experimental rooms, wherein the painters were given a free hand at informal expressionistic decoration.

The Polish Pavilion achieved as much a unity and a distinctiveness as
did the Austrian.  Here was newness with a more nationalistic flavor.
Though the exterior of the building, with the exception of one decorative

Polish Pavilion at the Decorative Arts Exposition, Paris, 1925.   Joseph
Czajkowski, architect.   [By courtesy of *l'Architecte*, Paris]

feature, might have been imagined by a Viennese or a Scandinavian architect in a fanciful moment, most of the interior decoration was of a heavily
rich sort that bespoke an East-of-Europe origin, a sort of peasant-art
vigor out of the near-Oriental peoples, though manipulated at times
with a Baroque-like touch.   It is just as well to note that among the
schools of decoration (surface decoration as distinguished from the architectonic sort) there is one that affects the peasant-art broadness, vivid-
ness, and simplicity.   It has given us some pleasurable moments in an
isolated way — like peasant-art stage-settings or batik shawls — but no
architecture has grown up related to it.   And this Polish style, so attrac-

An early phase of Frank Lloyd Wright's individualistic ornament, as seen in the Midway Gardens, an amusement park in Chicago. [By courtesy of the editors of *Wendingen*]

tive in an exotic way, seems at this time to hold no hope of an influence on universal architecture. We are down now, indeed, to a consideration of personal idioms and frankly applied modes of ornamentation.

For one such mode a world validity is claimed. As yet I have seen but the first suggestions of it in architecture (or perhaps I should say in Western architecture — for the Saracens were masters of one phase of it), but on paper it has extraordinary attractiveness. And indeed all the arguments for its universal use seem logical and convincing — when comes the master-builder who will make it integral to structure. It is the purely

Drawing by Claude Bragdon illustrating projective ornament as
applied to architecture.   [From *Projective Ornament*, by Claude
Bragdon, by courtesy of the author]

mathematical mode known generally under the name bestowed by Claude
Bragdon: *projective ornament*.   When modern art in all its branches is
toying with the abstract, working toward the eternally impersonal, there
is good reason to believe that mathematics in Bragdon's higher understanding of the word will underlie whatever the new architects achieve
by way of a surface language of ornamentation.   Bragdon has coupled his
own advocacy of the system with pleas for the generous use of color.   He

Projective ornament as an enrichment to architecture: drawing by
Claude Bragdon.  [From Bragdon's *Architecture and Democracy*]

has further pointed out that a true decorativeness, including ornament and
its color, arrives only out of the psychologic inwardness of the builder, of
architect, and of user.  If the spirit of man be not ready for a mode so
truly universal, if the consciousness of the time be not crystallized toward
a world-order, then the mathematically true expression will fail of arrival.
We shall then continue in a bare or material architecture, unenriched with
ornament, or else fall back on the old rag-bag of Greek acanthus, phallic
egg-and-dart, Gothic foliage and gargoyle, etc.  Those who are interested
in following out the idea of geometric projections of higher thought, in

Interior of the *Stahlkirche*, Cologne, Germany. Professor Otto Bartning, architect.
[From *Die Stahlkirche*, by Dr. Paul Girkan]

ornamental symbols and cosmic ideation, as basis for a new world beauty in ornament, may do so in the chapters on the subject in Bragdon's admirable volume of essays *Architecture and Democracy*, and in his monograph entitled *Projective Ornament*.

Unfortunately Bragdon abandoned the practice of architecture (in favor of writing and stage designing) before he had put into buildings conspicuous creative examples of his " system." Since we are concerned at present with the new building that is, I content myself with reproducing two examples of his suggestive drawings.

A Frenchman, Auguste Perret, has insisted on the mathematical bases of architectural design; and perhaps has hurt himself with the decorative wing of French Modernists by decrying the millinered stuff. But beyond the products of a genius for engineering, working in new uses for reinforced concrete, he has failed to add to the forms of modern architecture. His creations in concrete decorative detail have been heralded widely as the true crystallization of the machine-age style in ornament. But I have studied his "effects," particularly in the church at Le Raincy and the Orientation Tower at Grenoble, and it seems to me that the genius for structural adjustment is not matched by even an unusual talent for decorativeness. In short, the concrete patterns seem rather lifeless, meaningless, and — certainly, for this age — too colorless.

The Le Raincy church, being a stimulating effort after honest structural means in church-building, but failing to touch imaginative heights, or even middle ground, in decorative appeal, brings up the really serious question of what are appropriate surface forms in a transitional world; when religious sects and other institutions out of mediævalism persist into these machine-times, what are the logical garments for clothing them? The city will move on inevitably to different modes of expression: shall the ancient church, as long as it hangs on, cling to the old architectural dress, or shall it try to invent raiments for itself not too different from the surrounding business buildings, factories, hangars, and house-machines? Some of the answers are outlined in a later chapter. Meantime here is a picture of another "Modernist" church, at Cologne; not so strikingly new in idiom as that at Le Raincy, and perhaps more successful because simpler, more filled with the glow of color, more atmospheric — though inventing no new stylistic idiom.

One other personal decorative note demands illustration. For many years those of us interested in modern architecture knew the work of Robert Mallet-Stevens only in published drawings; and even today, when one may seek out certain of his actual buildings in Paris or at the

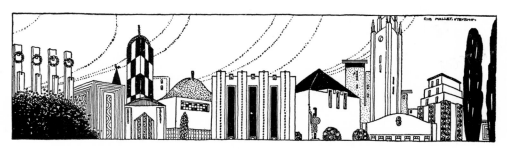

A modern city as visualized by Rob Mallet-Stevens

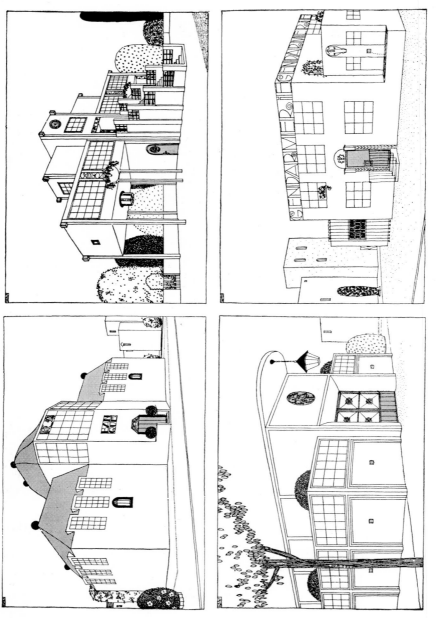

Four buildings for a modern city, by Rob Mallet-Stevens: a bank, a school, a garage, and a police station. [From Mallet-Stevens' portfolio of designs entitled *Une Cité Moderne*]

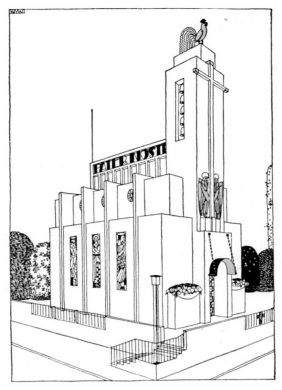

A church for a modern city: Mallet-Stevens' design for
his *Cité Moderne*.

smart resort cities, we may find his designs on paper more completely
expressive of a decorative thing he wants to do. Frankly indebted to
the American Wright, and having more in common with the posteresque
Modernists of Vienna and Munich than with any other closer associates,
he still added an individual fantasy, an unmistakable personal decorative
touch. The style of those early compositions was almost toy-like in its
simplifications and playfulnesses. The little cross-section of " a city of
tomorrow," for instance, is intriguing and joyous, though we know it
could never happen like that in any adult town dedicated to the uses
of today. But how charming, how disarming! In a portfolio of building designs for an imagined *Cité Moderne*, there is a whole series of pos-
teresquely simple garages, banks, villas, etc., in this toy manner. Even

Main doorways of the school at Celle, Germany. Otto Haesler, architect. [By courtesy of *l'Architecte,* Paris]

the church in this series is naive and frankly fantastic; though the playing with abstract line, with " edges," is a direct foreshadowing of the actual architectural work Mallet-Stevens is doing, as instanced in the Alfa-Romeo Garage in Paris, and in many catchy shop-fronts just now echoed in New York.

This method of playing the horizontal and vertical accented edges against each other for conscious decorative effect brings us back to the school of designers who stem off from Le Corbusier's sort of basic simplicity into manipulation of masses, of wall surfaces and openings, in balanced design of broad unadorned elements. The school building at

Doorway in an apartment.  Bruno Schneidereit,
architect, Berlin.

Celle is a notable example.  But here we have passed insensibly — as perhaps Mallet-Stevens himself did in ten years of thinking — from a thing that is at least half a matter of surface ornament to a thing structurally expressive, and decorative out of elementary usefulness, sculptural massing, and an intuitive feel for linear composition.

There is a whole school of architects, of course, who strip back to this sort of simplicity, and *then* touch in just a suggestion of ornament out of some past mode: sculptured figures with primitive heaviness were used effectively for " relief " in Germany for a time; and Gothic bits may lighten a façade rigid with upright lines; or a Neo-Rococo spray of ornament may save a wall or a window-frame or a proscenium arch from a too-severe aspect.

The Neo-Rococo touch is most in vogue at the moment.  The most engaging examples, perhaps, are in the theatres designed by Oskar Kaufmann in Berlin.  The auditoriums and foyers and promenades are touched with reticent outcroppings of playful ornament here and there, usually

Entrance to an office building, Topeka, Kansas, illustrating ornamentation of the sort initiated by Louis Sullivan.  Designed by George C.
Emslie, Chicago.

in the midst of sensuously lovely color.  The highroad to the future does
not lie in this direction; nothing so decadent as the Rococo or Baroque
could supply the motives for the future.  But until a sound new ornamental language is encompassed, we may on occasion be thankful to the
Kaufmanns who titillate our senses with just a suggestion of sophisticated
ornament as a cap to severe modernity.  It is, indeed, the fastidious way
in which the bit of decoration is touched in beside studied simplicity, that
counts.  The doorway of a dressing-room, by Bruno Schneidereit, illustrates the point exactly (page 223).

As a close to the chapter I return to America, to two men who have

View showing decorative detail of Bullock's Wiltshire Boulevard
Department Store, Los Angeles, California. John and Donald B.
Parkinson, architects.

been concerned with the search for an ornamental mode appropriate to
the new constructive architecture, one theoretically, the other in every-
day practice. For be it recorded that the pioneer Louis Sullivan worked
out in a series of drawings a complete system of ornamentation, in plates
nobly brought to publication by his old enemies the academicians — who
saw in this work if not in the polemic utterances of the veteran radical,
a permanent and safe contribution to architectural progress. In contrast,
one of the younger American Modernists, who outgrew his Beaux-Arts
training to get back to stripped commercial building, and then went
forward to essays in wholly "logical" decorative elaboration, has pro-

Ornamentation at tops of skyscrapers, designed for effectiveness at long range.   Ely Jacques Kahn, architect.   [Photos by Sigurd Fischer]

Ornamentation at top of a skyscraper, by Ely Jacques Kahn. [Photo by Sigurd Fischer]

duced, in place on building tops, what he considers reasonable skyscraper ornamentation. Ely Jacques Kahn has, indeed, felt his way toward a severe flowering of decoration on a half-dozen notable New York business towers. There is no Viennese lightness here, no attempt to lighten or make elegant or graceful what is essentially heavy, sturdy, business-like. But there is enrichment for the eye, appropriate " relief," just a suggestion of flowering. And that is the ultimate function of ornament in architecture — never to be the main thing, but to emphasize essential composition, to reinforce the characteristic design that the architect has put into the building. I think that even Ely Kahn would agree that in these ornamental outcroppings are but the faintest beginnings of a style, the earliest sprouts of a plant that may grow in quite different directions from any suspected now.   The point is that here is an elaboration of architecture that grew out of the actual new way of building, that was not thought of at all, separately, before the place for it was there, to be filled.   That is the beginning point of the only honest kind of style.

And so we are back again where style is not a sense-provoking garment, a seductive robe, thrown over a structure, but the flower of the structure itself.   We cannot, however machine-logical our intentions, live permanently with an architecture negating stylishness, insistently undecorative.

But we can demand of all the seekers after a style that they be more than poster artists, couturiers, Beardsleyesque illustrators, or stage-setters. They must begin with a religion of *building,* and decorate out of architectural imagination and living emotion for the fullness of " architectural form."

Duplex cottage in a group development at Hollywood, California.   R. M. Schindler, architect.
Illustrating " wrinkling " of the surface stucco as the only ornamental touch.

# CHAPTER VI

## *HOME*

APPARENTLY the home is in a bad way. There are those who attack family life as an evil, on economic, social, and even on moral grounds. There are those who point out that the physical house is oftener than not inconvenient, inefficient as a machine, dark, and tuberculous; even while factory, store, and office are taking on the habiliments of lightness and cleanliness and precision in service. And indubitably the æsthetic aspect of home-building suffered an alarming relapse after the arrival of industrialism — and " Victorian home" is an epithet of opprobrium that is almost universal instead of British in its intimations of gloom, bad taste, and futile showiness. It is a bit difficult to see why the industrial revolution, besides bringing with it a first crop of dirty and dingy factories, should have brought in the degradation of domestic architecture as well. Some argue that the raising of traders, shop-keepers and money-changers into the seats of the mighty — the creation of an all-powerful bourgeoisie

— corrupted taste and led to a demand for the pretentious and the cheaply gaudy; but that argument is at least partially answered by the certainty that throughout most of history "lower-class" architecture has been better than that sponsored by princes, priests, and professionals. (Distinctly peasant building is attractive wherever you meet it, almost.)

More to the point is it that irresponsible landlordism, grasping at cheapest mass-production methods, prostituted both the art and the mechanics of house building for the sake of pecuniary profit. But perhaps a still deeper relationship between architecture and civilization is to be blamed for the corruption that ate into domestic building in the nineteenth century: a materialistic, faithless, sentimental age could not produce other than a false and draughty architecture. Certainly the high-ceilinged rooms overcrowded with bric-a-brac, the false fronts, the iron ornaments, and the rest are eloquent of a period of separation of art from living, of divorced spiritual and "practical" activities.

And yet home remains home to the great majority of individuals. They refuse to take too seriously the predictions of those who prophesy the extinction of family life; they opine correctly that the architectural shell can be thrown off and another grown, one that fits the new life both functionally and æsthetically. Nor can anyone justly claim that a new world architecture has been born until evidence can be brought that peoples are beginning to live, at home, in a different sort of house. The skyscraper may be an answer to a different sort of economic need, invented by chance in America by virtue of leadership in business; but if we continue to build English, French, and Mediterranean dwelling-places, we confess that it *is* a chance, that our Modernism and our creativeness go no deeper than a surface necessity, are unrelated to spiritual impulse, are a shoot only, not a main growth. Our homes may well become the final test of our honesty and our inventiveness, and of our craving for or indifference to beauty.

Recorded history of architecture, to be sure, has dealt extensively with everything except the home, has been almost silent about the mere dwell-

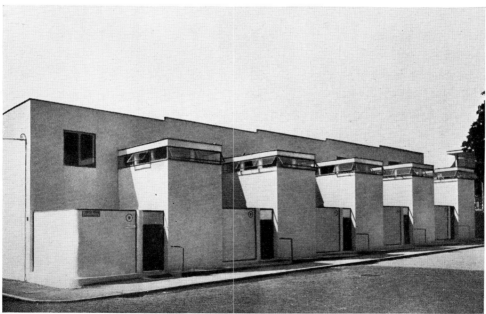

Above, a house by Le Corbusier (who originated the slogan " the house as a machine ") and P. Jeanneret. Below, group of houses by J. J. P. Oud. In the Weissenhof suburb, Stuttgart, Germany. 1927. [By courtesy of *l'Architecte*, Paris]

ing-house — a fact quite understandable when we realize that all our records have been written in the kingly and mock-democratic eras, when
architects, critics, and rich patrons were alike concerned with the elaboration of building rather than its fundamentals.   When the designers of
buildings codified their art according to systems of decoration, it was
natural that the writers should pay first attention to those structures affording room for grand displays of ornament, for pretentious draping of
architectural gew-gaws.   Today we see through the display and pretension — and we begin to believe that in most periods of architectural
practice the home was about the only place touched by the breath of
honesty.

It is likely that in the future all else in the history of the building art in
England up to 1930 will pale into insignificance beside the fine achievement of English " cottage " architecture, as practised more especially in
the sixteenth and seventeenth centuries, and as revived in the early years
of the twentieth.   Personally, I find more that is admirable in French
architecture among the peasant houses of Normandy and Touraine than
in the much-touted monuments among palaces, opera houses, and
churches (the ancient Gothic cathedrals alone excepted).   Even in Italy
a ramble through the farm-house country is more inspiring than a study
of the squares of Rome.   It is necessary to return to the fact, however,
that in France and England — and the United States — practically all
domestic architecture for a century past has lost the peasant simplicity,
has aped in small the display elements of chateau and casino and theatre:
has been as dispiritingly uncreative, dishonest, and tasteless as the church
building and the libraries.   Within three or four decades, to be sure, the
Eclectics have brought back *taste* to a notable extent (except possibly in
France) ; but the servile-mindedness of their contribution is only too evident in the copied motifs and types.   One could wager fairly safely on
the proportion of French chateaux, Colonial houses, English cottages, and
Italian villas to be found in any " high-class " Long Island or Westchester
suburb developed between 1900 and 1925.

Houses at Breslau, Germany.   Heinrich Lauterbach, architect.   [By courtesy of *The Architectural Record*]
Illustrating the trend toward greater " openness."

House in Dessau, Germany.   Walter Gropius, architect.   [1926]

Our business just here, however, is to discover whether there is a 1930 home architecture that is as much a product of direct thinking as were the peasant cottages, that is as beautifully simple — even while serving the purposes of the newly complex " house machine."   You will remember that we talked somewhat of the house as machine in an early chapter; that we found that life in the machine age demands living-quarters built around a network of functioning mechanical servants.   What progress has been made in capturing an old elemental simplicity of design in conjunction with this new home mechanism?

Already in the new age we have come to believe that to inhabit a wasteful and inconvenient house is scarcely short of being immoral; and some of us have arrived at the further conviction that the unbeautiful imitational grandeur of high ceilings, stuffed furniture, and cluttered parlors is a harmful influence that we have no right to impose upon ourselves or our defenceless children.   I, as husband and father in a co-operative

Beach house, Balboa, California.  R. M. Schindler, architect.  [1926]

family, stole many hours per day for many years from my wife, by failing to provide the latest convenience-equipped dwelling-house; and it may be that society in the future will judge that in thus enslaving her unnecessarily I was more guilty than if I had committed those crimes of violence or violation of property rights that are already commonly revenged upon the individual.  Of course if she had arrived at an adequate realization of machine-age independence and morality in those days she would have refused servitude — would have stood upon the worker's inalienable right to have the most efficient tools known to his trade.  (Fortunately the crisis is no longer an acute one in this particular family — evaded by three years' wandering.  But mind you, if *your* wife should insist that it is immoral for her to continue running your establishment without the latest electric aids, we shall both be on her side.)

And the architect must begin with a belief in that new morality. He is no longer to be hired to put a partitioned shelter over us, with picturesque additions. He is to begin with the house as a running machine, designed for scientific service and for tempered refuge from heat in summer and from cold in winter, for convenience in cooking meals and washing dishes, for automatic laundering, for easy and pleasant cleansing of hands, face, and body, for immediate and efficient carrying-away of waste, for controlled lighting, for the most comfortable disposal of the beds, chairs, tables, books, etc., that are necessary to the living of the good life. As contrasted with the architect of one hundred years ago, the house designer of today is thus faced with a problem of disposing his walls and floors and roofs in accordance with a network of wires, sockets, pipes, ducts, and machines, an amazingly complex fabric of time-savers and work-eliminators.

The architect who still considers these things as conveniences *carried into the house,* rather than as the basic conditioning factors of his designing, will never be more than a hang-over from the old age into the new. For it will be basic to the new civilization that the time once devoted to sweeping with brooms, to the carrying in of ice, and to washing of clothes by hand will be gained for activities having to do with the enrichment of living; just as already the saving has been made of the time once given to the filling of lamps, the shovelling of coal, and the carrying of water.

The universal foundation for the good home is in the cunning with which these problems of comfort, utility, and efficiency are met. Peasant homes have been good in general because the builders began by meeting directly and sensibly the problem of shelter, then a simple problem uncomplicated by any consideration of (uninvented) machinery; and lower-class architecture remained good until the inconvenient spaciousness, the complicated ornament, and the general " spread " of display buildings began to be copied into cottages. Really bad home building, as we have noted, became well-nigh universal in the nineteenth century, by reason of departure from this first law of simple answering to a need, to a function.   It seemed more important to ape the luxuries and wastefulnesses of the aristocratic: that was the way to prove one's standing.   (Duplicating machines just then made cheap the imitation grandeur of turned balusters, machine-stamped mouldings, lathe-work grills, scroll-saw edgings, iron stove ornaments, etc., etc.)   At one leap, so to speak, the house arrived at wasteful largeness, cluttered-up and therefore easily dirtied surfaces, picturesquely unsanitary complication.   And indeed, the average " picturesque," over-angular, high-standing Victorian house was immoral on both counts: inefficient and æsthetically abortional.   And the housewife either was a slave herself or stooped to the undemocratic device of employing slaves and occupying them with avoidable work.

THE modern English house, which is the first of the individual types that I shall treat of, did not grow from this conception of the house as a machine, but out of a revivalist spirit born almost wholly of æsthetic considerations.   (My chapter plan is to discuss in turn five phases of the new home building: (1) the English cottage; (2) Frank Lloyd Wright's triple contribution to progress; (3) the extreme Rationalist or Functionalist house-machines, as seen especially in Germany and France — with the mentioned Weissenhof suburb at Stuttgart as chief exhibit; (4) by way of contrast, the " individualist " theories, and practice, of that lone California pioneer, Bernard Maybeck; and (5) back to the less radical, the compromised Modernism of the now accepted " Californian Style."   Then, of course, will come some consideration of the mass-home, the modern apartment building.)

In England, at about the time that the Mackintoshes and the McNairs were almost creating a new style of interior decoration, touching at once upon the Japanesque, the *Art Nouveau,* and the Beardsleyesque — all to no lasting purpose in England — a sturdier group of designers were going back to the rediscovered " English Cottage " for inspiration, for an old simplicity, for actual building models.   If the architects thus employed had done no more than revive an old style, a very beautiful one, their work

Chaplain's House, St. Mary's Home, Wantage, England.   M. H. Baillie Scott, architect.
About 1900.   [From *The Studio* special summer number, 1901, by courtesy of the editors]

still would have been important — though not necessarily significant in
the record of Modernism; for the old English cottage was infinitely
superior to the seventeenth-eighteenth century Renaissance and the
mongrel Victorian products.   But it happens that a few architects went
farther.   They rationalized the ancient style, simplified motives, arrived,
about 1900, at a stripped product that almost contacts with the Modernism of a quarter-century later — though with only casual variations
of the fundamental forms, the masses and arrangements and motives
which characterized the sixteenth century "originals."   They at least
pointed forward to a geometric simplicity.

There is little use in discussing whether the eminent group of architects concerned deserve the name " Modernists," or only " Near-Modern-
ists."   What is important is that here was the first extensive phenomenon
in domestic architecture looking to stripping away Victorian preten-
tiousness and falsity; and an early thrust toward elemental forms.   Here
was a point at which a new ideal of craftsmanship entered into home
building.   Regrettably, the impulse ran out, after twenty years or so,
during which many " garden suburbs " took on appealing prettiness;
so that today the names that loomed large in the first decade of the new

"The Orchard," Chorley Wood, Hertfordshire, England. C. F. A. Voysey, architect.
[From *The Studio* special summer number, 1901, by courtesy of the editors]

century are (so far as the rest of the world is concerned) still the greatest names in recent English architecture. M. H. Baillie Scott, C. F. A. Voysey, and Edwin L. Lutyens were giant figures. They brought to their designing not only the true architect's understanding of building art, but deep penetration into the social values of good housing. With them should be named, perhaps, that artist and writer who became spokesman for their modified ideals, C. R. Ashbee; and curiously enough, in view of later developments, a promising young designer of interiors and furniture, among them, was named Frank Brangwyn.

If you will look over the files of *The Studio,* and particularly the " special numbers " devoted to architecture,[1] between the years 1898 and 1910, you will gain an understanding of the aims and accomplishments of an apparently considerable group of designers, among whom Voysey, Scott, and Lutyens were leaders. The whole " Renaissance " was accomplished with true British reserve: there was not the emotional drive of Wright's insurgency in America and Wagner's revolutionary campaign

[1] See particularly *Modern British Domestic Architecture and Decoration,* edited by Charles Holme, London, Paris, and New York, 1901. C. R. Ashbee's *Where the Great City Stands: A Study in The New Civics,* London, 1917, goes beyond architecture in the limited sense: is a book of prime importance for those interested in a new structure for society.

in Vienna, of the same years. But quietly and thoroughly these British " Arts and Crafts " architects erected houses, based on old English forms, but shaped cunningly to new needs, and with a stripping down in the decorative elements. The two illustrations indicate at once the origin of the architects' " inspiration " and the elements added creatively.

If today we let the clearly historic aspects of these houses disturb us — since we are seeking the truly modern contribution — let us remember that in 1910 such simple forms, such craftsman-like directness, such reticence and sureness in decoration, were strikingly unusual, were notable steps forward. This is the counterpart in domestic architecture of the Gothic-enveloped skyscraper: a stylistic mode out of the past happened to fit perfectly a new need for expression. In the hands of the three named architects the idiom not only was simplified, rationalized, but was stamped with individual creative manipulation.

Studying the English homes of the years since 1910, I have felt that England has not lived up to the promise implicit in the work of those pioneers. There has been recession rather than progress: a heavier leaning on the past, and less creative adaptation — so that many of the garden suburbs take on a somewhat monotonous " old English " air. Designers seem to have taken refuge again in the revival of picturesque detail and quaint effects. Still, there is nothing in the whole range of Eclectic architecture, nothing else based directly on revivals, that is so charming, so pretty, as a good block of English houses. Forms are fundamentally simple, surfaces clean, massing and proportion often very stirring, detail appropriate; and the interiors are relatively plain, quite uncluttered. If England is to preserve her traditional reserve, her immemorial belief in " every man's house his castle," her conservatism in adopting new forms — and since the war she has shown little inclination to rival the striving, the experimentation, of Germany, Russia, and America, in the arts — then this is near an ideal house form. But we, with conceptions of *a new open life,* a machine-age way of living, we may pass on from the English cottage, with perhaps a wistful glance backward at its homely

Houses by Frank Lloyd Wright, of the early " prairie " period.

prettiness, with regret too that the followers of Voysey and Baillie Scott did not take that one step farther, that would have put them into direct contact with the engineer-architects of today, with the builders of the Weissenhof houses.[2]

The several "styles" in domestic building created by Frank Lloyd Wright are so distinctive, so striking, that commentators are likely to tag him as a stylist without due regard to the economic and practical idealism underlying his creativeness. While not to be grouped with the extreme left wing of the Functionalists, who want a "use" reason for every detail that goes into their design — who are, indeed, consciously anti-decorative — Wright is extraordinarily the practical thinker before being stylist. His mind strikes directly through to the functional justification for every element in architecture. He was thinking of the house as a machine to be fitted to certain purposes, long before there was this decade's talk about machine-age living and machine-age æsthetics. No one else asked so searchingly, "What is a window for?" or "What is the use of a bedroom?" or "What function does a moulding serve?" No other architect has had quite the same passion for the right material in the right place, the same loving concern with the beauties of wood or metal or glass in appropriate positions. No one else, except his teacher Sullivan, has so vigorously resisted the placing of style before practical attention to function. And yet no one else has so created a style or styles based on the forms born of modern construction.

If Wright has erred, it has not been in failing to think directly, in accordance with modern conditions and needs, but in believing that the rest of mankind, and particularly clients, wanted directness, openness, simplicity, and a machine-age precision and austerity; when as a matter of fact most people are still visioning for themselves, in their houses, a reflection of French regal luxury, a stuffed-brocade softness, a lush and wholly feminine ease. As long as education remains what it is today, in Europe

---

[2] While reading the proofs of this book I have run across photographs of several English houses designed by Thomas S. Tait; as attractively simple and machine-like as could be asked. But they link obviously with Le Corbusier and the German Functionalists, and not with any tradition in England. An illustration will be found in the last chapter.

The Coonley house, Riverside, Illinois.  Frank Lloyd Wright, architect.  [1908]

and America, teaching a separation of hard practical living and spiritual exercise, holding up an ideal of art and the home as a fort and refuge from life, not as a machine of living, we shall have a " public " that resists simple beauty and straightforward design, that clings to falsity, cushioning, and fleshy display. Wright's early houses, in their elimination of clutter and fussed-up furnishings and historical architectural display, foreshadowed much that is characteristic of the best living thirty years later: a certain athletic spareness, openness, direct designing to purpose. Equally his " style " was a long step on the way toward that geometric abstraction so in vogue among the latest European " radicals."

If we look at the photographs of those houses that were Wright's first distinctive achievement, we can identify in them motives that have persisted through thirty years in competition with English gables, Colonial pillared porches, French windows, and the other historical elements and tag-ends that are the domestic architect's more usual stock in trade. But if we need to go only to the nearest suburban development to see faded reflections of Wright's " prairie type " house, we still are most likely to find it at its best back where he practised in those early days: most notably in the Chicago neighborhood.

The outstanding characteristics — speaking of the " looks " first — are the low-lying masses, the finely sculptural proportioning, the masterly designing of the few decorative units, so that windows are concentrated into bold compositional motives played against unbroken surfaces; and most noticeable, the accenting of the horizontal lines, with spare relief in the very slightly sloping roofs. (Doesn't " Victorian " connote to you sharp gables, ungainly height, restless up-sticking points and ridges? This was the most notable American revolt against that sharpness and restlessness.) The pictures show, incidentally, how stucco, glass, and wood were played up for their own virtues — not tortured into uses for which they were materially unsuited. In the Coonley house, too, there is an example of Wright's use of all-over pattern — sparingly, cunningly,

Houses by Frank Lloyd Wright, illustrating the extremest examples of horizontal accent effectively applied, with an enrichment that does not at all harm wall-sense.

In the early years of the century, just the appearance of these houses was so radical, so revolutionary, that orthodox sensibilities were shocked; and when it was discovered that the interiors were equally different, were almost " plain," low-ceilinged, without plaster ornaments or elaborate chandeliers, the conservatives simply knew that the man who built them was crazy. But today, without believing that *everything* that Wright did was a beautiful flowering of the new craftsmanship in house design, we may note these significant gains: Negatively there was the clearing out of the usual clutter of ornamental detail, of showy carved or slick lathed woodwork, of stuffy furnishings, etc., etc. The stereotyped mouldings, the elaborately pigeon-holed mantelpieces, the what-nots, the overstuffed chairs, the glittering brass-and-crystal chandeliers, the imitation Renaissance ceilings — all these were eliminated. Constructively, there was a new cleanliness, a simplification of surfaces, a sense of spaciousness and openness inside and out, and a restful, decorative beauty directly conceived out of the uses and materials of the day.

If Wright had done nothing else for American architecture, through the example of that early work, the nation would be deeply indebted to him for this: more than any other one man he pulled down the skyline of the residence sections of the entire western country. From Chicago to the coast, there has been in a quarter-century a steady tide toward lower and less restless forms; if not always, or even usually, toward the accented horizontality introduced by Wright, then at least toward similarly low-lying masses, toward sculptural outlines fitting to the plains country. You may find turreted French chateaux in Arizona still, and stark high Colonial houses in California; but it is pretty well understood even by the general public that these are " old-fashioned " — either the last gasps of a dying generation of architects, or individual fancies of unimaginative emigrants from the East, or of *nouveau riche* families clinging to some early conception of what is genteel. However illogical do-

The more sculptural style developed by Frank Lloyd Wright when he began to work in concrete: the Barnsdall house, Olive Hill, Los Angeles, California.

mestic building may still be in some aspects, at least it has, in the mass, come down to a peaceful communion with the earth — and Wright is most to be thanked.

But the " prairie type " was only one of his creations in the " home " field.   (You will remember that in this early period he designed that memorable industrial-mercantile structure, the Larkin Building in Buffalo; and in another direction we shall note later his pioneer Unity Temple, a challenge to the historic church builders.)   If we want to differentiate, isolate a second type, we shall find it chiefly in Los Angeles, where Wright projected a group of buildings, only partially constructed up to this time, with new characteristics shaped at once to site, to utilization of a different building material, and to his own matured decorative talent.   The central structure at Olive Hill, Los Angeles, the building which was constructed as a residence for Aline Barnsdall though now the home of the California Art Club, is the most typical; but the drawings for some of the cottages (and a theatre) planned for the same group give more richly the sense of the fullness of the architect's vision, and the great variety of his inspiration within a single group-vision.

The forms here are squarer, the masses heavier, the Modernist simplification carried farther; though Wright, having stripped back to bare structural forms and logical composition, never leaves the final result bare.   These blockier houses are relieved not so much with long horizontal roof-lines and banded windows as with variations in the proportioning, and with touches of creative ornament emphasizing the more important masses.   Both the compositional heaviness, the greater squareness, and the type of ornament are conditioned by the concrete utilized in building the group.   People used to make the criticism of Wright that his domestic work was always so similar that it could be identified with ease wherever found.   The prairie type had, indeed, certain distinctive characteristics. But looking back from a time after his later achievements, one may well feel that it was not a limited æsthetic or the learning of a formula that stamped the buildings alike, but a thoughtful consideration for certain

Scenes at the Barnsdall house, Olive Hill, illustrating how Frank Lloyd Wright ties together building and garden.

Cottage for Miss Aline Barnsdall, Olive Hill, Los Angeles, by Frank Lloyd Wright.    Unlike the original
Olive Hill group, this later cottage is rich in colors.

materials and a sense of " the lay of the western land."   As soon as he took
up poured concrete as a medium, his " style " altered to fit the new
material.

Then came a third " type " of creative design.   Interested intensely
in the social aspects of contemporary architecture, Wright experimented
toward "unit " house building.   And he came to a method which he
feels will go far, in certain localities, toward solving the problem of over-
high building costs.   He developed a process of constructing walls of
pre-cast concrete slabs, saving labor, and at the same time permitting
extraordinary decorative effects of a large elemental sort.

Starting from the view-point that concrete ("conglomerate ") is indeed, in its usual appearance, an " inferior " building material, without
the distinctive qualities that characterize woods or stone or most metals,
Wright points out that it can be given æsthetic character only when the
imagination of the architect acts upon it — within the limits of its natural
capabilities (but never to imitate cut stone or other material).   Its " im-
pressibility " when wet is such that concrete slabs can be made to take
designed shape and plastic pattern according to the creativeness of the
controlling artist; and color can be bred into the conglomerate organ-

Two views of houses in California, by Frank Lloyd Wright, illustrating distinctive character gained by use of pre-cast concrete blocks and slabs. [See also photo at head of Chapter VIII]

ically.  The deadest of architectural materials when handled without creativeness, it becomes ideally the artist's medium when adequate imagination is used in its manipulation.

How far Wright has advanced toward a new decorativeness, in the use of pre-cast slabs, is indicated in the several photographs herewith. Again the ornamental language and the larger form have changed in accordance with the limitations and the capabilities of a material medium. The architect's answer is logical, direct, organic — and again creatively inspired.  Color comes in generously; and there is more of applied ornament, simply because the new method makes duplication of patterned design easy.  To duplicate these illustrated houses in stone would be inordinately expensive, to build them of solid concrete and then decorate the various parts with the all-over patterns would be laborious and costly — and in neither case would the result be other than false and patently labored. But now, cheaply and facilely, the specially trained workmen may put up such distinctive and attractive buildings swiftly — almost mechanically — under the guidance of the creative architect.

After all I prefer to run the risk of being classed with those who over-emphasize Wright's stylistic achievement — I end each time with praise of the over-values, the decorativeness, the distinction of his work — rather than to dwell at length on the utilitarian or social aspects. I think the reason is that I know that the world is coming without great struggle to an acceptance of the machine-idea in house design, to the Functionalist view-point for a new beginning.  In the two years since I started writing this book I have seen a great slide toward the rational ideas of Le Corbusier and Gropius, Van der Rohe, and Oud.  But I see nowhere else in the world so rich a contribution as Wright's *beyond* what I have called " stripped architecture."  He has brought a compelling architectural beauty to more types of building than any other modern architect — in addition to being the most direct thinker, the pioneer practical worker, with solid foundations on an understanding of function and materials.  As for his being a " stylist " or not, one may note finally

Detailed bits from the two houses shown in the preceding plate.  Frank Lloyd Wright, architect

House at Dessau, Germany.   Walter Gropius, architect.   [Photo by Lucia Moholy]

that he himself has made the illuminating statement, somewhere in his writings, that we should all be seeking " not styles but style."  To bring style into everything one touches is a far greater achievement than to create a style — which every Tom, Dick, and Harry can imitate.

But let us go now all the way to the other extreme: let us examine the houses which at first glance, even self-consciously, remind us of precision, organization, and a mechanical austerity.  There are anti-decorative Modernist architects — unbending Functionalists and Rationalists — who damn out the decorative Modernism of Wright and Hoffmann almost as bitterly as they assail the weakly historical Eclectics.  They find their gods in the machine, and they even set up actual machines as better models for house building than any prototypes in the field of architecture: they insist upon the efficiency, the plainness, the clean strength, the reasonable directness, of automobiles, airplanes, and steamships, of electric ranges and refrigerators, as a new starting-point and a final inspiration for home building. They want the noticeably machine-house. Some of them claim to be anti-æsthetic; others set up an æsthetic of their own, denying decorativeness, scorning ornament, but recognizing " art " values in proportioning, sculptural massing, precise adjustment, and right coloring.

Germany particularly harbors a large number of the Functionalists; though the Swiss-French Le Corbusier has been writer-spokesman of the movement. The Germans — particularly the *Bauhaus* group — have made extraordinary progress in introducing into all the chief cities of their country what we may call first models of machine-houses. Meantime Le Corbusier's barbed and argumentative essays have gone out into many lands to stir alert minds and perhaps to break down defences of the conservatives.

In regard to the home, Le Corbusier believes that the engineers, the real pioneers of a modern building, were too concerned with bridges, railways, steamships, etc., to bring their logic to bear on the house problem, in the early days. Only now are we going back to ask, " What is a house for? " or " What is a room? " When we look at the old house and its furnishings, its inconveniences and its stuffiness, we know that only such fundamental questions can bring us back to sanity, and that only the machine can give us the cue to our new building.

" The existing plan of the dwelling-house takes no account of man and is conceived as a furniture store. . . It kills the spirit of the family, of the home; there are no homes, no families, and no children, for living is much too difficult a business." So writes Le Corbusier in *Towards a New Architecture*. And again: " Truth to tell, the modern man is bored to tears in his home; so he goes to his club. The modern woman is bored outside her boudoir; she goes to tea-parties. The modern man and woman are bored at home; they go to the night-clubs." And his conclusion is: " Every modern man has the mechanical sense. The feeling for mechanics exists and is justified by our daily activities. This feeling in regard to machinery is one of respect, gratitude, and esteem. Machinery includes economy as an essential factor leading to minute selection.   There is a moral sentiment in the feeling for mechanics.   The man who is intelligent, cold, and calm has grown wings to himself.   Men — intelligent, cold, and calm — are needed to build the house and to lay out the town."

Now I agree with this absolutely — as a beginning point.   That is, I believe that progressive peoples are fast becoming, in Le Corbusier's sense, *machine-minded,* and that there is a sort of new morality in a special way of living, in the mechanized world, and that houses must first of all be calculated to serve efficiently.   But the moment we have got that, when we have *got it underfoot,* then (I believe) we have also a new problem of individual artistic creation on the top of the machine foundation.   For the enrichment that art brings into life, the efflorescence, is beyond the cold intelligence and calm analysis that Le Corbusier lauds.

We may, however, while we are sojourning among the Functionalists, pause to list precisely the functions that the machine will serve.   What are some of the details of the house before enrichment?   First is that battery of service pipes, wires, and mechanical contrivances.   I must have warmth and coolness when I need them, baths at will, sanitary plumbing, clean effortless heat for cooking food and cold for preserving it, sockets for electric attachments that will clean floors and run sewing-machines or electric irons or Victrolas, special controlled electric lights for reading or dining or music; my walls and floors must be sheer and clean, signifying absence of unnecessary mouldings, chandeliers, hangings, curtains, etc., and elimination of a great amount of legged furniture, carpets, etc. (built-in furniture, fitting the house, will largely replace the individual pieces now almost universal — preventing the present museum or junk-shop atmosphere of the average home).   I shall demand windows designed directly to the problems of supplying fresh air and tempered light — flexible, like automobile windows.   I must have a spaciousness, too, that has been unknown to Victorian buildings: not the forbidding spaciousness of high ceilings, but free and open *living* space.   I want this openness to extend beyond the walls, to porches, sun-traps, sheltered garden ter-

Two views of a house in Paris, by Le Corbusier and P. Jeanneret.  [By courtesy of *l'Architecte*, Paris]

Villa on the River Var, France. Djo Bourgeois, architect. [By courtesy
of *l'Architecte*, Paris.] See also the view of the same house at the head
of the chapter.

races.  Within the house I shall want many set-in drawers, shelves, lockers.
(Life is only *half-orderly* when we have our usual desks, bureaus, mantelpieces, bookcases, library tables, and hat-trees, all inviting the casual
laying-down of miscellaneous objects.)

Perhaps you have here arrived at the point of exploding with that question which every avowed Modernist must meet sooner or later: *"Are we
then to live in hospital rooms?"*  Frankly, many of the earliest Functionalist houses had that bareness, that overemphasized whiteness.  But,
no, even in the hands of Le Corbusier or Gropius or Oud (because they
are artists) there is already an overvalue, a thing added beyond mere practicality.  Le Corbusier, though ruthless in regard to ornament, holds by

Group houses in Paris, by Rob Mallet-Stevens. [By courtesy of *l'Architecte*, Paris]

A house in the Weissenhof suburb, Stuttgart, by Joseph Frank.   [By courtesy of *l'Architecte,* Paris]

*proportion* as the precious thing that the architect adds beyond the engineering.   Mass, profile, contour — these the designer may play with. And you see in the photographs how Le Corbusier himself has played with them.   Gropius, too, whatever may be his faith in absolute rationalization, does get a decorative effect — not soft, not rich in " relief," but somehow austerely, mathematically decorative.

The Weissenhof suburb at Stuttgart is a group exposition of the work of the Functionalists of Germany, Austria, Holland, and France.   As one gazes at the houses, they compose so much better than the average home development that one at first forgets all criticism.   The return to fundamental building forms, the peaceful horizontality, the air of open living, the great deck spaces, the sweet cleanliness: these all register with telling effect.   But frankly there seems just a *tinge* of hospital-like monotonousness and regimentation about it; and when I look at a series of photographs of the interiors of these houses (no one invited me in) I find that a certain number breathe a definite sick-room bareness.   Others, how-

Two views of the Weissenhof suburb at Stuttgart, Germany. [By courtesy of the German Tourist Information Office, New York]

A concrete, metal, and glass " Functionalist " house in California: the Lovell
" health house " in Los Angeles.   Richard J. Neutra, architect.   [Photo by
Willard D. Morgan]

ever, seem to me to have captured the true homely atmosphere together
with the look of mechanical efficiency.   The best ones go on to creatively
designed livableness with architectural enrichment.

In summary, the Weissenhof achievement seems to me our best *doctrinaire* demonstration of a radical machine-age sort of housing toward
which the world is drifting.   It is a model of stripping back to fundamentals, an extraordinary exemplification of calm intelligence applied to the
house problem — and with a very general grasping of the architectural
values of sculptural proportioning.   But I know that I am not completely
satisfied because I find myself saying, " Now if Frank Lloyd Wright or
Joseph Hoffmann built me a house in the midst of this group of houses,

The Lovell house is built by a new method of construction in concrete and standardized metal posts, with standard unit windows set in. The building is to be completed by certain foliage masses not evident here. Richard J. Neutra, architect. [Photos by Willard D. Morgan]

At left, corner and tower of Oasis Hotel, Palm Springs, California; at right, detail of a California residence. Lloyd Wright, architect. [Photos by Will Connell]

equally simple in form, *but with something else that they are capable of giving artistically,* then I should be happy here." In short, I want all the virtues of these geometrically simple, these gratefully honest buildings, but with something of colorfulness and human intimacy and brightness added; and I know that the " richer " house I vision would lie happily among these. Functionalism is the starting-point of a new architecture, but it seems to me that other pioneers have already shown us glimpses of a road beyond.

What I miss is, in a sense, individualism of expression. Some commentators feel that the machine-age gains are to be made only at the expense of individuality. But my whole conception of the coming age is based on this: that man, as the machine lifts more and more of routine labor from him, will progressively come free for imaginative flights, for spiritual adventure, for individual creativeness in the field of the arts. The human soul is the great central creative fact in a universe which is slowly being conquered by science. Man's spiritual being and his æsthetic enjoyments and productions are the only things that science does not pretend to explain. The creative artist cannot go forward without reference to the changes effected by science in the material ways of living — otherwise the organism would be violated, the link of art with life broken; but the scientific regimentation of living must be *for the liberation of man's individuality, of his creativeness.* The Functionalists seem to me to want to limit the legitimate æsthetic values for which machine-age directness of thinking and machine-direct methods of planning can free us. They offer a corrective to the old destructive separation of function and form; but after establishing the usefulness of the building, they seem prone to forbid the mysterious processes of the soul by which artists, in the most creative periods of history, have made life boundlessly better worth living.

At any rate, individuality is a thing not to be overlooked. In house building it may be of two sorts: speaking unmistakably of the designer, or of the owner. You can seldom mistake a Frank Lloyd Wright house; therein the individual genius of the architect asserts itself. I want to talk here, however, of the other sort: the individuality of the client *built into his house*. And I can find no other examples so striking as the structures put up through a period of thirty years by that pioneer of the Far West, Bernard Maybeck.

You can usually pick out a Maybeck house too — there is that much of the designer always in it; or perhaps it is only because, in conservatively orthodox surroundings, he is almost invariably unconventional, original, colorful. His reflection of the owner's character goes not so far as the making of unoriginal, colorless homes for unoriginal people. But Maybeck does believe this: that there is in every client some ideal, or taste, or way of life, to which it is the architect's business to fit the house like a garment. It may be a streak of mediæval mysticism, it may be a Louis XIV courtly feeling for display, it may be a maiden shyness — for each there is a logical house. It may be a material thing that furnishes the clue: clients have a real love for a certain rocky hillside site — then assuredly the building will have the very " feel " of that site in its lines and masses and coloring. Or perhaps a woman betrays in her silks and furs just what sort of home atmosphere will be right for her; or a man ruthless in business suggests in his whole bearing that power over lives is his chief purpose and pleasure — that too can be dramatized in a home. The *human* element is Maybeck's first concern. He once told me that if when he had finished the house the owners completed the home scheme perfectly *in their own gardening,* he felt that he had been successful. Find the spirit of your client and architecturally dramatize that. Fortunately colorless and timidly conventional people don't go to an architect so different from the " Will-you-have-Colonial-or-Spanish " type.

It is not surprising that Maybeck's houses range through an extraordinary variety of " effects." But always there is creative handling of the materials, generally there is elimination of the old clutter inside and out, there is a fundamental sense of values gained out of massing, out of line and contour — and usually there is color. I think no other architect in modern times has used color so freely.

Three houses in " The Californian Style," with strong Spanish influence.
Above, house in Montecito, by George Washington Smith. [Photo
by J. Walter Collinge, by courtesy of the Plans and Planting Committee,
Santa Barbara Community Arts Association.]   Middle, the Osuma house
in Rancho Santa Fe; a century-old California-Spanish house restored.
Below, the Millard house in Rancho Santa Fe, by Lilian J. Rice.

In a considerable series of houses in the Berkeley neighborhood, designed for his neighbors with tastes like his own — for simple living, for color, for the pleasures of the garden, for bungalow-like unconventionality — Maybeck has achieved one of the most distinctive monuments reared by any contemporary architect. If the other half of his practice is better known in pictures, that is because the world has been more interested in the showier things. Maybeck believes that it is perfectly logical to employ, for instance, Roman surface motives when the client's spirit and " feeling " are Roman. The celebrated Fine Arts Palace at the Panama-Pacific Exposition and the Hearst Gymnasium at the University of California are examples; and the amazing independence of the designer in disposing the borrowed motives goes far toward reconciling us to the incidental harking-back to history. (Strict historians say that he invariably *misuses* the classic details: jumbles them and sets them up in relationships wholly without precedent — and there is some sort of paradoxical originality in that.) But my own view is that his domestic architecture is by far his greater contribution. I am sorry that available photographs do no justice to the houses; and I am representing Maybeck's work only with the clubhouse illustrated a few pages forward and with two distinctive churches in a later chapter (pages 273 and 329).

But if Maybeck and Wright are the most original figures — the only world figures — in the California architectural scene today, it is something else again that is implied in the term " the California Style." We mustn't confuse it with the old Mission Style that was an earlier push in the same direction — but abortive. Nor need we judge this more recent development by the less creative practitioners who still get their detail from Spain, Morocco, or other Mediterranean lands — though there is such confusion of the historic elements and what has " gone native " that no one will ever get them into separate niches.

At any rate, here is a development that is important to us not by reason of a sudden revolutionary overturn, not by the emergence of an unaccountable genius among architectural plodders; rather, a slow-moving

Three views in Palos Verdes Estates, California, where Mediterranean type or California Style houses are obligatory. Top photo, house at right by Kirtland Cutter; at left, by Clarence E. Howard and Charles H. Cheney. Middle photo, house at right by Edward Cline; at left, by Arthur Munson. [Photos by Padilla Studios]

body of architects, thoroughly respectable and recognized, gradually settles down to one historical style, the Spanish and its Colonial approximations, as a " source," slowly rationalizes that in accordance with climatic conditions, available materials, and modern use-demands, and in the end shows forth to the world a body of work only very faintly flavored with historical idioms and allusions, and very admirably serving the purposes of today's mechanistic living. This is the only achievement anywhere that is comparable to the rationalization of the English cottage as witnessed in the work of the Voysey-Scott-Lutyens group — and that, as we have seen, has apparently given birth to no later, more modern movement, whereas the California phenomenon seems to be only at the commencement of its most creative phase. And yet already it fits more snugly into the pattern of modern architecture.

The reason why these two originally old types of building are manipulated so readily into a contact with new-born Modernism lies, of course, in the original fine simplicity of the forms, the sculptural massing of the house-bulk. In the case of the Spanish antecedents of the Californian house, there are also these considerations: the patio arrangement, of rooms around a garden-court, contacts directly with modern ideals of openness and outdoor living; and the low-lying masses, so often with flat roofs, conform perfectly to climatic conditions and are congenial to the materials easily available where the development has occurred, besides lending themselves to those elementary compositional effects, geometrically pleasing, that are so dear to the Moderns. And indeed, in travelling that beautiful stretch of country from Berkeley and San Francisco to Santa Barbara, Palos Verdes and San Diego, one senses a unity of aim in architectural design unknown to any other locality; with so many pleasing — even brilliant — simple houses, that the trip is a constant delight.

But not to give too much space to the Californian Style — because it really is not so significant as Wright or the Functionalists — we may sum it up as the most attractive contemporary development of American domestic architecture, even where historic-mindedness determines its

Three examples of the simplified California house. Above, cottage at Montecito, by
Reginald D. Johnson; middle, cottage in Santa Barbara, by Carleton M. Winslow.
[Photos by Jessie Tarbox Beals and by J. Walter Collinge, by courtesy of the Plans
and Planting Committee, Santa Barbara Community Arts Association.] Below,
house in Palos Verdes Estates, by Roy Kelley.

details; and where rationalization of its elements has gone the farthest, as the most effective mass-push toward a type for good living in the mechanistic age. The Western architects themselves applied the name, " the Californian Style," because they thought their achievement had become distinctive enough to warrant official recognition of an advance beyond reflected Spanish, Mediterranean, or Mission, or Pueblo; but still in a great deal of their work they prove themselves Eclectics at heart — in a pinch they bring out their postcards from Algiers or their books on the Romantic Architecture of Spain. A half-dozen practitioners, however, may now be counted upon to continue the stripping toward Functionalist simplicity and then to add creatively, stylistically, out of their own truly Western originality. And we may believe that then the understanding of " Californian " may be widened to include some of the basically similar work of Wright — and that of two or three architects who have been his disciples on the coast. I may add that Maybeck twenty-five years ago was doing work that might reasonably be placed in any book of the most creative " Californian " buildings — as witness this Faculty Clubhouse at Berkeley.

Many times I have mentioned " openness " as an ideal of the new home building. I use the word with more than a spatial connotation. It seems to me clear that there is going on a freeing process in regard to both our physical and our mental lives. While the old walled-in house, the essentially castle-refuge sort of structure, is giving way before less-confined living space, women are discarding most of their clothes, and human minds are freeing themselves slowly of old superstitions, old limiting religions, old narrowly selfish motives. There is a general coming-forth — which seems to me calculated for the better health and the greater happiness of mankind. I want the architect to feel this wave of liberation before he begins designing the houses for the new age: to feel it as a background for his reasoning, his talks with his clients, and his sketches. I have little hope that any present-day breeze of freedom will blow out of their confines those architects who earnestly continue to multiply " the

The Faculty Club, Berkeley, California. Bernard Maybeck, architect. About 1903

charming old houses "; and I am particularly despairing about the group that regularly reproduces the picturesquely decayed. But the younger architects, the students especially, they are living the fresher, cleaner, open life; they will see surely that these developments we have been talking about are of their time, of their environment — of their gained freedom.

Apropos, I may add that there is a place in Tallmadge's *The Story of Architecture in America* where he makes clever fun of the " Arts and Crafts " people: " The Arts and Crafts theory was exactly the dish for the palate of the studios, the tea-rooms, and the rostra of the social settlements and community houses — a pinch of reform, a spoonful of socialism and æsthetics to taste, and over it all the flavor of Toynbee Hall and of England's intellectuals made it a highly delectable entrée. . . As I interpret the improvement in the applied arts since 1891, architecture led the way and the industrial arts that made any progress followed in its train. As it stands, the Arts and Crafts movement left us Elbert Hubbard and the Roycrofters, a host of ' uplift ' societies (most of which are defunct now), thousands of ' lytle shoppes,' mission furniture, art jewelry, pyrography. Its effect was not in sum total deleterious (Bertram Goodhue seems to have been a disciple) . . ." etc.

However we may deplore the affectation that brought in the thousands of "lytle shoppes" and arty tea-rooms, we should be able to see through to the truth that the Arts and Crafts movement brought about, in this country as in Europe, almost the first honest thinking about the arts in ages. And as for architecture leading the way during the last forty years, that should be said in confession, not in praise. The professional architects *did* lead — that is the explanation of the Frenchified aspect of Fifth Avenue, of our servilely showy public monuments, of our mixed suburbs. Incidentally those leading, controlling architects crucified the man who most truly thought and created with craftsmanlike honesty, Louis Sullivan, for a quarter-century they blanketed the work of the artist-craftsman Frank Lloyd Wright, for years they laughed at the few exceptional originators like Maybeck. They were away worshipping their gods: Palladio, Wren, and the showy Beaux-Arts Frenchmen, and they ignored every good influence out of native craftsmanship and creativeness.

Tallmadge, it seems to me, convicts himself and the professionals for whom he speaks: convicts himself and them of snobbery, of blindness. Over-page from the above quotation, he inserts an illustration of an American house, with the descriptive line, " Discriminating taste, common sense, and wide knowledge underlie the best of American houses today." It happens to be an excellent transcription of English domestic architecture, in its larger forms and masses. But close study reveals that the window-glass is done into tiny diamond panes, the roof-slates are purposely unevenly spaced, manipulated into quaint crooked lines instead of straight ones, and even the chimney-pots breathe " English " at you. Now if the conscious manipulation of naturally straight roof-lines into ancient-looking crooked ones isn't the exact architectural equivalent of naming one's shop " The Lytle Shoppe," I don't know affectation when I see it. Isn't it silly?

The " open " house, as seen in the Weissenhof suburb, Stuttgart, Germany. Above, Adolf Rading, architect; below, Hans Poelzig, architect. [By courtesy of *l'Architecte*, Paris]

Apartments in Paris, by Rob Mallet-Stevens.   [By courtesy of *l'Architecte*, Paris]

What we need is more creative architecture, in our houses, with exactly those elements of honesty, simplicity, and originality which the true Arts and Crafts leaders visualized — based today on mechanistic facts of living; and less snob architecture that holds by the sanctified professionalism of the past while not above adding novelties of affectation and quaint allusion.

THE machine leads us to ever greater speed, efficiency, intensity, and concentration.   The intensity and concentration of city life make more and more people want to live in one central area, the speedy electric elevator makes it possible to stack up their "houses" ten, twenty, thirty stories high, one on top of another; the while the greater efficiency of heating the group dwelling, and of the other "services" therein, furthers the extension of *apartment* living.   The apartment skyscrapers of the teeming cities, and the lower apartment blocks of the nearer suburbs — these

Apartment house in the Weissenhof suburb, Stuttgart, Germany.   Peter Behrens, architect.   [By courtesy of *l'Architecte*, Paris]

are indeed a phenomenon of our time.   No one can foresee how far the drift toward swarm life will carry us, how far the individual house will be superseded by living barracks.   There are two agencies apparently working in opposite directions: first, the automobile and the airplane make transportation so effortless that dwelling away from the centre of activities is less and less a deprivation — while radio and television carry entertainment and "cultural things" to country and city alike.   But the greater ease of running the mechanics of housekeeping *en masse,* the advantages of central heating, the economy of installing group plumbing, the saving of building costs where one foundation and one roof serve fifty intermediate homes: these considerations lead on to ever greater apartment houses.   One residential "block" in New York now provides more than one million square feet of floor space.   The latest hotel in the city provides more than 2500 rooms (with 2500 baths).

The mass-apartment structure partakes of the nature of the skyscraper and the commercial building at one side, and has many features

Three typical Dutch apartment buildings. [From photographs by Walter T. Steilberg]

The Panhellenic Tower: a skyscraper apartment
building in New York. John Mead Howells,
architect.

of the individual home at the other. As we have explored both those
directions of modern building, we may be content with merely a glance
at this variation. As a living-machine the apartment, in its stricter con-
finement, its concentration of service elements into restricted space, often
surpasses the simplifications and the rationalizations of the Modernist
individual homes, even as designed by the Functionalists. It is truly amazing how the mechanical servants are arranged in one and two room apartments: plumbing, electricity, heating and cooking apparatus, laundry
machines, refrigeration. And here we come to a place where it is almost

Typical experiments in modern apartment building. Top left, a block in Cologne, by Wilhelm Riphahn. Top right, a block in Berlin, by Rudolf Fränkel. Lower left, a block by Ernst May, in Frankfort. Bottom right, the Jardinette Apartments in Los Angeles, California, by Richard J. Neutra: an experiment in continuous banding of steel-casement windows.

Sideboard in a Berlin dining room.  Harry Rosenthal, architect

impossible to plan other than built-in furniture; at least it will be, if the drift toward ever greater concentration continues.  Thus economic pressure aids what a new æsthetic tells us is desirable: an absolute stripping back to use-essentials, as a new beginning point.

The problems of air and light for great apartment buildings determine forms and methods, but not in ways radically different from those already posed by the business skyscrapers.  The more interesting variations have come where architects have approached the mass-dwelling problem in the light of the new ideal of open-air living; and perhaps the most intriguing examples architecturally are buildings wherein the addition of balconies determines the exterior design.  The photographs here illustrate some of the remarkable " effects " achieved by playing up the balcony-lines.  For the rest, there are skyscraper apartments hardly to be dis-

Four photographs of balcony arrangements in Berlin.  [By courtesy of the Architectural Record]

Hallway in apartment of Mrs. Alfred L. Rose, New York. Ely Jacques Kahn, architect. [Photo by Samuel H. Gottscho]

tinguished, by any outward softening, from the commercial office towers, and there are pueblo-like terraced crag-houses, and a few compositions like Peter Behrens' multiple-dwelling at Weissenhof that are like seventeen Functionalist houses modelled together by an artist with a fine sense of sculptural design.

As a matter of fact, when we get down to the apartment in " the big city," the designers are likely to forget, perhaps of necessity, ideals of open-air living: anything but a pile of cubicle-rooms costs too much. After the machine-servants have found place in the cubicles, the main differences become those of " interior decoration." Whence the amazing multiplication of Modernist " decorators " — not fundamentally architects at all — in the New York and Chicago of the last twelvemonth.

Furnishings in New York apartments, by Paul T. Frankl, pioneer among modern decorators in America

A German living-room, by Emil Fahrenkamp

I conceive it as not my duty to go into interior decoration separately in this book. (I hope there has been some thought about it integral to my main story along the way.) But let us note that the impetus of Viennese Secession stylization has been carried on, largely through Paris, till a distinctively modern mode is recognizable whether one meets it in New York or Cannes or Prague.

The elements of this surface decoration — too often considered separate from the containing structural architecture — are these: walls are kept as unbroken as possible, and rich spots of decoration are played against the resulting broad areas. In the larger masses, wood is often played up for its own sake, its natural beauty preserved and exhibited but not forced into intricate compositions; or wall-paper of delicate all-over pattern is spread over large unbroken walls. The decorative " spots " contrasting with these simpler background elements are concentratedly rich, are sensitively touched in to set off the larger " air " of the room. The keynote bit may be a piece of modern furniture,

Above, two views of men's smoking-room, Arizona-Biltmore Hotel, Phoenix, Arizona, showing interior use of the type of pre-cast concrete block originated by Frank Lloyd Wright. Albert Chase McArthur, architect. [By courtesy of *The Architectural Record*.] Below, unconventional interiors by R. M. Schindler (at right); and by Lloyd Wright, (at left — photo by Will Connell).

or a hanging over the windows, or a panel of frank decoration over a doorway.

The " sense of style " arises no less from the vitality and sensitive smartness of the outstanding motif than from the harmonious adjustment of major and minor elements, the balance of broad simplicity and exquisitely contrived inset. Sometimes a structural line, smartly emphasized, carries

Carrying the " feel " of the site into the house: above, exterior, and below, interior of living room, in Frank Lloyd Wright's country house, Spring Green, Wisconsin. Frank Lloyd Wright, architect.

the main burden of decorativeness; other times the scheme is built around an introduced element: the pattern of a hanging, the design of a bed, or even the prevailing color of milady's wardrobe. But always unity of impression, a pervading, all-determining modishness, is basic.

The varieties of modern interior decoration, of course, despite the beginning with simplicity and the ending with precise adjustment, range from the Functionalist self-proclaiming simplicity, through the restrained elegance of the Viennese Secession rooms, and on to the fuller, more voluptuous French practice. But almost invariably, in all varieties, color plays a more generous and more sensitive rôle than in ages past. And perhaps it is color that compensates for the Victorian and Renaissance values lost in ruthless elimination. Color makes the house human and intimate for us. And it is in the realm of color, of consciously designed color backgrounds to living, that the next great advance is likely to come. It would indeed be a sin to carry over the drabness of the old house into the new age. The automobile with its firm but soft coloring and its flashes of bright metal may again afford us a clue.[3]

[3] As I read the proofs, it strikes me that I have been more arbitrary and theoretical in this chapter than in any other. I might well have broadened my list of types and directions of modern endeavor to include the " Santa Fe Style " house, a modern rationalization of pueblo forms, and as attractive and appropriate in its restricted district as the California Style in its larger one; and the distinctive " bungalow " type associated with the names of Greene & Greene, as seen particularly in Pasadena; and finally the latest experiments of three notable " radical " practitioners in Southern California, Richard J. Neutra, R. M. Schindler, and Lloyd Wright. Photographs of their buildings find inclusion, at the last minute, though it is too late to treat of their contribution in the text. But then, a book like this is never completed: with the corrected proofs dispatched to the printer, and every page crowded, I find new names and new work constantly arriving at hand, particularly in the pioneering of Kiesler and Lescaze in New York, of Bruce Goff in Oklahoma, of a whole school of initiators in the Southwest. One can only ring down the curtain and say, " We have shown as much as we can." For the rest, you must consult the architectural magazines, which almost suddenly have " gone modern."

# CHAPTER VII

## WORK–PLACES AND NEW MATERIALS

IT IS, if you will, a paradox that the world's factories are increasing in number, size, and importance, the while man reduces, by the advance in mechanical mastery of nature, the amount of work to be done. The explaining factor is the continual decrease in the length of the work-day, in the number of hours that the individual man or woman spends " at the machine." But, however one may juggle the three elements — factory, machine, and labor — the fact remains that " work-places " are emerging as a major consideration in architecture as they never have in the past.

In olden times, let us say until 1800, manufacture was carried on in the home. A few trades brought their workers together before that; particularly where the early hand-power machines became essential: a master-printer and his assistants must labor in association where the press stood.  But overwhelmingly, the individual shoemaker, or jeweller, or seamstress did piece work, and workshops were in houses.

It was the application of steam power to the machine that marked the revolution to a factory system.  As soon as power could be applied to multiple machines (the steam engine turned a shaft which could be belted to a dozen or a hundred looms, lathes, cutters, presses, etc.), it became profitable to bring the workers collectively into one building.  Home work and piece labor went out; factories, the six o'clock whistle, and massed labor came in.

Almost everything about the industrial revolution thus wrought was wrong, except the efficiency with which steam power did the heavier work.  There were cruel exploitation of workers, devastatingly long work-days, speeding-up tactics — and bad buildings.  That was the period of capitalism at its ugliest, most uncontrolled.  Work became a horrible burden; and our schoolbooks to this day echo the notion that work is something to be escaped from at the earliest possible moment: that the successful man retires to moneyed ease and the better things of life.  At first laborers struggled in vain under the nightmare of factory existence.  Then slowly, through nearly a century, they fought for better conditions, united in unions, and finally, by struggles verging on civil warfare, gained (in progressive places) a working-day of reasonable duration, and working conditions not too inhuman.  Today Labor controls some of the most humane governments; and in most of the Western world labor unions have manœuvered into positions from which they can treat with still-controlling capital for a fair share in the world's comforts.  At this juncture Modern Architecture arrives, to assure that the all-important work-places will be light, clean, sanitary, even pleasant.

The first modern factories crept in despite the architects.  More than in any other direction of architectural design, the engineers here pioneered, with the aid of a very few rebel — " Bolshevik " — architects.  The " profession " was uninterested in factories at all, or else regarded the problem as one of masking: a particularly difficult problem because what was to be

Model for a commercial building in concrete with banded windows, Berlin. Emil Fahrenkamp, architect

masked seemed ugly beyond redemption, and because the leeway for stylistic decoration was strictly limited. In an earlier chapter we have explored the æsthetic implications of the subject: on the one hand learning how the anti-industrialists failed to find any inspiration or stir to creation in labor or industry or machine; on the other discovering how a few "insurgents" took the machine itself as the starting-point for their designing, and how they created the first examples of a world architecture as simple and efficient as our commoner mechanical organisms, and stamped with the revealing idioms of metal-smooth surfaces, long clean lines, powerful massing. We also found a machine-design tidiness to be a part of the factory-architecture expressiveness.

We need not retrace our steps through the ideas and examples of that chapter on machine-conscious architecture. The thought about tidiness, however, affords us a new point of departure, from which we may explore some of the *social* aspects of the new world architecture as it relates to industry. What is it that people need in their work-places? Is Mod-

A factory in Charlottenberg, Germany.  Hans Hertlein, architect.
[1926]  Note the clean, hard lines in the addition, as compared
with the original building at back.

ernism to deck the shops and factories in faded reflection of regal luxury,
or with some new attractiveness that breathes of the life and outlook
of today?  Are factories really becoming " pleasant " places?  (Then
later we shall turn technical and examine the potentialities of those commoner *materials* that are associated with the factory idea rather than
with " noble " buildings like palaces, libraries, churches, etc.)

Our new morality tells us that the work-place, like the home, simply
*must* be attractive.  If only in an austere way, without breathing the
least air of cushioned ease, luxury, or " spread," nevertheless, it must be
almost sparklingly clean, bright, solidly efficient — nay, beautifully utilitarian.  For some generations yet, work will be a main concern of human
beings.  Factory work and shop work will be the commonest kinds —

though there is no drawing a line between these sorts and "office" labor.

The new philosophy of living — very vague as yet, but slowly taking a recognizable world shape — tells us that it is no right thing to admit work as an evil: that, just as the building is an organism, so the individual life is an organism, and that to divide it into work and pleasure (structure and façade, you might say), into toil and refuge from toil, is fundamentally wrong. If labor is the dominating factor in one-half of our hours awake, then labor must be controlled, geared to good living.

And just as the modern engineer-architect is revolutionizing the house, so that the old-time home drudgery of women is well on the road to elimination, just so he has made a beginning toward revolutionizing collective work-places — in the interests of the good life. Just as the inefficient house, the unmechanized house, is immoral, so is the dirty, ill-lighted, badly planned factory immoral — even though decorated with a whole row of Corinthian columns or a Tudor battlement effect to make it falsely "look pretty."

There is, of course, a right "feel" in factory architecture that is different from the "feel" of home or library or church or club. Openness, tidiness, a heavy solidity (subconsciously connoting safety as well as machinery) — these are qualities entering into it. But somehow it is *lighting*, scientifically efficient lighting — even a margin of cheerful lighting — that has most to do with the drift toward a different industrial architecture. It was natural that the engineers should be the pioneers who first expressed simply and directly the other things that stir us (the non-factory workers) so deeply: in elementary sheds they installed the powerful travelling cranes, the immense elevators, the belt conveyors, the nifty (and inviting) package chutes. But it was also the engineers who brought in generous light.

Unnamed American engineers created many a building that might justly be illustrated here. You will remember that Le Corbusier gave them credit for initiating a movement toward simplification, honesty, and

This and the illustration at the head of the chapter show buildings in the Toledo Scale Company development, Toledo, Ohio.   Norman-Bel Geddes, architect.

powerful expressiveness that has been felt beyond the oceans.   But —
partly because I still feel that the engineer's achievement, in architecture,
is usually only half a triumph — I prefer to pick up the story a bit later,
when a few architects have become architect-engineers.   Here again is a
chapter that would be incomplete without mention of Louis Sullivan,
who made form express function; and in his time there was also the Dutch
pioneer Berlage, who was abused from one end of the architectural world
to the other because he utilized an honest idiom (which has since become
quite respectable in industrial-commercial building), the idiom of tex-
tured brick as an *inside* wall.   There was, too, Frank Lloyd Wright, who

Kahn and Feldman Factory, Brooklyn, New York.  Ely Jacques Kahn, architect

first notably caught the accent, the epic power, of the machine in the architectural design of the Larkin Building, in 1903: a building simple, massive, efficiently lighted — and, it happens, with brick walls through and through.  It was Berlage, incidentally, who wrote of " the business-like character " of the Larkin Building, noting that " the offices — in their brutal mass — display the unflinching strength of industrial life in these times."   (Wright, significantly, was a student of civil engineering before he turned to architecture.)

But let us turn quickly to the more usual practice of today, a quarter-century after those pioneers.  This Brooklyn factory is typical of thousands of checkerboard designs: glass, steel-casemented, set into the simplest arrangement of concrete piers and floors.  In this case there is notable expressiveness of the separation of the manufacturing space from two units of grouped service elements: the two larger concrete masses housing stairs, elevators, wash-rooms and toilets for the workers.  The building is obviously fire-proof, obviously well-lighted, obviously based on thoughtfulness for purpose.  And one need not stretch his imagination to believe that workers go to this factory happier-minded (in gen-

Control room of the Klingenberg Factory in Germany.   Klingenberg & Issel, architects

eral) than nineteenth century laborers went to their dirtier, darker
work-places.

That generosity with light: note how it is expressed in the several other,
almost random, examples illustrated above and below, in a warehouse,
in a power house, in a department store, in a mill.   Note how it is signi-
fied in the great window areas of the machine-room of the Klingenberg
Works, and intensified in the white tiles of walls and floors.   If the workmen are to rule the world, as they should in the next phase, then let us
hope that there is a symbol in the lightness and openness here; let us even
believe that the new architecture here again reflects a world drift to open
minds, light let in, the life of unconcealment — darkness conquered.

The progress in industrial architecture recently has been widely international.   If the American engineers and the few pioneer American functional architects broke the trail first, the most spectacular progress along

Two studies for the Toledo Scale Company buildings, Toledo, Ohio. Norman-Bel Geddes, architect. Construction in concrete and glass.

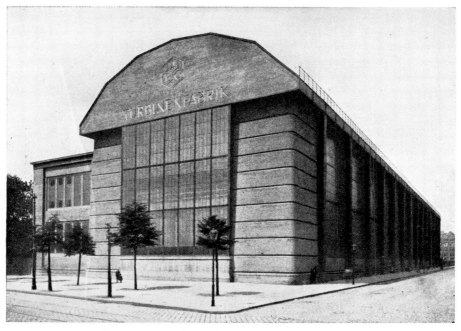

Power house in Berlin.  Peter Behrens, architect.  [1909]

it has been made by the Germans, since the war.  And indeed, the first notable run of buildings conceived with particular engine-room tidiness and generous lighting, in conjunction with engine-room massiveness, is to be credited to Peter Behrens.  It is a curious circumstance that we first encountered Behrens's name in connection with our study of the search for an outward style, in some early experiments in pattern applied to the outside building walls of expositions.  But later he came to this other extreme, to decorativeness out of proportioning and severe cleanliness.  His tidy buildings are to be encountered in many an industrial suburb where a quarter-century ago one expected to meet only the dirt and litter of uncontrolled and hurried exploitational industry.

The Germans and the Dutch more than any others have drafted their foremost architects into the service of the great manufacturing and power-distributing concerns.  After all, Wright's Larkin Building was in the nature of an episode — his legacy to the world is preponderantly

Buildings of the Neumann Mills, Zittau, Germany.   Emil Fahrenkamp, architect

Army Supply Base Warehouses, Brooklyn, New York.  Cass Gilbert, architect

in other fields; and although so distinguished a " regular " architect as Cass Gilbert has been drawn into industrial work, with interesting results, the Americans are to be credited rather with the pioneering in this field than with the later achievement at the hands of a large group of architects.  The notable German practitioners include, beside Behrens, Wilhelm Kreis, Erich Mendelsohn, Hans Poelzig, Curt von Brocke, Paul Bonatz, Adolf Abel, Max Berg, Otto Bartning, Fritz Schumacher, Bruno Taut, Max Taut, Emil Fahrenkamp, and others — an imposing list upon which the internationally educated observer will find many names to stir pleasant memories and expectancy.  I have chosen some examples of Fahrenkamp's designing as representative illustrations of the best recent German practice.

In Holland, too, industrialism has blossomed in new and becoming garments.  Ever since Berlage built the massive Bourse in Amsterdam, a landmark of the insurgency of the nineties, his uncompromising faith has gained converts among the younger Dutch architects.  The severe symmetry and fine cleanliness of the bath-house by Willem Dudok (page 101), and similar qualities in factories by the same architect and de Klerk, Oud, and their associates, indicate that the Hollanders have got beyond the somewhat doctrinaire Modernism that made their originality mannered and sectional for a time.  And you may travel the country over and find innumerable evidences that the architects are meeting logically and joyously the problems of humanized work in a mechanized age.

Van Nelle Tobacco Factory, Rotterdam, Holland. J. A. Brinkman and L. C. van der Vlugt, architects. [By courtesy of *The Architectural Record*]

The good burghers of Dessau, in Germany, speak of the Bauhaus there as " the Glass Box "; and out of their merriment over a sort of building that had not existed on sea or land before, we may find an indication of the measure of opposition and of welcome that the avowed Modernists are meeting. For the Bauhaus architects and craftsmen are the most avowed machine-age people of all those working in Central Europe today; and the city of Dessau, despite bourgeois suspicion and merriment, actually aided financially in the erecting of the glass-box group of buildings.

Before speaking of the Bauhaus buildings as " work-places," I shall diverge to tell something of the ideals of the Bauhaus organization; for no other school of radicals in Germany is quite so outstanding, none other quite so uncompromisingly Rationalist.

The Bauhaus group originally formed around the architect Walter Gropius, and included such famous artists as Wassily Kandinsky, Paul Klee, and Lionel Feininger. A revolution in architecture and craftswork has been at the heart of its aim; and the one touchstone of its teaching has been appropriateness to use in the machine age. If a chair or a window-lock or a house were not first of all fitted to use, and possible of mass reproduction by machinery, it had no right to the Bauhaus birthmark. The organization is both a school, with international student body, and a loose association of practising designers. Latterly, I think, the less practical artists — mere painters and the like — have felt that the drift of the school toward ever stricter tests of utilitarianism and mechanization has rather squeezed their work out, as something not wholly logical in the machine age (though all the original members keep at least an " ideal " association with the school).

In this connection I remember a Bauhaus student telling me, when I paused to admire an exhibit of pottery, that the school had finally dropped pottery-making because it seemed too near to mere æsthetic exercise, and because individual pieces could not be mechanically duplicated. In short, too artistic! The students certainly have been convinced of a change in living to be accomplished by the machine, have become rationalists, have been cured of any possible adherence to the styles of the past. I gathered that even the Viennese Secession sort of thing, with its essential or incidental search for a style, was out of favor with them. Like the Russian Constructivists, these young radicals were not content merely with a stripping process and then progress toward a new and modern style; they were definitely anti-decorative. The word " æsthetics " was something of a red rag. What they wanted was that the chair or the lock or the house should be " right," in its perfect usefulness, in its economy, in its place.

When I talked over the point later with the Bauhaus " masters," mentioning that I found the student attitude toward the æsthetic values and toward decorativeness a bit puzzling, among workers who frankly practised in the field of the arts, I discovered that there was far less of doctrinaire intolerance and limiting theory among the masters than among the disciples. " After all, they are very young yet," was the verdict; " and perhaps at first they need to be extreme — to cure them of any taint of the stylistic creeds of the ages before machinery." And I learned here,

The Bauhaus, Dessau, Germany. Walter Gropius, architect

as once before I had learned while studying the compositions of the Russian and German Constructivists, that an avowed " anti-decorative " bias may mean merely search for a different sort of decorativeness, not of the surface but of the skeleton, of construction. A fine scorn for ornament may mean a passionate search for an appealing quality in the nature of form revealment. Disregard of æsthetics may mean allegiance to a new æsthetic of declared solidity, flashing cleanliness, and expressive massing.

For plain as they are, the works of these Bauhaus students are appealing as an automobile is appealing, with a decorativeness grown out of utilitarian make-up and emphasis on characteristic mass and line. Feeling that the world was fed up with too much directly contrived beauty, with conscious ornament, they try rather to let the hand follow out the direct constructive line, adding no over-value that is not born of a subconscious feeling of material rightness. The designer must be rational workman first — engineer — and then if some inspiration of an " artistic " sort stirs within him, he must turn it into reinforcement of expressive mass, into accenting of the revealing line, and not into ornament. And let me record — though I count their scorn for æsthetics and decorativeness

Detail of rear of Bauhaus, Dessau, Germany.  Walter Gropius, architect

merely a different sort of æsthetic and a passion for a deeper decorative quality — for *organic* decorativeness — let me record that I believe that no other school anywhere is giving to its students a firmer foundation for creative endeavor in the fields of modern architecture and craftswork. No school can create genius or talent; but no other is so likely to leave unblanketed the native creativeness which the student brings with him, or so likely to open a clear vista to the possibilities of naked beauty in the materials and uses of the machine age.

But let us return to the work-place that is called the Glass Box and to

Office and shop building at the *Werkbund* Exposition, Cologne, 1914.    Walter Gropius, architect.

the masters — particularly to Walter Gropius.    Even before the war he had shown himself a devoted searcher for new architectural truths growing out of logical use of modern materials, out of functional efficiency, and out of consideration for the workers.    This building for the offices and shops of the *Werkbund* Exposition at Cologne in 1914 is said to have been the first instance of walls constructed of all glass-and-metal in Germany.    Even earlier, in the " Fagus " factory at Alfeld, Gropius had expanded the windows until they almost claimed all the surface of the main façades; the few brick piers that carry the roof being so slender (and slightly inset) that they were lost in the expanse of glass. It is easy to see how Gropius's mind, reaching after the full decorativeness of glass as an architectural material, arrived at the designing of the Bauhaus, after these earlier essays. And no one can stand looking at the fine mass of the Glass Box, with its long horizontal bands of concrete contrasted with the immense areas of glass grill, without feeling that a new reach has been made toward a strictly rational twentieth century beauty-in-building. When one thinks back to nineteenth century factories and workshops, the lightness-with-strength here, and the cleanliness, become doubly notable.

Now I have heard it whispered that this Glass Box, though grown out of a philosophy of use, though held up as the type example of a new architecture developed from a strict logic of structure, fails a little of its practical purpose. It is said that an all-glass building traps an intolerable amount of heat in summer (though the Bauhaus students avowed they had felt no discomfort); and we Americans may be certain that in our climate of great extremes, an unmodified duplicate of the Glass Box, without an elaborate system of shades and screens, would be impossibly furnace-like. Still other critics say that this method of building (shown so clearly in the picture opposite), with concrete piers and floors and roof practically independent of the glass screen, is really not economical or logical; and the ever-ready carpers even say that after the building was finished, it became necessary to find a way of linking up the several floors tight to the glass — lest a hammer dropped at the edge of the top floor go clattering down three full stories.

But why cavil? It would be miraculous if Walter Gropius, fulfilling a new vision, even one rather theoretically developed on a creed of economy and practicality, found no adjustments necessary when his building first stood there in concrete and metal and glass. What is truly important is that he contrived out of those materials, using each in characteristic ways, a structure that somehow expresses the power and the cleanliness

Detail of Bauhaus, showing floor construction in relation
to glass walls.  Walter Gropius, architect.

of the new industrialism, the massiveness and the precision of the machine,
as an automobile or airplane or steamship would express those things —
and at the same time a building that affords a constant pleasurable " feel "
to its workers.  No one else has quite so convincingly advanced the doc-
trine of naked functional architecture.  And if the Bauhaus people prefer to talk about something called " a rightness " in their designing, in
place of æsthetic values, we may know that the truth and the decorativeness of their work will flow into the stream that is modern architecture.

Gropius is but one of many architects who have foreseen a great new architecture growing out of metal-supported glass. Anyone who has realized the drift toward greater openness, toward increased light and air in buildings — accompanying a world drift toward the open life — will have some vision of "the house of light" and of glass in enormously increased expanses. Architects like Wright and Bragdon, who never fail to see the spiritual significances behind material architecture, have remarked on the appropriateness of the increased utilization of glass in this hour when man is between an ancient darkness and a new enlightenment. Bragdon, mentioning "great rooms serving diverse functions lit by vast areas of glass," in place of the old partitioned cell-like structures, believes that "this breaking down of barriers between human beings and their common sharing of the light of day in fuller measure, is a symbol of the growth of brotherhood, and the search, by the soul, for spiritual light." It is illuminating to note that Bragdon has been a leader among those artists who have experimented fruitfully toward a new art of mobile color, a visual art of moving colored light in space, comparable to the art of music in the field of aural sensation. Color, light, openness — and brotherhood — seem inextricably bound together in the search.

Frank Lloyd Wright has used glass creatively over a period of thirty years. In the first place, as we have seen, he concentrated window units into accented compositional areas, gaining effects entirely different from those of the older architecture with deeply recessed windows; and beyond that he has used ornament in glass as no other gifted modern has. But let him speak his own vision of the possibilities of the medium:

"The sense of glass as the crystal has not yet to any extent entered into the poetry of architecture. It is too new, for one thing. For another thing, tradition did not leave any orders concerning it. It is strictly modern. Therefore, let us try to understand what it is. The machine has given to architects, in glass, a new material with which to work. Were glass eliminated now from buildings, it would be, so far as our buildings have gone, only like putting our eyes out. We could not see out or see into the building. We have gone so far with it as to make it the eyes of the building. Why not now combine it with steel, the spider's web, spin the building frame as an integument for crystal clearness — the crystal held by the steel as the diamond is held in its setting of gold — and make it the building itself?

" All the diversity of color and texture available in any material is not only available but imperishable, in glass. . . The prism has always de-lighted and fascinated man. The machine gives him his opportunity in glass. The machine can do any kind of glass — thick, thin, colored, tex-tured to order — and cheap. A new experience is awaiting him.

" Then why are modern cities still sodden imitations of mediæval strongholds . . . ?

" The glass and bronze building is the most engaging of possibilities in modern architecture. Imagine a city, iridescent by day, luminous by night, imperishable! Buildings — shimmering fabrics — woven of rich glass — glass all clear or part opaque and part clear — patterned in color or stamped to form the metal tracery that is to hold all together to be, in itself, a thing of delicate beauty consistent with slender steel construction — expressing the nature of that construction in the mathematics of structure which are the mathematics of music as well. Such a city would clean itself in the rain, would know no fire alarms — nor any glooms." [1]

By turning to the chapter on " houses " you may judge from the illus-trations how windows have grown — in size and in importance as units of composition — from the earliest work of Wright to the latest creations of Le Corbusier, Frank, and the Dutchmen. And you may see how many another factory builder besides Gropius has massed glass to secure greater light to machinists and craftsmen, before the Glass Box at Dessau capped the progress with a newly decorative structure of glass and concrete. And even then we have only the faintest suggestion of the richer achievement that Wright has written of. The book frontispiece shows a " project " that shadows forth on paper some of the jewel-like brilliancy and deli-

[1] From an article in the series entitled *In the Cause of Architecture*, by Frank Lloyd Wright, in *The Architectural Record*, July 1928.

cacy that he visions for his " city iridescent by day, luminous by night, imperishable." As in the Glass Box, the outward walls are conceived as a thin screen only, in this case fabricated of sheet-copper and glass, unbroken by weight-carrying piers. The floor weight would rest on an independent skeleton of interior concrete piers, with floors cantilevered out to the copper and glass surfacing. Incidentally the building materials are all so standardized in the planning that the whole structure may be put together from mass-production units. But what interests us most at this moment — at the end of our exploration of generously lighted workplaces — is the extraordinary use of sheet-metal and glass. Of the screen system as shaped to this project, Wright has written:

" The walls themselves cease to exist as either weight or thickness. Windows become in this fabrication a matter of a unit in the screen fabric, opening singly or in groups at the will of the occupant. All windows may be cleaned from the inside with neither bother nor risk. The vertical mullions (copper shells filled with non-conducting material) are large and strong enough only to carry from floor to floor and project much or little as shadow on the glass may or may not be wanted. Much projection enriches the shadow. Less projection dispels the shadows and brightens the interior. These protecting blades of copper act in the sun like the blades of a blind."

Although we may pause for a moment over the more ephemeral " Glass House," which was connected with the Austrian Pavilion at the Paris Exposition of 1925, and may think back to the " Iron House " built at Leipzig in 1913 and to the intriguing *Stahlkirche* at Cologne, we must note that in general glass has come into greater use in architecture by virtue of the strides forward in *combined steel-and-concrete* construction. To be sure, the advance in machine methods has infinitely increased the quality and the range of glasses available to the builder; and the greater freedom in the manufacture of metal framing makes it possible to suspend thousands of small panes or a few immense ones wherever willed. But the greater availability of glass is due most to the steel skeleton and reinforced

Drawing, by Frank Lloyd Wright, of St. Mark's Tower, an apartment building projected for the Bowery, New York City. Typical of the revolution in architectural forms brought about by new building materials: a concrete "stalk" rising at the centre sustains the weight of cantilevered floors, while the walls are mere screens of glass in light metal framework.

Design for a commercial building with walls of glass and cantilevered concrete bands.   Mies van der Rohe, architect.   [1922]   [From *Internationale Architektur*, by Walter Gropius]

concrete methods of building, whereby the weight of a structure can be carried at will to a relatively small number of supports.   In the old methods of masonry construction, the lower stories of high buildings could not be pierced with openings large enough to permit great expanses of glass.   The only case in history of extensive use of windows was in buildings without floors — cathedrals; had these immense shells included a series of floors, as practically all modern buildings do, the buttresses would have swollen to such size that the windows would have been of little use.   Now, as Gropius and Wright have shown us, the weight of roof and floors may be thrown entirely on supports far inside the suspended outer walls.   Here, too, is a project for a massive factory designed with floors cantilevered out to ribbons of concrete and glass.

But the virtues of steel and concrete range far beyond any such exceptional case as that.   The steel frame, of course, made possible that greatest epic of the new architecture, the skyscraper.   And it serves us magically in a dozen minor ways, such as clearing out the posts, once such a nuisance, in our theatres, and raising heavenward with a refreshing ease and majesty

Glass pavilion of the Austrian Building at the Decorative Arts Exposition, Paris, 1925: a "stunt" in glass, by Joseph Hoffmann.

the slender spires and webs of our broadcasting stations. Concrete has revolutionized architecture in other and even deeper ways.

Fewer than 10,000 barrels of cement were used in 1870 and 176,000,-000 barrels in 1928 — a sign that man has found new ways to use this material, and that concrete now serves more economically a dozen major building purposes once left to stone, brick, and wood. A building up to a score of stories in height may be constructed wholly of reinforced concrete pillars and floors; and usually the floors of higher (or lower) steel-framed structures are of that material. Beyond that are the possibilities of cutting down costs of solid walls, through the ease of concrete pouring, and the construction of whole buildings by the laying up of pre-cast concrete blocks and slabs.

If you will look about you, in any city or town where you may happen to be, you will find concrete casting going on in half a dozen forms. Only yesterday, in this little Swiss town, I happened on a con-

An experiment in concrete block forms and ornamentation, as set up by Frank Lloyd Wright, to test values appropriate to the Arizona desert. [Note the different forms when designing is conditioned by canvas and wood materials, at right]

crete "works." By means of an electric hoisting gear, cars of gravel were being drawn up out of an old gravel-pit. And right there on the ground had grown up an industry whereby building materials and a dozen by-products were being mass-produced. Always in these places you will find a utility man or two pressing out the solid concrete blocks with which so much rural building in Europe is now accomplished: artificial squared stone, in effect. Less simple, but perhaps more important to architecture, the hollow blocks are being made of concrete, on the pattern of the " hollow tiles " long manufactured of baked clay. But beyond these more usual products, there were, piled in this concrete yard, building slabs of varying sizes, concrete pipes, concrete culverts, concrete manhole-covers, concrete fencing, concrete brackets, concrete tanks. From where I sit writing, I can see one of those concrete fences across the road; and our neighbor on the other side has a concrete wind-break to protect his dwarf orchard: cast grooved posts at six-foot intervals, and slabs of concrete slid into the grooves till a solid seven-foot wall stands

Four concrete halls in France. Top left, bathhouse interior, by L. Bonnier. Top right, school gymnasium, by Payret-Dortail. Below, two views of the central market hall at Rheims, by E. Maigrot. [By courtesy of *l'Architecte*, Paris]

Two examples of new architectural values to be gained in re-enforced concrete: a scenic studio and a garment factory in Paris.   A. and G. Perret, architects.

between the trees and the weather.   When the material can be shaped to such special uses, it is easy to see why it is displacing less pliable and less imperishable substances in building.

It is no part of my plan to go into the technical details or possibilities of the new types of construction; in this bird's-eye view of the world's new architecture we need know rather what are the things that architect and engineer are able to compass in a larger way with any material or method.   And so I am leaving it rather to my illustrations than to my text to suggest the conquests made in the name of concrete.   Here are halls which are made to stand up, to support vast roofs, by virtue of concrete arches and vaults — by no means undecoratively.   What need now to build those gaunt nineteenth century brick factories, with scattered small windows?

Auguste Perret is a leader of those who have developed a modern technique in reinforced concrete (*beton armé,* it is called in France).   Indeed, Perret has escaped entirely the *couturier* softness with which we have reproached French Modernism, in earlier chapters; and he, assisted by the engineer Freyssinet, whose hangars at Orly are shown in another chapter, and a bridge below, has served to establish France as a leading country in the inventive adaptation of concrete to new functional purposes.   Perret also has attempted a system of ornament in cast blocks (you will remember the church at Le Raincy) — but where he only made

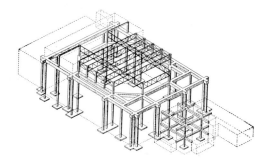

Exterior and concrete skeleton of the theatre,
Exposition of Decorative Arts, Paris, 1925.
A. and G. Perret, architects.

a beginning toward beauty in that direction, he really stirs us with his achievements in structure. The concrete skeleton of the temporary 1925 Exposition Theatre in Paris, shown here in its naked state and in the finished auditorium, afforded another example of weight carried independently of the main walls; and in the church at Le Raincy and other permanent structures there are striking feats in support and suspension.

The concrete construction work in this congress hall at Breslau is nearer

Exterior and Interior of the Centennial Hall, Breslau, Germany.  Max Berg, architect.  [Photo above by courtesy of German Tourist Information Office, New York; below, from *Die Baukunst der Neuzeit*, by Gustav Adolf Platz]

to the heavy solidity which has been thought expressive of the medium up to this time (though Perret, and Wright in some of his California houses, and the Austrians, have proved that concrete can be characteristically and honestly used and show a face not at all heavy or unaspiring). But we must turn again to the German Erich Mendelsohn for study of an architect who — at one time in his checkered career — felt that a new building aspect might be coming out of the moulded forms of poured concrete, and tried to express the heavy fluidity of the material in exterior design. You will remember his sketches, and the look of power and grandeur in them. Here are great vitality, directness, structural truth, massive creation. Mendelsohn reminds us, too, that there is another freedom gained by the new materials, steel and concrete, a radical departure from the four-square architecture of stone: if function or site or light-considerations demand a slanted wall instead of a perpendicular one, it is wholly possible — and economical in the building. " Sculptured architecture " and " spatial design " are terms that take on new significance when considered in relation to metal, glass, and concrete.

Mendelsohn's one notable design in this mode, that came to actual construction, is the Einstein Observatory at Potsdam. One feels that in it the architect has allowed himself a little too much revelling in the modelling for its own sake, playing in rounded forms because he has newly found a material that lends itself to rounding. And so the Einstein Tower becomes more important as an indication of a new freedom than for intrinsic architectural values. There are those who consider it a monstrosity — the rounded and bulging masses and slanting lines offending all eyes trained to classic squareness. Without being as extreme as that, we may consider it considerably less than a masterpiece of the new architecture — but interesting as warrant of other changes to come, of capabilities still to be mastered.

An exceptional use of the modelling possible to concrete is illustrated in the pictures of the Fiat factory in Turin, where a testing track for automobiles was built on top of the 400-yard long manufacturing and

The Fiat automobile factory, Turin, Italy; showing portion of track on roof, and interior court.
Matte Trucco, engineer.  [By courtesy of *l'Architecte*, Paris]

The Einstein laboratory and observatory, Potsdam, Germany.  Erich Mendelsohn, architect

assembling shops.  You may see how concrete has lent itself to the shaping of the turns — where stone would have been an impossibly expensive material.  The other picture of the Fiat works may serve to bring us back to the more usual uses of reinforced concrete, with glass, in neatly utilitarian service of industry — and so back to the " work-place " as an architectural entity.

There is, however, one proof of the great potentialities of construction in both steel and concrete, which I wish to bring in at this point.  Some recent bridges indicate that we have mastered materials that promise achievements in building which our limited structures today hardly hint at.  Of course it is no new thrill that we feel when a simple bridge

The Hunter Street Bridge, Peterborough, Canada.   Claude Bragdon, architect; Frank Barber, engineer.

is made to span a gorge or a river.   Always the throwing of a pathway
over space, if accomplished honestly and economically, has given back an
emotional stimulus.   The ancient bridges of the masonry days, even in the
worst periods of neo-this and neo-that in ordinary building, were likely
to be finely simple.   Travelling the roads of Italy, France, and other
countries where the centuries-old bridges are likelier to be repaired and
reconstructed by local masons than replaced with structures of the iron
age, one is continually delighted with arched spans of beautiful proportions and grace.   The tall masonry bridges of the Alpine railroads are
likely to be equally a source of surprise and pleasure.

The structures of the early iron age are in general less exciting — notable and interesting in the same way that the Eiffel Tower is, novel but
somehow not ultimately satisfying.   There are glorious exceptions, chiefly
creditable to the engineers rather than to the architects.   It is rather with
concrete that a twentieth century era in bridge building opens.   Innumer-

The Grandfey Viaduct, Fribourg, Switzerland

able simple decorative structures are being built over gullies, creeks, and canyons, often without the once inevitable Roman balustrade; and even the larger rivers are being spanned with roadways not framed by ornamental-architectural approaches. The inspiring lines of great metal spans and daring concrete arches are still occasionally spoiled when an Eclectic architect persuades a town board or an engineer to " do something artistic "; but we are better off in that respect than ever before. Honesty and economy become increasingly respectable. The stability and poise and grandeur of the engineered structure are not so often fussed up with purely showy architectural elements. The architect becomes basically engineer.

Of the examples shown here, the bridge at St. Pierre de Vauvray in France, by the engineer E. Freyssinet, offers the latest instance of daring simplicity in the new materials. The duplicated single arch, of concrete, from which the roadway is suspended, is 260 feet in length. The other illustrations are rather representative of the usual run of modern practice, where engineers and architects have freed themselves from the desire

Above, bridge in Ulm, Germany. Paul Bonatz, architect. Below, bridge built partly of concrete blocks cast on the Wright system, to harmonize with total building development, Phoenix, Arizona. Albert Chase McArthur, architect. [By courtesy of *The Architectural Record*]

Bridge at St. Pierre de Vauvray, France.  E. Freyssinet, architect

to show off architecturally.  Thus the poetry of geometry displaces the makeshift of ornament.

When architect-engineers can spread before us achievements like these — to say nothing of the new suspension bridge over the Hudson River at New York City, with its central span of 3500 feet — what may be the wonders they will ultimately construct in multiple-buildings, in aërial towers, in apartments over the waters?  Work-places!  We come back to them with a sinking feeling.  They are still commonplace, even the best of them — mere intimations of wonders that the architects are sure to encompass within the century.  To work with the crystallized wonders of machine-age imagination all about us — that is a social ideal far beyond the " pleasant " lighted factories with which the chapter began. In this branch of Modernism, too, the mind leaps forward to glories and to grandeurs that as yet are only hinted at.

There are men who believe that the trend toward urbanization of society will continue indefinitely, and that economic necessity, coupled with the possibilities of ever greater feats in steel, concrete, and glass

Imaginative drawing of skyscraper offices and apartments on immense bridges, by Hugh Ferriss. [From *The Metropolis of Tomorrow*, by Hugh Ferriss, by courtesy of the publisher, Ives Washburn]

fabrication, will result in " scientific cities," compounded of skyscraper units on a scale hitherto unknown. Each skyscraper will house, in its thousands of apartments, the population of a present-day town, together with the shops and services needful to that population. There are, however, strong influences working toward decentralization also: increasing ease of transportation, and extension of cultural advantages, by radio, moving picture, etc. Ultimately, too, when some sort of Communism displaces Capitalism, the land will be released to those who want it — and the Nature instinct is strong. But whatever comes, meantime, in new ways of collective housing, new materials and engineering are ready.

# CHAPTER VIII

## *HOUSING THE SPIRIT OF MAN*

THERE are those who count the gains of the mechanized age as wholly material, and the coming of a machine-hard architecture and bigger windows as a fair advance for business buildings and factories only; and those conservative ones hold that we should preserve the old-time refuges for the uses of the Spirit, making the houses of God and the halls of learning and the theatres in the image of the past. Yes, they say, we are in for an age of industrialism, committed to " stripped " buildings for our offices and our workshops, and even to houses that are sanitarily plain and simple; but surely there is no need to cut off an occasional escape into decorated playhouses, into traditionally showy churches, into historically masked libraries and colleges and clubs.

In short, it used to be thought that fancy architecture was for the special purpose of dressing up churches, theatres, and other places of " special occasion " importance; and now some people, pathetically aware that they are to be deprived of the pale reflections of glory and of luxury in their work hours and their home hours, cling to the idea of a continuing historic refuge in *communal* structures. We may need, they say, the machine-age house and shop, for the uses of the modern athletic, machine-tending body; but where spiritual values and concerns enter in — why, then the Spirit demands the old mystery, glamour, and decorative cushioning.

Alas, alas! when shall we learn that Life too must be conceived as an organism? When shall we give up the vague hope of a terrestrial refuge, when stop dividing our lives into duty and pleasure, into work and escape from work, into " commonplace " and spiritual activities? The idea of refuge architecture is a relic from a defeatist age, when man was considered a poor humble creature, destined to a life of sorrow and care, subject to punishment by a vengeful God and His priests on earth: when the individual could only hope for an occasional *escape* into beauty, serenity, and spiritual peace.

If the new architecture be not based on the truth that man in his own creativeness may shape his whole life, his work, and his recreation — his house as well as his temple — on the truth that he need admit no defeat, seek no refuge, may bring the light of the Spirit into all that he touches, then it will indeed be no new world architecture. If I have found, have in this book set forth evidences of, a new *universal* art of building, it is because the Spirit of Man is coming forth, because a new religion of courage, faith, human power, of the divine and miraculous *in the man himself*, is taking form.

Let us see just how far we may go out to meet those defeatists and conservatives and romanticists. After food, clothing, and shelter, *then* structures dedicated to the uses of the Spirit. So much is true: man may not make consistent spiritual progress without the " necessities " cared for.

First Unitarian Church, Berkeley, California. Bernard Maybeck, architect. About 1900

Only with the coming of a margin of unharried leisure for conscious culti-
vation of beauty, for philosophic and scientific speculation, for spiritual
adventure, does he need an architecture beyond elementary shelter. But
today no man goes to work to build his own house, to weave his clothing,
to lay up a store of food. Complex ways of living, specialization in industry, modern machine-transportation and distribution, make his supply
continuous and afford him a share in that margin. Not only does he
share in time that can be devoted to strictly cultural and recreational
interests, or to direct spiritual pursuits, but if he is alert and wise, he can
exert a choice of occupation, for his working hours, that will enable him
to carry back the spiritual, the courageous, the adventurous over-values
into his "commonplace" work.

The escapists, of course, are visualizing the new home and office and
factory as too stripped, plain, severe, too consistently utilitarian, too little
enriched; just as they visualize a balancing refuge-architecture, churches
and the like, with too much of the luxurious and now unmeaning enrichment of the past. If architecture truly is a fixation of man's thoughts,
emotions, and aspirations, let us remember this parallel: the new world

thought or world religion will mean nothing unless it reaches back from universality to the intimate recesses of each man's soul; and the new monumental architecture will mean nothing unless it has definite kinship with a man's dwelling-house, his garage, his workshop. Man's spirit must transform his home before it can be significant in church, meeting-hall or " art building."

Having said so much — in defence of the organism, of the unity of the spirit — then let us concede that in communal buildings, by virtue of their largeness, of the greater numbers of people they serve, of their more intensive service to the inner man, a greater degree of enrichment is legitimate, a little decorative spread justifiable — but of the sort creative out of its own time, its own artists. If a building's first purpose is to house the activities that directly enrich living, then in that building the flowering will be more intricate and more colorful. And indeed, if cathedrals were once made beautiful for the glory of a distant and mysterious God, there will be temples again, of our own devising, glorious with some other beauty, when we have finally brought clear what we are learning about Divinity-in-Man.

Of course, palaces are out, in any alignment of the structures on which men will expend their finer architectural creativeness. We shall lavish our best not on the dwelling of the king or the rich man, but where men congregate. We have no clue yet to the Church of the future — though the older churches are so much with us still that there is an architectural problem there, which we shall address in a moment. Theatres already are stripping themselves, and new forms, clean-cut and simple, and reflecting a new phase of stage art, are emerging. Universities are still timidly Eclectic, with notable improvement in tasteful dressing, as befits the academic folk who have now caught up with the progressive thinking of a quarter-century ago; but many of the elementary and high schools are being transformed into generously lighted factories, clean, bright, unmasked. There are a few art galleries, too, where the spirit dwells, unstifled by period decoration, uncluttered and harmonious, and libraries

Two views of the Boston Avenue Methodist-Episcopal Church, Tulsa, Oklahoma.  Rush, Endacott & Rush, architects; Bruce Goff, designer.

almost machine-like in their efficiency and co-ordinated service to read-ers.  These are some of the varieties of communal building that are with us, trembling on the verge of a plunge into deepest Modernism; and a few, a very few examples begin to show traces of æsthetic achievement.

THE Church and modern architecture — the most baffling of all our juxtapositions of ideas!  Does the Church belong to the new age at all?  Is the Church failing?  Is there a modern spirit in the old Churches that might be a starting-point for a new-age ecclesiastic architecture?  Is there growing in the world a spirit, a spirituality, universal, too broad to be called a " religion " — in the narrowed sense to which existing sects have limited the word?  And will this new human-divine spirituality sweep mankind out of the old church edifices, and stir architects to build newly

St. Anthony's Church, Basel, Switzerland.   Karl Moser, architect.   [By courtesy of *l'Architecte*, Paris]

glorious congregating-places?  Is the machine age to know only a spiritual Renaissance — will it be re-birth or more glorious birth?  Whither is the Spirit leading?

   If it is to be a new birth, for the first time a religion broad enough for all the world, stripped of all the idolatries, mythologies, and magic formulas that prevent men from facing life fearlessly and clear-mindedly, then it surely has something to do with the world drift toward the open life and open-mindedness which we have noted.  To that extent perhaps the beginnings of a world spiritual movement have already affected architecture — for openness and light are fundamental to the new building in all types. But assuredly the new religion as such is too unformed, too tentative, too slight — even though inevitable and beautiful and nascent — to be reflected in new " churches." We have come to the problem too early. All we can hold up as examples are efforts of isolated parishes of the older sects, Catholic and Protestant, to create houses of worship combining certain traditional motifs of religious building (particularly the aspiring line and the colored window) with certain rational principles and some of the simplicity of strictly modern building. We have before us some very interesting compromises.

The Catholics of Basel have built a large church in concrete, that is half factory-like and half mediæval. It exhibits some amazing capabilities of the poured-concrete medium, provides some beautiful moments of lighting when the sun strikes through the vast expanses of colored glass at just the right angle, and admirably brings back simple wall backgrounds for the pomp and ceremony of the Catholic service. But neither is the building greatly attractive as an architectural entity (I tried to visualize it as a meeting-place *if* we had a religion distinctly of today), nor does it fit with any interpretation of Catholicism that I have been able to find. The architect is by all odds the ablest of the Modernist practitioners in Switzerland, with a number of very interesting structures to his credit; but I cannot believe that in this building he found *a reason for architectural creation.* He put up a modern building, structurally; but he found no goad to his imagination, to his inventiveness as artist — I looked long at the tower, and said to myself, " If we can't make more than this out of long hard lines and simple proportioning and a bit of decorative flowering, then perhaps the soft Eclectic maskers are right." But I know in my heart that when Karl Moser or another is religiously stirred, deeply, when the new wave of spirituality brings him an ecstasy, a serenity, a soul-communion of today, then he will write out that beauty in the architectural elements of some new cathedral. Meanwhile here are something like the bare bones of one. And meantime, the Catholics seem strangely

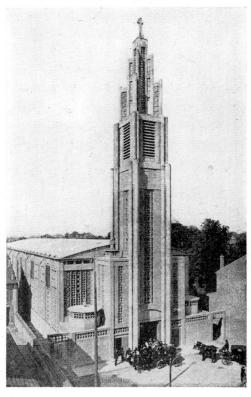

Church at Le Raincy, France.   A. and G. Perret, architects

out of place in the light, pitilessly open place; the idol-worship, the burning candles, the incense, the kneelings and hushed prayings, are curiously
hollow without the architecture of mystery, of refuges, of confessional
booths, of dim recessed chapels, that have been Catholic since the early
Fathers crystallized Christianity into a set mould.

Nor is Auguste Perret, with his celebrated concrete churches at Le
Raincy and Montagny, more successful — even though he is more decorative.   You will remember that he evolved a much-discussed system of
" machine-age " ornamentation in concrete castings.   On my way back
to Paris from Le Raincy I made this notation: " The church is a big barn
of a place put up easily and logically, with interesting use of concrete

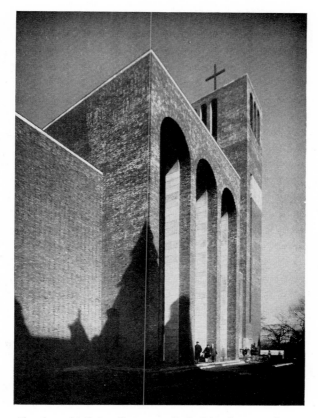

Church at Mülheim, Germany. Emil Fahrenkamp, architect.
[By courtesy of German Tourist Information Office, New York]

pillars to carry weight. A good effort, pleasing enough, honest, a stirring try for a direct building out of these times — but sadly needing richer *feeling.*" I think I had not at that time considered at all deeply the source from which that " feeling " must come: had not arrived at any conclusions about a new church architecture in relation to a modern spiritual overflow. I saw the building as a modern structure and was enthusiastic about the ways in which a new material had served an honest sheltering purpose: the small sections of solid wall, mostly on the front and tower, are mere sheets of solid concrete blocks, laid up like brick; the main walls are of glass (fairly rich) set in concrete cross-bars and arabesques; the roof weight is carried independent of the walls by inside pillars. But I

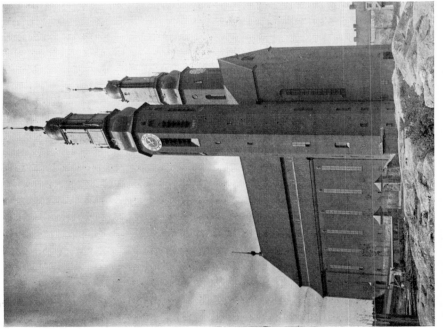

The Högalid Church, Stockholm, Sweden; showing typical Swedish "moderate radicalism" in simplification. Ivar Tengbom, architect. [By courtesy of Swedish State Railways Bureau, New York]

noted even then that the interior seemed too light, too open, for a religion of mystery and refuge. (Even from a design point of view alone, without regard to religious purpose, less glass and more solid wall would seem an improvement.) The designers of the furnishings, moreover, in an effort to be modernly simple, have cut off all imagination, all touch of individuality. M. Perret's concrete-cast ornament is different, and of today's materials — but my last notation was, " No logical ornament seems to be flowering richly out of the organism." Somehow I cannot get away from the idea that this decoration was evolved only from thinking about the material, and failed to be born of the spirit, that complementary source of true creativeness.

In neither of these cases does there seem to have been reconsideration of the meaning of the building, the meaning of the activities to be housed; as, for instance, Frank Lloyd Wright thought back to the significance of the dwelling house, or Mendelsohn to the significance of the modern factory. Perhaps if we look back to sources we shall have to agree that in our era only a church leaning on the idioms of ancient ecclesiastic architecture can be right. You know that a great many church members today, if you say that you could not believe the things they repeat in their creed or prayer, will tell you that the Church does not expect you to believe those things literally — that they are only " forms." Perhaps equally the architect designing a church, must run in a lot of traditional forms, insincerely — because there is no new Church yet to create fresh and believable forms. The elder Church is with us, he says, and (like one's grandmother) one must respect it. And not wanting to lose the church — or is it his job? — he arranges an echo of past glories.

At any rate the most successful of the essays toward modern church architecture seem to me to be tinged with that sort of compromise. A number of the Swedish churches have been rationalized down to simple forms, with a certain relief in decorative idioms from the past. The architects Ivar Tengbom, Lars Wahlman and Sigfrid Ericson are a progressive group not easily matched in any other country; unless we except the

The War Memorial Church, New Ulm, Germany: façade and view from nave. Dominikus Böhm, architect. [This and next two plates from *The Western Architect*, September, 1928, by courtesy of the editors]

The War Memorial Church, New Ulm, Germany. Dominikus Böhm, architect

Danish, with P. V. Jensen-Klint and Kaj Gottlob as leaders. A little more
" radical," more expressive of new materials, even while leaning back
upon some traditional " effects," is the German Professor Dominikus
Böhm, who made the Catholic Church at Bishofsheim an amazing illustration of the impressive values of concrete. His also is the War Memorial
Church in New Ulm, with its heavily monumental front, and its interior
with forest-like dimness broken into by bursts of light. Professor Böhm
is credited with a method of building in reinforced concrete without the
use of wooden forms, gaining greater variety of line, greater plasticity,
by getting away from the limitations of the lumber usually used to hold
the concrete mass in place until dry. There are those who believe that
the concrete parabolic arch, as seen in these two churches, will replace the
Gothic masonry arch in the ecclesiastic architecture of the future.

Catholic Church in Bishofsheim, Germany.   Dominikus Böhm, architect

And indeed, here is an impressive architectural expression born of a material economically used.   Here is architectural adventure, daring.

In America a pioneer Modern church was designed in concrete, as long ago as 1908.   Here was no echo out of the past in either material or "style."   Indeed the Unity Temple in Chicago, designed by Frank Lloyd Wright, and almost as much a landmark in its field as was his Larkin Building in the industrial field, is as rational, as honest, and as organic as anyone might wish; and yet a decorative entity as well.   It was perfectly appropriate to its purpose as a Universalist meeting-house; if it founded no world-tradition of new church building, that is because the occupant-church was not big enough.   Chicago too claims one of the latest and

The Unity Temple, Chicago: a pioneer " radical " church building, and the first monolithic concrete structure of its type. Frank Lloyd Wright, architect. [1907]

most interesting examples of compromise between very modern and historic, in the Church of St. Thomas the Apostle, by Barry Byrne. This building, historically reminiscent in the few decorative motifs, is yet intriguingly rationalized, and in some aspects attractively simple-rich.

But it is in Tulsa, Oklahoma, that the most provocative American example of different church building has emerged. The Boston Avenue Methodist Episcopal Church there is of a form that anyone would recognize as " church-like " at a distance or close-by, inside or out. Its style begins with the accenting of the aspiring line. But its detail is daringly new, its ornamental idioms fresh and vital, its masses fairly well sculptured and perfectly expressive of plan. But why for the *Methodists?* — that I couldn't answer. Incidentally the plan of the building illustrates a trend of life even within the most traditional and institutionalized of the

The Boston Avenue Methodist-Episcopal Church, Tulsa, Oklahoma. Detail in social lobby, and main portal. Rush, Endacott & Rush, architects; Bruce Goff, designer.

The Boston Avenue Methodist-Episcopal Church, Tulsa, Oklahoma.
Rush, Endacott & Rush, architects; Bruce Goff, designer.

sects, that toward combination of educational and social activities with preaching: the "club" and school features of this building balance, to the left of the tower, the church auditorium to the right. Significantly, a "Social Lobby" runs through the building between these two main units. There has been a great deal of talk about humanizing the old Protestant churches; in so far as the process has prevailed, architecture has kept up.

When Protestant architecture has not aped Catholic, the churches have in general been bare. In the four hundred years since Luther, no true style has been born — and certainly meeting-houses in America have been as dismal, as mongrel, as unoriginal as anything in the whole range of our architectural misfortunes. It has seemed to me that the Christian Science

Side portal of Christian Science Church, Berkeley,
California.   Bernard Maybeck, architect

Church, the only great sect founded within our own lifetimes, has usually
and regrettably lapsed into the barren Protestant mode of church building, has been unadventurous, uncreative, colorless.   Strangely modified
classic temples have had a vogue where large structures were raised.   The
most notable exception, perhaps, is that curiously attractive church in
Berkeley, erected many years ago from designs by Bernard Maybeck.
Although it is far from the simplicity that we think of as modern, it
affords a rich pleasure to the eye of the passerby, a sense of a fresh decorative aim successfully achieved; and I am told that the interior is richer
in color than any other contemporary church.   By way of contrast, I
may add that the Unitarian Church in Berkeley, designed by Maybeck
even earlier, is one of the prettiest simple and logical meeting-houses in
the whole range of non-conformist church architecture.

For the sort of passive structure that the Christian Scientists apparently
want, this design by Eliel Saarinen seems to come as clean and as near
architectural richness as one could wish.   Yet one asks what there is here
to suggest spiritual exercise, to remind one even vaguely that religion lives

Designs for a Christian Science Church in Minneapolis, Minnesota.  Eliel Saarinen, architect

Interior of the *Stahlkirche,* Cologne, Germany. Professor Otto Bartning, Berlin, architect. [This and photo opposite from *Die Stahlkirche,* by Dr. Paul Girkan]

in the region of high serenity and deepest ecstasy. As a contrast — and our last church — I am adding pictures of the Modernist chapel erected in connexion with an exposition at Cologne. This metal-and-glass building, whatever else may be said of it, achieved an atmosphere, a richly colorful evocation. The designer had been stirred, conceived an individualistic thing, brought it richly to completion. It is architecturally organic, of one piece decoratively, colorful, evocative of mood. One can imagine sitting for an hour in the building and discovering that the architecture itself invites the soul. But this *Stahlkirche* is, I believe, no longer

The *Stahlkirche*, Cologne, Germany.  Professor Otto Bartning, architect

in use: was built as a model and a suggestive experiment, in connexion with a temporary exposition.

The whole church problem in relation to architecture is, indeed, muddied by the uncertain, controversial, and negative position of the various "religions" in the contemporary world.  The only entities important in a broadly international view, the Jews and the Catholics, are bound together in ways not deeply spiritual — rather in material, intellectual, and emotional bonds.  The Jewish bond is racial, the Catholic political-superstitious.  To neither one of these, nor to any Protestant sect, can we look for an art that is spiritually expressive, vital, or more than a vague echo of a glorious past.  I cannot believe that a living Church, in the larger sense, can be expressive of the Spirit and fail to create an art of its own time.  Art is the very flowering, the tangible flowering, of the creative soul come to ecstasy.  Conversely, no age without an art is in

tune with Divinity.   And if architects today build us no modern
churches, in new forms of beauty, it is because their souls have nowhere
touched upon Divine revelation and mystic creativeness.

Personally, I count the processes of artistic creation and æsthetic enjoyment as far closer to the absolute of spiritual experience than most
people suspect — certainly closer than any clergyman would admit.   In
the fields of revelation, of ecstasy, of personal identification with the
Divine, of contact with the infinite, of realization of perfect blessedness
— in these realms of spiritual re-creation and purification and exaltation,
which we call religious, the arts are the channels, the ways inward and outward, the expression and the joy.   And I think that we shall hereafter
discover our artists closer to our priests and " ministers."   I find myself
spiritually attuned more often after a concert, or a tragedy of Euripides,
or after an hour in a room of Cezanne and Gauguin paintings, than after
a sermon.   I do not know the means by which Divinity lives in an Isadora
Duncan, how it communicates to an audience when she dances; nor do I
know what it is that leaps up within me when I see a Lehmbruck statue
or hear a Wagner prelude.   But I do know that then I touch upon what
is divinely pleasurable, contact with the final mystery, the everlasting
serenity, the spiritual that is timeless and outside space.

ALL our modern art and modern architecture is growing out of our first
gropings toward a soul-expression of these times, for which we shall find
a philosophy and an æsthetic.   And we are as likely, so far, to detect the
early sprouts of it in buildings constructed for the arts as we are in any
contemporary churches.   Of course the art buildings have been, in times
past, illustrative too.   What more expressive of nineteenth century religious thought, or lack thereof, than the shallowly lush theatres, the
mausoleum-like art galleries and the cold north-lighted studios?

In the theatre, if anywhere, the architectural richness may appropriately reflect colorfulness, joy, and imaginative fancy.   But who was it
decreed an interpretation of joyousness that is fleshy, superficial, and

The *Werkbund* Theatre, Cologne, Germany. Henri van de Velde, architect. [1914]

gaudy? The better Eclectic architects still give us reflections of the dignified frumpery and fat obscenity of the Paris Opera, while the average
movie-level architect wallows in cheaper exhibitions of unrestrained ornament and catch-penny gilding and red-plushing. Now I am not one of
those who say lightly that the theatre is going to be the church of the
future: the casual utterers of that thought are usually thinking of some
intellectualized and moralistic variation of our amusement-theatre of
today; and you must go back a long way in the history of the stage art
before you will find drama, acting, or theatric ritual — or theatre buildings — worthy of the religion, the spiritual life, that is coming. But I do
believe that we of the theatres, in our own way, working from a foundation stripped of all the frumperies and vulgarities of the nineteenth
century realistic and trivially diverting types of drama, will shape an in-
strument that will provide one of the channels to the soul, that will reveal
instead of portray, that will contact Divinity. I foresee a new " playhouse " beginning with the cleanliness, simple proportions, sweet rational-
ism, and characterfulness of the Modernist architects — and functionally
beginning with a simple architectural stage for setting out the actors and
dancers, as against the proscenium-framed, picturizing stage of today —

Portals of two Berlin theatres: at left, the Nollendorf Cinema; at right, the *Volksbühne*. Oskar Kaufmann, architect. [By courtesy of Ernst Was-muth Verlag, Berlin]

Project for a People's Theatre, Amsterdam, Holland.  H. Th. Wijdeveld, architect

and going on to colorful richness and atmospheric mood in the auditorium and social-rooms: a theatre that will be, indeed, not less than a new cathedral in its appropriateness to the uses of the soul.  This will be an integral unit in the new City of Art.

If the church-builders have hardly hinted at a church for the new world-order, the theatre-builders have little more than cleared the way to beginning foundations.  For let us admit that if we yet lack prophets and priests of a modern religion, we have no more than a visionary pioneer or two and some timid or hampered practical experimenters where our artist-prophets of tomorrow's theatre should be.  There is little chance for the combination to come right, wherein the prophetic-creative artist and the inspired architect achieve a stage and auditorium in tune with the wisdom of tomorrow.  Most so-called Modernist theatres are surface applications of Modernistic architectural idioms to basically old-fashioned theatre structures; and many a so-called progressive theatre organization is housed in a feebly traditional playhouse because it couldn't bring its experimental production ideals clear enough to afford a starting-point for a distinctive or positive theatre design.  Thus the New York Theatre

The Municipal Theatre, Jena, Germany.   Rebuilt by Walter Gropius and A. Meyer

Guild inhabits a pleasantly reminiscent building, without character; even the Pasadena Community Theatre chooses a Spanish house as most "suited" to its ideals and purposes.   And the few real thrusts toward something else are — well, thrusts.

There was some intimation of a new spirit in Van de Velde's theatre for the *Werkbund* Exposition in Cologne: the building departed diametrically from the Italian-French tradition, was democratically simplified in auditorium-plan, was provided with a "reform" stage, and achieved in the exterior design a real feel of "people's theatre," with a strain of machine-like heaviness.   One could hardly have asked for more of the *Werkbund* suggestion in 1914.   Walter Gropius, in the rebuilding of the City Theatre in Jena, accomplished the most noted return to an

Inside the Ziegfeld Theatre, New York: a "revue" theatre
with simple masses enriched by gay all-over decoration.
Joseph Urban, architect

utter simplicity of forms and a decorativeness growing out of creative
handling of naked masses.  Auguste Perret, in the temporary theatre for
the Exposition of Decorative Arts in Paris, 1925, set up an interesting
example of structural simplification, in reinforced concrete, and eliminated the proscenium-framed stage in favor of a tri-partite platform;
but the building was conceived without any relationship to a production-
need, and proved nothing — unless to students of structural engineering.
Frank Lloyd Wright made plans of a theatre for Aline Barnsdall, projected for Los Angeles; and the exhibited plaster model of the building led
American stage artists to look forward to the most revolutionary — and
the most beautiful — big theatre so far brought to public notice; but for

Project for the Max Reinhardt Theatre, New York.    Joseph Urban,
architect

some eight years the plans have awaited execution.    H. T. Wijdeveld drew
intriguing designs for a radical People's Theatre in Amsterdam.    Max
Littmann of Munich, working by evolutionary change rather than revolutionary, became leader of the architects who simplified and democratized
the theatre structure between 1900 and 1920; and he designed that attractive and stylish playhouse which is illustrated back in Chapter V.    His
place has been usurped by another German, Oskar Kaufmann, who has
built the most attractive " styled " houses in recent years, adding to a
generally simplified structure a glow of warm color and an amusing dash
of Neo-Rococo ornamentation.    His auditoriums afford the most alluring atmosphere achieved in any theatres I have attended anywhere; and
although they indicate little regarding the broader aspects of future

Project for an opera house and studio building, New York.   Joseph Urban, architect

theatre building, they prove that the Modernists can evoke, without strings of gilded sausages, a gay, even a joyous mood that will somehow always belong in the halls dedicated to the theatre-god Dionysus.  Unfortunately the atmosphere and the color do not photograph well, and I can render the architect scant justice here.  Something of the same combination of rich colorfulness and simplification of forms has been achieved by Joseph Urban in the Ziegfeld Theatre in New York.  In a revuehouse, the extravagant and fanciful decorations are wholly in place — though the stage again tells us nothing progressive.  Urban's design for the projected Reinhardt Theatre in New York, however, promises crystallization of certain more advanced theories of a Modernistic theatre,

Model of a theatre building for a repertory company, bringing into one composition a large theatre, a small theatre, a children's theatre, and a cabaret and roof garden. Norman-Bel Geddes, architect. [Photo by Maurice Goldberg]

and the outward clothing of the building is as interesting a variation of Viennese stylization as any recently laid on paper. Urban too has made striking designs for an opera house integral to a great city skyscraper, and has designed other theatres with new and even startling implications.[1] As a leading designer of stage-settings, though first trained as an architect, he is fitted to think from the theatre production outward to an appropriate architectural shelter, as the usual architect, who only stands outside the playhouse looking in, can never do. Another designer, who begins even farther back with conceptions of complete new productions — drama, stage, and method of presentation — is Norman-Bel Geddes; and his "projects" for theatres are the most provocative, prophetic, and intriguing of any of the radical thrusts so far.

[1] See *Theatres,* by Joseph Urban. New York 1929.

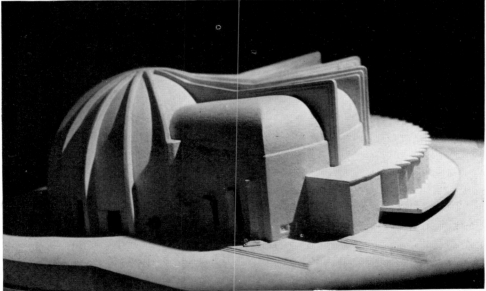

Model of theatre specially designed to house Norman-Bel Geddes' production of Dante's *Divine Comedy:* a non-proscenium theatre with a semi-circular Greek-type auditorium facing a domed stage. Norman-Bel Geddes, architect. [Photos by Maurice Goldberg] Note scale of building in relation to figure in upper photo.

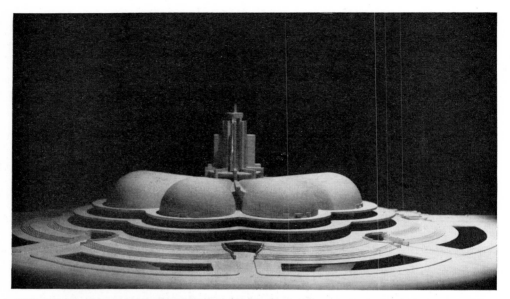

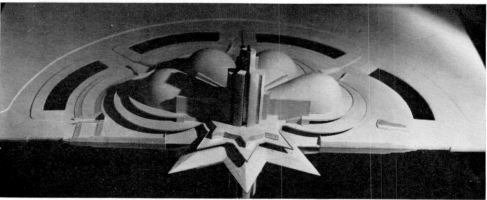

Model for a temple of music in a waterside park. Provision for an audience of 10,000, an orchestra of 200 pieces, and a chorus of 600. The tower houses a carillon, offices, dressing rooms, and studios. Terraces provide promenades and parking space for 1720 automobiles. Norman-Bel Geddes, architect. [Photos by Maurice Goldberg]

Model for a theatre of the circus type: with auditorium surrounding a central circular stage. Norman-Bel Geddes, architect. [Photo by Maurice Goldberg]

But when all is said and done, we are working but tentatively and haltingly toward the new world theatre as yet. Most of the progressive houses actually built are compromises, to accommodate old forms of drama; or else they are essays toward the sheltering of that machine-canned and immature cousin of the immemorial drama, " the pictures." We may pause over certain examples of auditoriums conceived as expressions of the spirit of the machine-projector and of the movie mass-audiences: more particularly over Mendelsohn's Universum Theatre in Berlin, and Kiesler's Film Guild Cinema (interior only) in New York. But — this chapter so far has been particularly full of buts and howevers, from which you may read my lack of conviction about our success in housing the spirit of man beautifully — we can detect in these buildings only the first signposts toward a different road. If theatre owners could once make up their minds to give Frederick Kiesler — one of the pioneer Functionalists of Europe before he migrated to New York — a completely free hand in the design and creation of a theatre, we should have an example to point

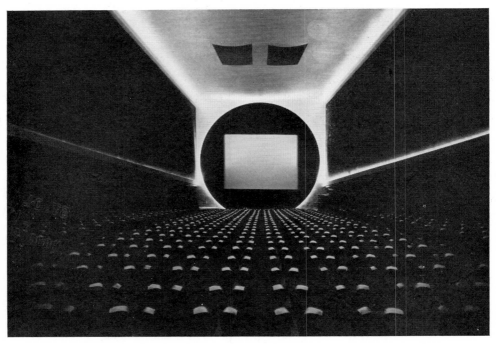

Above, the Universum Cinema Theatre, Berlin, Germany. Erich Mendelsohn, architect. Below, the Film Guild Cinema, New York. Frederick Kiesler, architect

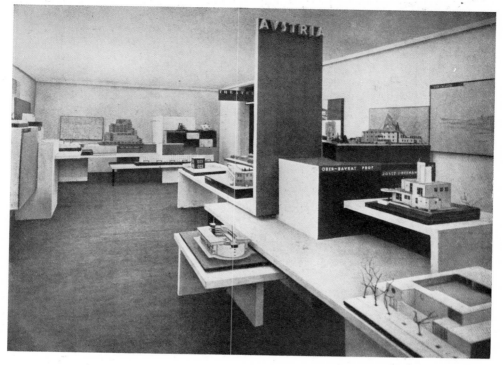

Austrian room at an exposition in Paris.  Arranged by Frederick Kiesler

to: in this case, a ruthlessly severe example, in line and mass, but finely colorful, with an enrichment of its own sort.  The trouble is that Kiesler's conception of a stage and auditorium is indissolubly bound up with a wholly revolutionary vision of the theatre art; and like Geddes, he will be able to give us of his best only when he is free to create from the beginning — not as slave to an amusement-peddler on Broadway.  Geddes' fecund genius has afforded us already the most intriguing set of drawings and models for " different " stages and auditoriums seen anywhere.

In setting forth the hope, nay the faith, that in time the world's art galleries, concert halls, and crafts museums will be spiritually important to us, and at the same time will architecturally express beauty, created out of our own life and era, I again find myself armed with only the slightest proofs.  Most of the evidence has come and gone with temporary expo-

The trend toward intimacy and simplicity in exhibition gallery and school. Above, photograph of exposition building by Joseph Hoffmann at Paris, 1925. Below, the Oak Lane Country Day School at Philadelphia, by Howe & Lescaze. On page 327 is a building, by Frank Lloyd Wright, suggesting equally radical, but more monumental, possibilities.

The Roerich Museum and apartment building, New York.
An art center under a residential skyscraper.  Corbett, Harri-
son & MacMurray and Sugarman & Berger, Associated
Architects

sitions.  Recognition that the graphic arts of today should have appropriate backgrounds has meant that a certain number of architects brought
simplification and sheer surfaces and harmonious coloring to the exhibition rooms.  Vienna led the way, with alluringly simplified galleries,
touched with elegantly reticent ornament — or sometimes luxuriously
dressed in stylish patterned surfaces.  Germany followed, with rather
soberer backgrounds; and you will find a dozen well-set-out exhibitions
in the Rhine cities and Munich, Dresden, and Berlin, to every one in England or America.  Holland and Scandinavia are both progressive, and

Main portal of the art gallery in the group of Exposition
Buildings, Düsseldorf, Germany.   Wilhelm Kreis, archi-
tect.   [By courtesy of German Tourist Information
Office, New York]

Paris sets forth its really modern shows with its own effective if somewhat dressmaker-y accent.   But of outstanding examples I can offer exceedingly few.

The older galleries and concert halls simply denied the spirit.   They
were dead places, and deadening to the art within them.   There was
nothing to evoke " the Presence."   Today we go back far enough in elimination to still the deadening forces; and we begin to create mood, vaguely
but unmistakably.

UNIVERSITIES and schools should be includable in a classification of buildings devoted to the deeper pursuits of humankind.   If I confess that I
found but one university building, or project for the building, related

Porch of an exhibition gallery, and Planetarium, Düsseldorf, Germany. Wilhelm Kreis, architect. [By courtesy of German Tourist Information Office, New York]

to the subject we are studying, I may follow with the statement that I believe that just about represents the place we have come to in education. The higher learning today is either traditional or material. It comes not from the inner soul. An inspirational teacher is a menace; a creative artist at a university is a disturbing element. When we shall get away from historic and objective education, rise to spiritual evocation, to tending the flame of creation that is born in the child (but almost invariably snuffed out by conventional teachers before he is ten) I cannot say. Perhaps this "cathedral of learning" designed for the University of Pittsburgh is reflective of some new trend in education. More likely it is a happy application of faintly Gothic meditation to skyscraper architecture, impelled by materialistic land values, without too great thought about what the higher learning has been, is, or may be. Anyhow, it is a striking

"The Cathedral of Learning": skyscraper building of the University of
Pittsburgh.    Charles Z. Klauder, architect

stunt-building, and has gained recognition throughout the architectural world as a novel, even startling thrust toward a machine-age expressiveness of something.

Still one wonders what would eventuate if a modern university were established, and a prophetic artist like Frank Lloyd Wright called in to design and construct the buildings.

Fortunately in turning to the lower schools, we return to fields where pioneering has already been accomplished. In this country as long ago as the first decade of the new century, the Gothic gables, small windows, and high-ceilinged, draughty rooms were being attacked and eliminated in favor of the lower, simplified and more intimate forms, with special attention paid to generous and controlled lighting. I remember in my own town the controversy over the " plain " buildings by Bernard Maybeck, who was considered by some to be bringing the schoolhouse down from the realm of cultured and fancy art to the plane of commonplace life. Too few of us recognized then that exactly such a pulling-down process was necessary — and was to be initiated throughout the world within a decade following. At any rate, school architecture in the Far West has gained immeasurably within the last quarter-century: has been brought back to a basis of functional planning, to architectural masses that lie easily along the ground, to simplicity and openness and lightness. Gone forever — I hope — are the forbidding piles of Gothic and Romanesque gabled masonry, with faithfully narrow windows. Gone are the adapted French chateaux and Rhenish fortress castles; and although we may not so easily discard the inconveniences of adapted English Collegiate Gothic, or escape a certain type of formidable red-brick-and-white-stone-trim bastard-Renaissance, we may take pleasure in a great many existent rationalized schools, and foresee a complete world shift in the matter. The underlying principles are largely those we met in connexion with our study of the modern house and the factory or " workplace "; except that some of us *want* to count the educational establishment as nearer to the things of the soul, and the schools as akin to " art buildings." If we bring them down to factory plainness at first, we may profitably meditate afterward on the ways in which a theatre or art gallery can be designed to invite the Spirit, and weave something of that atmosphere and enrichment into the schoolhouse.

The examples illustrated tend toward the factory simplification and tidiness, of course, rather than in the direction of complete and enriched Modernity. For one thing we know far more at present about minister-

Main front of public school at Celle, Germany.  Otto Haesler, architect

ing to the healthy athletic student body, than we do about playing up to the healthy creative inner being.  And it may be noted in passing that the modern ideals of physical healthfulness have led to the building of some distinctly Modernistic sports fields, and, in the United States, to an extraordinary crop of immense stadiums, a few of which have escaped the weakening hand of the Classic architects.  The fields at Nuremburg and Cologne especially, compact, logically planned, with decorativeness growing out of arrangement and simple concrete structures, without display, are models of form following function.

You may be so convinced by this time of the logic of stripping off the stylistic envelope lingering from other ages, that you find me too insistent on the point — as if I might be arguing excitedly for a thing practically accomplished.  But let us look back at the university buildings, anywhere, everywhere, even the ones being built today; and unfortunately we shall know that no breath of Modern rationalization has disturbed the dust back there where learning begins.  As my last word on the educational building, let me insert a bit of description I have just run across, concerning the new buildings of the branch of the University of California at Los Angeles.  Out there on the very rim of the Western world, where

The " window side " of public school at Celle, Germany. Otto Haesler, architect.
[This and photo opposite by courtesy of *l'Architecte*, Paris]

one might most easily expect some independence, an escape from the falsities and pretensions of warmed-over Italian-French culture, we meet, in this year 1929, the following example of deceit, servile-mindedness, and picking at the bones of antiquity:

" The motif of the campus as a whole is Italian-Romanesque, with some Spanish-Romanesque, and some early Italian-Renaissance in the interior decorations. In selecting this period and style, it was the purpose of the architects to obtain something that would unite the warmth and freedom that are characteristic of a southern climate with the proper air of dignity which should prevail on the campus of an institution of higher learning. . .

" Architectural monuments of this period which have come down through the centuries to our day are almost exclusively churches. Practically all learning and culture was concentrated in the ecclesiastical organizations, not to mention most of the wealth. . .

" Lack of proper material, lack of money, variety of available material, and limitations in the ability of the workers, led to the completion of buildings of such free design that their parts are frequently incongruous.

The New School for Social Research, New York:
designs for street façade and for theatre.
Joseph Urban, architect

Symmetry was conspicuous by its absence. On one church it may be found that the foundations date back to the Eighth Century, part of the nave or the apse to the Ninth, one tower to the Tenth, and a balancing tower of different width, height, and design to the Eleventh or Twelfth Century.

" But in spite of this heterogeneity, lack of perfection, and even crudity, the spirit of these ancient buildings looking backward to the Dark Ages and forward to the Renaissance, lends itself well to the needs of the new Los Angeles campus. . .

" Now as to the method of carrying out this motif. The facing materials of the new buildings are reddish brick and light terra cotta, arranged in a multitude of designs to reproduce in a modified manner the free spirit of the old churches without too great a loss of the symmetry to which our modern eye is accustomed. In most cases, where this lack of symmetry has been incorporated into the design, it becomes noticeable only after careful inspection. For example in the two towers of Royce Hall, which by the way, were undoubtedly inspired by S. Ambrogio's in Milan, a careful inspection reveals three arches in one tower and two arches in the other. Looking more closely still one sees that the pattern of the brick work and terra cotta is also different in the two towers. . .

" Though the exteriors of the buildings are striking and unique to a high degree, the decorative effects achieved on the interiors of the Library and Royce Hall are even more so. The Chemistry and Physics buildings, of course, are finished plainly, in strict accordance with the needs of the sciences which will be housed in them. They were designed as laboratory buildings of the most modern and practical type, without waste of time or money on decoration which would be both useless and inappropriate. But in the larger two buildings, and in the Library especially, much thought has been given to appearance. . . The ceilings are beamed in Spanish-Romanesque style, to which the tile may also be attributed. The inspiration for this work may be found in many old palaces of Toledo, Burgos, and other Spanish cities. The chief difference, perhaps, lying in the beams of the ceilings. In Spain they were of wood, in the University

An attempt to square " modernism " with some older traditions of school architecture. The Cranbrook School, Birmingham, Michigan. Eliel Saarinen, architect

Exposition building at Cologne, Germany. Adolf Abel, architect

Library they are of stained plaster-of-Paris, but so remarkably executed that only the initiated are aware that wood has not been used. . .

" The ceiling design of the auditorium in Royce Hall is taken from a later period. Garnsey characterizes it as highly developed late Renaissance. Then there are the windows. They are of the small-paned type in general, and a few are constructed of glass bull's eyes of pleasing orange shade. These latter windows are leaded, and pictorial designs are worked into the center of each. Another happy inspiration of the architects was the inclusion of two open cloisters on the north side of this building." [1]

Isn't it silly? Isn't is a joke, not without deeper tragic implications, that for a hundred years the modern-living Californians are to be saddled, at one of their highest cultural institutions, with these cramped relics of mediæval picturesqueness, instead of machine-like buildings, light, open,

[1] *The California Monthly,* May 1929. I really should complete the description by adding here one of the illustrations of the Byzantine St. Ambrogio's-Royce Hall, with its caption commenting on the impressive ingenuity of the architects, because, forsooth, they draped a pretty garden-temple around the smoke-stack — thus masking the one thing that might honestly have expressed function, the one modern thing in the whole piece of make-believe. The churches of the Dark Ages had no smoke-stacks — what, then, could the perplexed architects do?

and suggestive of the functions they serve? California boasts that it has outgrown the ox-cart stage of civilization more thoroughly than any other state, owning one automobile for every two inhabitants, and having arrived at more intensive airplane travel than any other section of the world. But the intellectual centres are still fairly impregnable to the machine idea, to the thought of life lived as a whole, to a union of spirit, culture, and conduct. The orthodox custodians of culture are still busy putting up defences against and refuges from Tomorrow. From California to the Atlantic Coast, the same hollow joke is being played by the academic institutions — and the high academic architects.

But the spiritual is going out into life, away from the refuge-churches, away from the cloistered intellectual centres. Our epilogue-chapter may succeed in summing it all up, in something about the City as Architecture, and Life as Art. Sometimes we get perspective enough to see the audience as drama, as unfolding play. If once we can glimpse architecture and mankind like that, in reversal, we shall realize from deeper planes the problems and the possibilities in housing the spirit of man.

The new architecture, conservatively and radically experimental: a gateway and, beyond, a pavilion at the *Pressa* Exposition, Cologne, 1928.

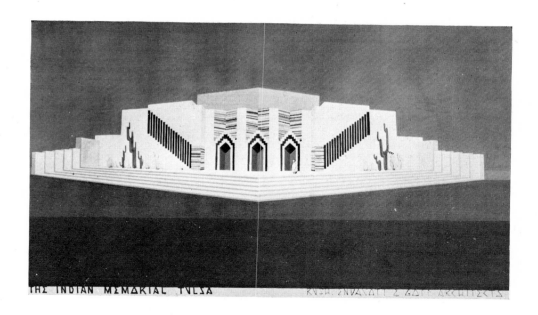

THE INDIAN MEMORIAL, TULSA

# CHAPTER IX

## THE CITY AS ARCHITECTURE : LIFE AS ART

NEW YORK, they say, has suddenly "gone modern." Shop-fronts echoing the latest Paris salon fashions are laid up with bewildering rapidity, the department stores have put in suites of softly Modernistic decorated rooms, and the Sunday papers regularly publish illustrations of catchy interiors by a new generation of "decorators." And, indeed, within a year there has been a landslide toward surface architecture "in the new manner." But I think the pioneer workers, the true visionaries, are a bit dismayed by this sudden popular conversion; and I am sure some of them resent the casual manner in which many Eclectic architects have "turned a hand" to Modernistic design — as easily as that. We need to build up some standards of discrimination, if our enthusiasm, our love, for the new art is to mean anything to the coming generations. For much

375

that is emerging today in the guise of a modern style is merely flashy, superficial, and amusing.

Here, as always, are two ways of approaching an art or a work. One is easy, the other at first difficult. The easy way, the common one, is to turn lazily from one's comfortable practice, which has always been in compliance with academic architectural teaching and the whims of one's clients, to supplying buildings with the fresh attractiveness of modish European wall-dressing. It is not at all difficult to catch the knack of the latest Parisian interior decoration, to learn the formula for the newest novelty in shop-fronts. The first rule for the architect working thus, transplanting a mode, is that he shall never look deeper than " appearances." He must remember that " something different " is what the public wants, and that recently some European artists have fortunately provided a variety of novel surface motifs and patterns which can be spread out appropriate to the business in hand. He must never let himself go down to the questions of organic unity, and spiritual expressiveness, because then he might find a disturbing dis-affinity for the imported French stuff in which he is trafficking.

The other way is longer, harder, but perhaps infinitely more satisfying. It must afford Mr. Wright and Herr Hoffmann and M. Le Corbusier a certain satisfaction, in the midst of the shallow Modernism of suddenly converted associates, to know that their own contribution is solid, secure, lasting; because, forsooth, they have lived their lives in conviction about this thing, testing, struggling, achieving, relating it to social progress, re-studying every law or supposed law of their own art, gathering inspiration and clarifying their perspective by studying men who are revolutionizing the other arts, keeping a perspective on humanity while trying to understand the problem of their client, watching world social, political, and mechanical-human drifts in relation to architecture. They are the ones who never forget usefulness as a test in their hurry for a new sort of " looks "; they accepted as fundamental that function would determine form: they never tried to create architectural " beauty " outside the or-

The simple and reticent modernism of the pioneer Joseph Hoffmann, as seen in a block of workmen's apartments in Vienna.  The building stands in an interior court.

ganism.  They knew better than to try to " dress " buildings with easily arranged clothes.

After many chapters of analysis and description of individual buildings and architectural types, I want, apropos of this, to return to the fundamentals touched upon in my opening paragraphs.  Because the one thing I fear most now is a deluge of too easy, too shallow, too soft a Modernism, superficially conceived, based on the narrower view, I want to end as I began, with a survey out over the world as it is, and with a glance back at the foundation stones of this art of architecture.

In the first place, most people do not see big enough. What chiefly made nineteenth century art so sterile, so trivial, was the narrowed viewpoint. Detail was more absorbing than depth or spirit or impression. Art, moreover, was made a separated, for-Sunday-enjoyment sort of thing — divorced from every-day living. Today the plea is, let art be an intensification of life. The artist must not study his art isolated from living; and true art enjoyment, æsthetic appreciation, cannot be experienced except as the values of contemporary life illumine the work. All other art is merely echo or pretension. Let us widen the view, push out the horizon, orientate art to the new conception of the world as unit.

Second, we must no longer work from the rim inward, but from the spirit outward. Architecture particularly has been starting with objective elements and working in — a very short way — toward creation. The true artist works from the inner light toward crystallized form, creates from spiritual conception to material finality.

In summarizing, I am going to review pretty thoroughly some of the eternal architectural verities, as they have applied to Greek, Gothic, and other indisputably great architectures of the past, and as they must appear in any lasting " Modern Style "; but since we now know more about what the modern architects have accomplished in the concrete, I am going to proceed with greater attention to the search for " a modern æsthetic." If I have talked a great deal about the machine as an influence, I have said very little so far about the element or quality in the art work that makes it beautiful to the beholder.

There are theories of modern art that emphasize the intangible thing called " form " as the first test of the degree of artistry of a painting, a sculpture, or a building. Perhaps the most suggestive of twentieth century popular books on æsthetics [1] sets up the quality "significant form " as a test for the visual work of art. Other commentators though no less certain that an indefinable but identifiable art quality differentiates the creative work from a merely inventive or arranged or imitative one, have

---

[1] *Art,* by Clive Bell, New York 1921.

quarrelled with the label but offer equally vague terms: one insists that a deep quality in the nature of contrapuntal organization is the true stimulus to the beholder's æsthetic sense, while another holds to " emotionally expressive form " as the exactest label. Again there are those who prefer the term " rhythm " or " rhythmic vitality." All these are efforts to tie a convenient tag to the quality that the artist puts into the work, the quality that lifts it above photography or illustration or (in architecture) tasteful echoing of dead masterpieces, and above mere walls and roof that stand up.

The quality of " form " in architecture is necessarily anchored in the building's use, grows with constant reference to materials and principles of construction, and flowers out of the architect's vision and emotion working over these basic elements. The style is properly the result of these things, not the conditioning factor.

In the light of this generally accepted Modernist theory of the arts, it will be seen why the new world architects decry modes of decoration and stylistic systems as beginning points, and why they discount Renaissances, and turn to the elemental principles of *building* for a new start, creating out of space, mass, functional line, proportion, texture, color, volume. With them justifiable decoration is organic, form is expressive, rhythm is functional. They do indeed manipulate the elements of architecture for the revelation of that unmistakable quality that warrants our calling them artists, not constructors; but their manipulation begins with the nobility of a serviceable plan, feeds on structural relationships, and ends with restrained playing (ornament) appropriate to the materials. The façade no longer steals away their affections *from the building*.

In Germany today there are schools where the architectural student begins by arranging cubes and other geometric solids for the values of proportion, contour, profile, and volume-relationship. It is a better starting-point than a study of " the orders " or other stylistic elements. For massive contours and gauged proportions may be magnificent and emotional and powerful, whereas surface decorative elements can be

Part of a workingmen's suburb, Frankfort-on-Main, Germany.   Ernst May, architect.   [By courtesy
of German Tourist Information Office, New York]

pleasing and little more.   The beholder sees the building first as a composition of masses in light.   Think of the Parthenon or Rheims Cathedral,
and it is rather the mass, the profile, the bulk, than the detail that stirs the
imagination in memory.   One may go farther in these masterpieces, analysing the decorative elements and getting secondary pleasure; but this is
supplementary, not the main thing — and only half-important if the
impressive construction were not its setting and its reason for being.   The
big simple mass is the first emotional factor: it stirs us by its bulk, its
horizontalness or verticalness, its amazing profiles, its rhythmic contours.
Nor can bad massing be wholly covered, disguised, by any amount of good
ornament.   (Even the lovely sensuous color and rich painting and carved
detail cannot save St. Mark's in Venice from a lingering impression of
squatness and disunity.)   Whatever else modern architecture lacks, it has
achieved, in the type examples, creative volumes and masses.

Then the Modernist goes on to the fact that elemental volumes and
masses mean a number of large, not-too-broken surfaces; and in treating
these surfaces, he believes that proportioning and rhythmic disposition
of the structural elements — skeleton, wall, and openings — are the more

Houses in the Rue Mallet-Stevens, a group development in Paris.  Rob Mallet-Stevens, architect.
[By courtesy of *l'Architecte,* Paris]

important half of the problem.  The larger light-and-shade composition of the building-mass may here be reflected in answering rhythms — always conditioned by the engineering and the building materials.  There may be repetition of the mass-contours, profiles, and directions of the whole; and there is the added value of texture-interest and foundation color.  Only after that comes a more detailed flowering in ornament.

Ornament, indeed, however intriguing bits of it may be on their own account, is in architecture merely the final touch, the appropriate enrichment, that sets out character the more fully.  When one speaks for more color in modern architecture, one is thinking less of *applied* coloring than of the native color of materials — a wider range of inherent color now being available than ever before.  For the rest, ornament, to be right, reinforces structure, completes rhythmic design, echoes in little, something already set out in large.  If you prefer to think of the structure as the plant, and ornament as the flower, the rare and precious blossoming for which all the energy has been gathered, stored, and expended, remember that no flower can be cut from its stalk without losing its beauty, its rightness, its power to give pleasure.

There is a group of Moderns who find the key to architectural design in a conception of *space enclosed* rather than of material mass with its secondary emphasis on surfaces — walls. This means a different approach to building rather than a different æsthetic. It is a method of making the architect think primarily of enclosed space as a means to better living; links up with the conception of mankind progressing toward the open life. Walls become boundaries of light, roofs are made to cover sheltered but not necessarily walled space. As a matter of fact, walls may be more important elements here than where façade design is the first consideration of the architect, and certainly the flat surfaces will be less broken up by openings: for now a wall is considered as a protecting boundary of living space, as a reflector of light, as a sun-trap. (There is a parallel in the theatre, where the old architectural stage gave way three hundred years ago to painted scenery, which now in turn gives ground before new conceptions of " a place for acting." If a Modernist does not advocate revival of a plain architectural platform for acting, he probably creates his productions out of visions of a " space stage." So some architects may be said to construct " space houses " out of a new conception of " a place for living.") In this new approach to architecture, the term " spatial relationship " takes on additional and fourth-dimensional implications.

There is one other " principle " central to our thought: a basic consideration in the architecture of the glorious periods of the past, and equally in the pioneering of the Modernists. Materials must be used *genuinely*. It may not be that every architect can attain truly expressive values out of the stone or iron or concrete that he works with; but at least there is a primal virtue in not covering up the nature of what went into walls and doors and wainscoting. Warning is doubly necessary in view of the popu-

The Barnsdall Cottage, Olive Hill, Los Angeles, California. Materials and site lending character to design. Frank Lloyd Wright, architect. [By courtesy of the editors of *Wendingen*]

The Barnsdall house (California Art Club), Olive Hill, Los Angeles, California: the values of monolithic material capitalized in outward expression.  Frank Lloyd Wright, architect

lar acceptance of some easy falsities, considered Modernistic because of their novelty.

A new material in the domain of an art is, of course, a baffling thing. If it be a fibre substitute for leather, its surface at first will be squeezed by designers and craftsmen into the uneven surface texture of leather. If it be steel panelling in a railway coach, its surface will for a time be laboriously painted and streaked to simulate grained wood.  If it be a hollow wooden column around an iron support, where a stone column used to be, the wood must be shaped for a time (say two hundred years) in image of the stone column.  Now it is a first canon of the modern æsthetic that each material, whether in painting, sculpture, theatre art, or architecture, has its characteristic virtues, its valuable potentialities, and that true art can arrive only by respecting those; yet men continue to be afraid of iron or wood or metal in a different-from-usual place, try to hide new uses — even take delight in clever imitation of one material's characteristics in terms of another (the lowest known form of appreciation).

Modellers, aping the freedom and sketchiness of brush-painting, are hailed as clever " sculptors "; light ornament is chiselled in hard stone; intricate stucco ornaments are cast in iron and riveted to stoves; a Swiss chalet is copied, exteriorly, by English or American architect and laborers, but the projecting beams and shaped board-ends are nailed on for effect, to simulate the original ones that grow organically out of the structure; and small minds applaud the huge columns added, uselessly, on the front of a State Capitol or a college library.  They pretend to be strong supports, carrying the weight, and the school-trained mind remembers something like them at Rome or Athens or Girgenti, and jumps to the conclusion that thus the demands of an art-loving people are met. These are common examples of clever transfer of values, of surface imitation, of plausible architectural lying.[1]

The incubus of this sort of thinking has been on the art of building since the beginning of the reign of the " selective " architects; nor were the habits of designers changed with the appearance of wholly new building materials capable of solving the new architectural problems arising out of the living, business, and transport of the machine age: materials, moreover, holding in their essential textures, capabilities, and strength the secret of, the stimulus to, the styles of the future.  Concrete came into wide use where stone had been; sometimes it was tortured into the semblance of rough-hewn stone, at other times merely lined out to suggest piled blocks, though occasionally it was moulded, carved, and smoothed

---

[1] Believe it or not, the room in which I happen to be writing this chapter has smooth plaster walls which have been painstakingly painted and stained into the semblance of an oak-panelled interior. Not an inch has escaped " improvement " at the decorator's hands. Indeed the Italian-Swiss artist responsible for the job has proudly signed his name in the key panel over the door.  And out there in the sun-room — whence one looks over the untroubled blue expanse of Lac Leman, and across to the serene majesty of Mont Blanc, he has painted and streaked and troubled a three-foot strip of concrete wall, from floor to window-sill, into a transparent and truly ugly semblance of veined marble.  He has even made it into a composition in two different colored marbles.  Horrible! doubly horrible!  I don't want to treat lightly the pride in work which led this decorator to sign his name; but I deplore his standards.  And yet how is he different, in the lack of artistic invention and integrity, from the distinguished architects who gave us that stained plaster-of-Paris beamed ceiling, " so remarkably executed that only the initiated are aware that wood has not been used," in the costly university library described in the preceding chapter? Some falsifiers are successful and some aren't, just as some highway robbers escape while others go to prison — but is there no higher morality?

Two views of a model for a revolving cafe-tower at an American Exposition. This aerial restaurant is designed to be as much an architectural "stunt" as was the Eiffel Tower in 1889. Three restaurants with wide terraces are supported on a slender, slowly revolving steel shaft, high over the Exposition grounds and buildings. Construction in glass, aluminum, and steel. Norman-Bel Geddes, architect.

into false pilasters, cornices, panels, and the like. The steel frame escaped the architect for a long period, became a separate thing from the architecture, but ultimately was dutifully hidden by façades nowise related to it. Metal doors and door-frames in skyscrapers were for long painted like wood. These three materials now for the first time are emerging *in expression*.

And indeed this is our great gain: the steel frame at last finds its dominating uprights confessed as piers in the necessary envelope; its rows of cross-beams, the secondary accents, noted story by story. Concrete, reinforced or armored concrete (with imbedded metal bars for strengthening), affords a frank solidity, a sculptural heaviness or blockiness to the building composition. The naked concrete arch, moreover, emerges with thrilling new implications, with startling promises. And sheet-metal contributes the flatness and brilliant finish inherent in its composition and shape. Glass, too, finds more generous place in building, until occasionally an entire façade is of glass and metal.  All this is true gain. It is genuine architectural progress: advance within the limits set by materials.  It affords an honest basis for going on to a flowering that will belong to our own times.

So much for our review of the æsthetic and of material considerations. Now let us turn to that other conditioning factor, social and human: let us return to *the world* as we viewed it at the opening of the book.  If we know in perspective the civilization of the nineteenth century, and feel vitally the changes accomplished in the twentieth, we may conceivably aid in the march on to an architectural achievement unexampled.

If one could get a fixed view of the human edifice in the year 1910, say, one would be struck by certain magnificent gains for humanity, over earlier centuries, and at the same time by an appalling instability of the whole structure.  And one might detect certain elements of confusion and of weakness, and others promising clarification and strength.  In the larger outline this is the world made up of a few powerful *states*: all that counts is civilization as exemplified in the commercially supreme European and American nations.  There are no longer any migratory barbarian hordes that might engulf civilized society.  The earth is so " opened up " that at last there is security except as nations that know better attack one another.

The " living " of most of humanity in the Western world depends upon commercial success of these dozen or so states; world equilibrium depends upon their finding success without goading each other to the fighting point.  A great international game is played, in which the securing of natural resources, the protection of a nation's own markets and the invasion of the other fellow's, and control by holding surplus capital, are chief factors.  It is a business game, and business men control government, material prosperity — and the arts.  Apparently everybody's happiness within the state is dependent upon prosperous trade (such is the interdependent structure of finance, credit, law, communication, and markets that even agriculturists are affected by " bad times," and of course all the workers in the factories). State consciousness is built up in a spirit called patriotism, which makes it seem right that one's own nation should corner prosperity, and punish any less-chosen state (within the reasonable precaution of never attacking one bigger than yourself). Fortunately science and invention, and ever-increasing tapping of Nature's resources, make possible an undreamed-of extension of wealth: of means to food, clothing, shelter, and enjoyment of the arts, recreations, and social amenities, so that all nations during the nineteenth century measurably have bettered the average standard of living.

But the business-man-state is jealous, pushing, even greedy. And inevitably the final reaches after world trade domination result in war. In 1914–1918 the entire edifice is near crashing to the ground. And apparently nothing in the social or trade practice since has made a final crash of the Western nations impossible or improbable. That fact is a background menace, whether one is considering at the moment the well-being of humankind or the emergence of a new architecture.

The arts, outside of literature, have not prospered under commercial civilization. For example, England, dominant imperialist nation for roughly two centuries, has never had a sculptor whose name anyone outside London can recall, nor a musician of world importance; and the only outstanding visual art of four centuries has been the French, which remains regal and ornamental — fluffy — even down through so-called democratic days. One has to go back to a few rather isolated artists of the Renaissance — Michelangelo alone in the sixteenth century, and *very* few between him and Giotto — and then back to early Gothic times, to find art that is original, strong, fundamental. After that everything comes perilously close to being just what the tradesman has always thought it: ornament, diversion, trimming — a sort of feminine cushion to the truly masculine activities of life.

Spirituality has not got along well under the later phases of civilization. All the individual religions had badly run down by 1900. Nation after nation pulled itself free from religious domination: evidence enough that state, *civitas*, had come to mean more than Church.   The only very great Christian establishment progressively lost prestige and power over a period of four centuries, until it weighed heavily, in temporal matters, only in the least progressive states.   The other Christian bodies, being too narrow to unite with similar-thinking groups within the Protestant wing, failed ever to become internationally powerful.   (Catholicism, to be sure, once was strong enough to create an architecture; but the Gothic has steadily declined since 1300, and never was a style for other buildings than churches; and doubly limited because appropriate only to a religion of refuge, mystery, and idolatry.   A Gothic-styled house is simply a *terrible* thing.)

Under this civilization, where religion was progressively weakening, and the arts put aside as a diversion for unimportant times, the true gods were economic and commercial.   Which means that man's faith, the driving force within him, was material.   In the nineteenth century, civilization reached its intensest point in material achievement, but headed straight for those devastating evils that only spiritual consideration and active belief in creative power within the human soul can prevent: war, and enslavement of great masses of people to controlling groups.   And we are so much within civilization today that these, the great nationalistic evils, make unstable the ground under the artist and the trader alike, under architect and artisan and builder.   These are the shadows that still lie over the new world we have glimpsed.   These are the confusing elements that give color to the statement that the larger revolution in living is yet to come.

But even while these confusing evils were shaping and growing, other forces were preparing for the after-time, were working toward clarification.   Most notably, the machine, at first manipulated to bring a different sort of slavery to the hand-worker, was being improved, expanded, brought beneficially to the service of all classes of men.   The machinery of the dawning industrial age, under early and mid-nineteenth century civilization, seemed to bring nothing but slavery to workers, further dirti-

Simplification in house design, as seen in Sweden.
Ernst Spolen, architect

ness to the surface of the earth, and noise and dust into all ears and all eyes. But the machine was then turned to the uses of cleanliness, domestic efficiency, ease of transportation, effortless communication, to multiplication of the arts, to the enrichment of individual experience. Man's physical coming and going, his problems of cleansing, of communication, of heating, lighting, were revolutionized. A *clean* world, a united world, could be visioned for all — even if the more fundamental problems of

A house typical of Swedish progressive but not radical designing. Cyrillus Johansson, architect. [This and photo above by courtesy of Swedish State Railways Information Bureau, New York]

A group of " radical " modern houses, as contrasted with the conservative modernism illustrated opposite. Above left, suburban house in England, by Thomas S. Tait of Sir John Burnet & Partners. Top right, architect's house in Frankfurt, Germany, by Ernst May. Middle left, house of cast concrete blocks in California, by Frank Lloyd Wright. Middle right, house in California, by Lloyd Wright. Bottom, two early experiments by R. M. Schindler in simplified cottage forms, in Los Angeles and Hollywood.

[1923–24]

food and clothing were entangled in trade exploitation and war. In short, the machine (the term includes all that man has been doing with coal, gas, steam, steel, oil, and electricity) helped everybody, and promised world freedom, even while it was serving such questionable purposes as taking all tools out of the laborers' hands and placing them (with control of living) in the hands of trade-capitalists, and making infinitely more horrible the weapons of war. And machinery, mind you, is only at the beginning, is yearly developing new efficiencies, new savings, new multiplications of the finer possessions, opening fresh vistas — until no one can doubt that, if world *organization* comes right, economic comfort is assured for all mankind, plus extension of the enjoyments of art and recreations. This is the main clarifying factor, the chief constructive thread that runs through that picture of unstable early twentieth century civilization. And anyone who conceives architecture without reference to the scientific-mechanical factor, who continues to consider architecture as a matter of styles, and not as an organism shaped within the larger machine organization of mankind, will inevitably fail, will see his ideas and his works crumble with the old human edifice. This is the basis of " understanding " in the new age, the spur to imaginative invention, the fundamental fact of ordered living. A beneficent mechanicalization leads out of the old confusion just as surely as a baleful mechanicalization helped at first to intensify it.

There are other clarifying factors. In the stricter domain of economic and political advance there is the emergence of woman into independence of various sorts; there is the even more epochal rise of labor to a position where the worker wields, if not great power, at least a potent threat to trade-civilization. This laborer escaped from the old feudal system long ago, in what seemed like a revolution; but where work service is recognized as the fundamental fact of life, that change is seen as merely a shift of mass-labor from one sort of dependence to another. Only with the emergence of labor organized to control (and ultimately suppress) national governments, did the people who do the hand-labor, who actually

The house for outdoor living: view from roof of house by Le Corbusier and P. Jeanneret in the Weissenhof suburb, Stuttgart, Germany. [By courtesy of the German Tourist Information Office, New York]

guide the machines of industry and create its products, become a force in the political-economic line-up. (This forecast of a possible workers' world — not a series of nations ruled by kings, priests, or business men — may give you an inkling why there is less than usual talk in this book about cathedrals, temples, opera-houses, palaces, and other " monumental " edifices of earlier eras, but a great deal about small houses, factories, schools, stadiums, etc.)

But there are other less tangible factors that we may search out for proof — or for hope and cause — of a new architecture. Most important, to me, is what I have called the drift to the open life. By this I mean the increase in open-mindedness, matched by a throwing open of the doors in physical life. As for the open mind, we are not yet unduly alarmed by the wave of tolerance and understanding, or any general casting-off of the religions of fear and self-negation; but comparing, for

Architecture designed for the open life: home of Frank Lloyd Wright,
Spring Green, Wisconsin. Frank Lloyd Wright, architect.

instance, with the time when the democratic tide first set in, man is extraordinarily unfettered in his thinking, in his daring, in his reach for truth.   Democracy largely failed as a political philosophy; at least in practice it came near being a wash-out; it transferred only the illusion of power to the *demos,* the people as an entity.   But the democratizing of education sensibly opened the mind: more people think *a little* than ever before.   Fear is less a driving force, mental curiosity more so, adventurous seeking commoner.   And — here the machine enters as an influence — there is a well-marked tendency to seek the open life: symbolized in less-cluttered rooms (the appalling Victorian decorated stuffiness giving way before both spacious and intimate arrangements, clean-walled), in the spread of motoring as the most popular of all " sports," in the increase of interest in gardening.   In a different aspect, the woman of today, wearing scarce a third of the clothes that her grandmother carried around, is a symbol of this " coming forth."   To live the open life, with mental honesty, fresh air in one's lungs, sunlight for tonic, color for enrichment, respecting only the barriers of mutual consideration: this may become with us a national ideal, and even seems to me a tide that is washing at all the shores of the world.

The architecture of civilization was not conceived for this open way of living.   It was an architecture of walls, not of space; of masonry, not of trapped sunlight and fresh air.   It was not conceived as a machine to serve man, as an aid to living the good life; rather as stylistic parade, as traditional " Art," as a walled place of refuge.   I think that not in the entire history of the Western world has there been such a radical, complete, and swift overturn of thinking about the place and purpose of architecture as has occurred (among the true artist-leaders of the profession) within the years you and I have been living.   I am sure there has been none based so directly on the purpose to bring the right buildings into the service of every individual, with so little consideration for display and upper-class toadying.

In short, we recognize, at the moment when exploiting civilization

The City Hall at Stockholm, Sweden, far famed as a monument of modern architecture, has the new basic simplicity but with reticent touches of traditional decoration — a sort of cautious modernism now becoming very popular. Ragnar Ostberg, architect. [By courtesy of Swedish State Railways Information Bureau, New York]

reaches to the ends of the earth, with its battleships, its competitive states, and its cultural modes — we recognize an epochal dislocation in the ways of living, the first prominent emergence of world thought, a well-marked current toward the " open " life, and the early signs of a different art of building. The universe of humankind, passing on from civilized life and institutions toward a socialized world-organization, judges the old architecture to have been logical for nationalistic living and ideals, but not right for the new age. And now a genuine and expressive machine-age architecture pushes through.

WE MAY take the City as an ultimate symbol. Before we can become final masters of the new world, we must make our cities Architecture in the largest sense. They must be true to plan, functioning as an organism,

Project for a waterfront development at Detroit, Michigan, showing public buildings in relation to controlled business skyscrapers.   Eliel Saarinen, architect

beautiful in unity and in every part, serving the common inhabitant practically and æsthetically, in his business of living the good life, the open life.

In the past all cities have negated most horribly the ideal of open living. They have escaped unity in every sense. They have known no singleness of design in themselves; they contribute but haltingly to the uses of him who tries to make a reasonable design of his individual life.

We have had, indeed, several decades of agitation about city planning, but the proposed regulation is ninety-nine hundredths timidly remedial, where only a drastic cutting off and building anew can be effective. " The city beautiful " was the first cry; and in those days beauty could not be conceived as having anything to do with common usableness. Park systems, *rond-points*, and focal palatial buildings, opera houses and museums, were to save the city for art. But the typical aloof æsthetes didn't get very far.  They made Paris a tourists' paradise, with the most wasteful spaces, the most vainglorious buildings anywhere; but you need only dodge down any back street to know that it is mostly show, and unrelated to the life and thinking of the people.  After the surface beautification idea, there came much talk about traffic plans, and then there were excursions into housing, playground provision, etc.  Finally arrived zoning; and it is recognized as the nub of the problem today.

But why not the City as Architecture — that is, as something built for perfect mechanical functioning in the service of man, with an over-value of sheer pleasure-giving beauty in the building?  Of course it will be a city of machines, and machinery can be made noiseless; but are our cities reasonably noiseless today?  Of course it will be clean, with a typical mechanical-era tidiness — like a power-house or an electric bakery; but forty thousand tons of soot are let loose in Pittsburgh's air each year, and on a cold day in London you can scarcely breathe for the heaviness of the coal-smoke atmosphere.  Do we go easily from place to place?  Ask the riders in the New York subways — or the New York surface cars.

No, we don't care enough yet for truly beautiful cities — beautiful as the automobile is beautiful — to take the necessary steps.  We should have to strip back, consider function and material and the human elements, and then go ahead idealistically — ruthlessly (and be cruel to the investors).  We should find ourselves cutting across the interests of so many powerful persons, political and clannish and commercial, that we would wisely say, the world is not ready for that yet.  We should see that the City itself will be the last to give itself up to truly architectural treatment, in a profiteering age.  We should see that the chaos and the disease and the poverty and the dirt are inevitable in a civilization based on getting, on war, on competition.  We may individually, even now, raise up buildings that are evidence of a new world spirit, of unselfishness, of a will to clean living.  But the City will be the last to succumb.

Yet that ideal of the City as Architecture is worth holding in mind, as an ultimate goal.  Thinking about it, visioning it, will make it come

Vision of a future city, with spaced skyscrapers, by Hugh Ferriss.  [By courtesy of the American
Institute of Steel Construction]

true some day.  Let the vision be of a city beautiful, clean-walled, glowing
with color, majestically sculptural, with a lift toward the skies; and let it
be simple, convenient, sweet-running, airy, and light.  Our children's
children may see it, so fast do thoughts travel these days.  And we may

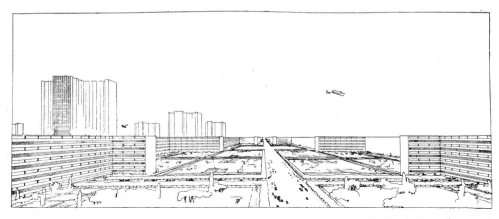

Sketch by Le Corbusier for a scientifically laid-out city, with all apartment blocks edged by parks, and business concentrated in separated skyscraper units. [From Le Corbusier's *Urbanisme*, by courtesy of Payson & Clarke, publishers of the English translation]

thank sincerely Hugh Ferriss and Le Corbusier and the others who are putting before us, in imaginative drawings, it may be idealistic, it may be mechanistic, suggestions of what the aspect of that City will be.

Meantime we may make our minor contributions, by insisting that our own immediate architecture be right. Having once seen what we have now seen, we shall be progressively impatient of inconvenience, falsity, or cultural make-believe in our living and working places. If we come to the new wisdom, which says that each man may make of his life a work of art, we shall know that the old buildings of the sham architects, the masked, overdecorated, dead buildings, are not for us.

We cannot live without architecture; we cannot live happily without architecture breathing beauty about us. Perhaps all that is noble in architecture is a reflection of that conviction of ours, about man being essentially noble, about his inborn power to create, about the good life being really a work of art. All we are asking is that the architects forget themselves, forget their traditional prerogatives of being aloof artists, forget their soft indulgences, and for a time serve us, normally, unostentatiously, in our machine-age living-pattern, to which we think we are now bringing a design.

# INDEX

## A

Abel, Adolf, 30, 72, 198, 300, 373.
Adler & Sullivan, 128.
American architecture, 60 ff, 86, 136.
American Institute of Architects, 198.
Anker, Alfons, 171.
Apartments, 276–288, 311, 377, 380.
Arch construction, 41, 56.
Architectural aesthetics, 33ff, 39, 115–6, 174–5, 302ff, 348, 378–387.
Architectural education, 32, 301ff, 379.
Architecture: history — *See under* Baroque, Byzantine, Eclecticism, Gothic, Greek, Renaissance, Roman, Romanesque, Chapter II.
Architecture and civilization, 4–5, 10ff, 44, 65, 119ff, 217, 229–234, 293, 327–331, 387–396.
Art galleries, 361–5, 373.
Art, modern, 5, 116–8.
*Art Nouveau*, 177–180, 237.
Arts and Crafts movement, 273–6.
Ashbee, C. R., 239.
Austria, 25–6, 181–194.
Automobiles, 78–9.

## B

Barber, Frank, 322.
Baroque, 52.
Bartning, Otto, 13, 218, 300, 346–7.
*Bauhaus*, Dessau, 104, 186, 255, 301ff.
Beardsley, Aubrey, 176.
*Beaux-Arts*, 55, 64, 126.
Bebb, C. H., 63.
Behrens, Peter, 166, 194–8, 209, 277, 283, 298.
Belgian style, 178.
Bell, Clive, 378.
Berg, Max, 198, 300, 318.
Bergsten, Carl, 213.
Berlage, H. P., 28, 84, 111, 201, 294–5, 300.
Bestelmeyer, German, 161.
Bliss & Faville, 63.
Blomfield, Reginald, 178.
Böhm, Dominikus, 338–340.
Bonatz, Paul, 100–1, 300, 323.
Boni, Giuseppe, 63.
Bonnier, L., 315.
Bourgeois, Djo, 211, 229, 258.

Bragdon, Claude, 34, 163, 216–8, 308, 322.
Brangwyn, Frank, 239.
Bridges, 91–2, 93, 321–6.
Brinkman, J. A., 301.
Burnet, Sir John & Partners, 391.
Burnham, Daniel H., 129, 140.
Business buildings, 9, 11, Chapter IV. *See also* Skyscrapers.
Byzantine architecture, 44.

## C

California style, 20, 23, 267–273.
Carrere & Hastings, 140.
Cathedral of St. John the Divine, New York, 120.
Cathedrals, 50.
Cheney, Charles H., 269.
Chicago, 24, 56, 205, 244.
Chicago Tribune competition, 63, 144–151.
Churches, 13, 33, 219, 221, 327–348.
City planning, 83, 114, 145, 219, 324–6, 396–400.
Civilization. *See* Architecture and civilization.
Cline, Edward, 269.
Color, 195, 197, 216, 252, 266, 288, 381.
Colosseum, 42.
Columbian Exposition, Chicago, 129–135.
Concrete construction, 58–9, 105, 205, 247ff, 263, 297, 306, 310–326, 335, 339, 356ff, 386.
Concrete slab construction, 24, 203ff, 250–3, 286, 323.
Constructivists, 302.
Corbett, Harrison & McMurray, 363.
Corbett, Harvey Wiley, 139, 363.
Cram, Ralph Adams, 62, 84.
Crane, Walter, 181.
Cutter, Kirkland, 269.
Czajkowski, Joseph, 214.

## D

Davidson, J. R., 212.
de Klerk, 300.
Department stores, 165, 169ff.
Domestic architecture, 8, 17, 23–4, 55, 78, 118, 196, 199–205, Chapter VI.
Dudok, Willem, 29, 101, 103, 300.
Duncan, Isadora, 137–8, 348.